Kijana

Also by Jesse Martin
Lionheart: A journey of the human spirit

Kijana
THE REAL STORY

JESSE MARTIN
WITH ED GANNON

A SUE HINES BOOK
ALLEN & UNWIN

First published in 2005

A Sue Hines Book
Allen & Unwin
83 Alexander Street
Crows Nest NSW 2065
Australia
Phone: (61 2) 8425 0100
Fax: (61 2) 9906 2218
Email: info@allenandunwin.com
Web: www.allenandunwin.com

National Library of Australia
Cataloguing-in-Publication entry:
    Martin, Jesse, 1981– .
    Kijana: the real story.
    ISBN 1 74114 429 9.
    1. Martin, Jesse, 1981– — Journeys. 2. Kijana (Sailboats).
    3. Voyages and travels. I. Gannon, Ed. II. Title.
    910.41

Edited by Margaret Trudgeon
Text design by Phil Campbell
Typeset by Pauline Haas
Printed in Australia by Griffin Press

10 9 8 7 6 5 4 3 2 1

To anyone who has ever wanted to be someone or somewhere better. And, to my crew, who each went on their own journey during Kijana.

AUTHOR'S NOTE

Throughout the book kilometres and miles are used to record distance. Distances on land are recorded in kilometres, while distances at sea are in miles. In this case 'mile' refers to the metric measurement of a nautical mile (1.852 kilometres), which is longer than the land mile of 1.6 kilometres.

CONTENTS

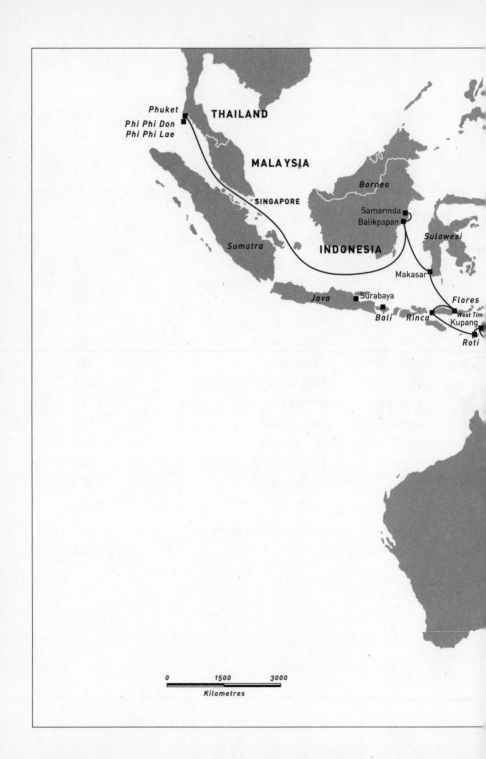

Phuket
Phi Phi Don
Phi Phi Lae

THAILAND

MALAYSIA

SINGAPORE

Borneo

Samarinda
Balikpapan

Sulawesi

Sumatra

INDONESIA

Makasar

Java   Surabaya

Flores

Bali   *Rinca*

West Tim
Kupang

Roti

0   1500   3000
Kilometres

KIJANA'S VOYAGE

INDONESIA

PAPUA NEW GUINEA

T TIMOR

Cape York

Forbes Island

Darwin

Nhulunbuy

Lizard Island

Low Isles, Snapper Island
Cairns

AUSTRALIA

Mooloolaba

Coffs Harbour

Port Stephens

Sydney

Melbourne

CHAPTER ONE
STILL DREAMING

ADVENTURE. HAVE YOU EVER STOPPED TO consider what that word means? Tropical jungles, exotic ports, sparse deserts and wild natives – they'd all surely figure in anyone's definition. They certainly did for me. In fact, these were the things I planned to see and experience on my ultimate adventure – sailing the seven seas with a group of friends. It was the stuff I'd been doing since I was a kid. For instance, the two-month 450 nautical mile journey on an open catamaran along the tropical Queensland coast when I was just 14. Or the five-week kayak odyssey with my younger brother, Beau, along the beautiful coast and villages of Papua New Guinea when I was 15. Then there was the time I flew alone as a wide-eyed 16-year-old to the crime-riddled South American country of Belize on the strength of a phone invitation to join a crew, which was a hell of an adventure, and the 11 months I spent at sea to become the youngest person to sail solo, nonstop and unassisted around the world. My visits to the boardrooms of Australia's most powerful companies were also nerve-wracking adventures, as was plunging into the bright lights of America's most popular television talk show.

But I now know that adventure means so much more than conquests and excitement. Adventure is actually another word for life. Think about it. Think of all the hurdles and obstacles thrown in your path as you do this simple thing called living – schoolyard fights, falling in love, losing your job, getting married, having kids, sickness, drugs, loneliness, death. These are all adventures.

It took a crazy experience called Kijana to make me realise that all the things that I thought of as adventures were really just a sideshow to the ultimate adventure – growing up.

But enough of the philosophy – let's get into the story – the story of Kijana.

I first became fascinated with the adventure of sailing in September 1995, a few weeks after my fourteenth birthday. That was when Dad, my brother Beau and I began a two-month journey, sailing a tiny 14-foot open catamaran along the north Queensland coast to Cape York. We were doing it pretty hard on that trip, camping out in the open and living off burnt fish. Yet I loved the thrill of the adventure and didn't want it to be my last.

We arrived at Lizard Island, a resort island, to find ourselves surrounded by luxury boats. I loved their nice comfortable cabins, with fresh water on tap, and the fact that they'd been sailed to this beautiful tropical place. I thought, hey, I'd love to get my own little boat and sail around the world doing all the stuff we're currently doing, except in a bit more comfort. My imagination sprang to life with images of exotic ports, meeting people, swimming in crystal-clear water, diving and catching fish. It'd be bloody sensational.

However, my plans weren't exactly greeted with the same enthusiasm by the others. When I told Dad I wanted to sail around the world, he said 'OK' as if I'd announced I was going to the shop to buy an ice-cream. I spent the rest of that trip making lists of what food and equipment I would need and reading boating magazines to find the boat I'd need.

By the time I returned to school in 1996 I had one thing clear in my mind – I was going to sail around the world. The notion of doing it nonstop hadn't been considered at that point. It was only when

I heard about 17-year-old David Dicks leaving Fremantle in February 1996 aboard his 34-foot yacht, *Seaflight*, in an attempt to become the youngest person to sail solo, nonstop and unassisted around the world, that the thought of doing a similar thing entered my mind.

Around that time a family friend gave me some books about others who had successfully sailed around the world. There was one by Tania Aebi, an 18-year-old from the United States who, in November 1987, returned from a two-and-a-half-year solo journey around the world on a 26-foot yacht. Another was *First Lady* by Australia's most famous female sailor, Kay Cottee, who became the first woman to sail solo, nonstop and unassisted around the world, completing her journey in 1988. They made for pretty inspiring reading. So inspiring, that as I read each book, the idea that I should attempt a solo voyage began to build in my mind.

By the time I'd finished reading, my decision was made – I wanted to become the youngest person to sail solo, nonstop and unassisted around the world.

I learnt that American Robin Lee Graham was the youngest to commence an around-the-world trip, at just 16 years of age, so I decided to up the ante and leave when I was 15. I set a departure goal of early 1997, by which stage I would be 15½ years old.

I was as flush with cash as your normal 14-year-old, so I set about raising some dough. I wrote to about 50 major companies seeking sponsorship. I got 24 replies – all of them rejections.

Undeterred, I decided to seek a crew position on an around-the-world trip to gain some experience. I did a two-week trial down the east coast of Australia with the skipper of one planned trip, but that voyage fell over financially for him, much to his and my disappointment.

At the same time I continued to seek sponsorship, until I realised that my dream of still being 15 when I left was becoming a very long shot. I then hit upon the idea of making documentaries to fund my endeavours. To do that I'd have to film something.

Of course, that could only mean embarking on another adventure. Flicking through *Australian Geographic* magazine I came across an account of a sea kayak expedition in Papua New Guinea. I was mesmerised by one photograph in particular, of a man in a kayak in beautiful crystal-clear water. I knew instantly that was where my filming adventure lay.

After making heaps of calls and letters, I managed to get $3000 in sponsorship from *Australian Geographic*, as well as cheap flights, some insurance and equipment. The bulk of the finance came from Mum, via a $4000 loan.

I needed a travel companion, so Beau, who is two years younger than me, stepped in after a mate pulled out. We left in September 1997, one month after my sixteenth birthday, paddling 150 miles over five weeks and seeing some amazing sights. It wasn't easy, and there were times I was terrified, but it was an adventure – and I loved it!

After we arrived home in late October I had a five-minute teaser tape of the trip professionally produced, which I was going to tout to television stations. Unfortunately, this took a bit longer than I expected and, as things began to move so quickly, the tape got a bit lost in my wake.

I continued my search for a position on an around-the-world crew, which led me to an Australian boat that had spent the previous three years meandering around the globe. In a few weeks it would be in Florida, in the United States, where it wanted fresh crew to sail the final six-month stretch to Australia. I was keen – very keen.

By this stage it was the end of 1997, which was crunch time for my education. I was due to start Year 11 the following year, the first year of the crucial Victorian Certificate of Education. If I was to embark on my final years of school I had to make a decision – school or adventure.

No matter how hard I tried to see the sense of doing my VCE, I ached to go on another adventure. It was an opportunity too good to miss, so I applied for the crew position.

It took a few weeks for them to reply. I remember how nervous I felt as I opened the letter. I also remember the disappointment when I read the rejection. They'd filled the spot and no longer required crew.

I was devastated. This had been my best chance, I told myself, and now it had gone.

That letter sealed my fate. I entered Year 11 in February 1998, determined to do the best I could. But about two weeks into the school year I received a phone call. It was the skipper of the boat in Florida – the new crewman had failed to arrive. Did I want to join them? They'd be in Belize, a small country bordering Mexico and Guatemala on the Caribbean Sea's Gulf of Honduras, in a fortnight. If I was coming I had to meet them there, he said.

I was beside myself when I got off the phone, having mumbled something about getting back to him. Then the reality of the situation sank in. I had already started school. If I were to embark on the trip it would probably put me too far behind in my schoolwork to catch up and allow me to make a proper go of VCE. Luckily, Mum knew how much I desperately wanted to go, and said she would support me in whatever I decided, so I went for it.

I only had a bit over a week to organise my schooling and equip-ment for half a year at sea. I scraped together some money, as it was going to cost $150 a week to crew on the yacht to cover food and over-heads. Once again, I had to borrow the money from Mum.

I flew to Belize on my own and somehow found the skipper in a dusty street. We set off for an amazing trip through the Panama Canal across the Pacific Ocean to the Galapagos Islands and Tahiti.

Dave, the skipper, was a lot more easygoing than most other sailors I'd ever met. He didn't care if I drank as much beer as I could hold and Dave never once told me to do my homework. But the best thing about sailing with Dave was that I learnt so much simply by watching him. He was far from the snobby sailor who relied on a plethora of electronic equipment to get anywhere. Dave ran a simple but effective ship, sailing as nature intended it. As I observed his methods, I realised I could do everything he did. It was commonsense. I just had to know which rope to pull. The idea of sailing around the world no longer seemed such a big deal.

By the time we arrived in Tahiti after three and a half months on board I decided that if I was going to have a serious go at the age record I had better get home and do it. I left Dave, flew home, and set about making my dream come true.

The preparation for the solo trip was a blur. I set a departure date of December, which meant I only had four months to get a boat, secure sponsorship, convince a yacht club to allow me to use their facilities and organise some publicity that, in turn, would hopefully attract some sponsors. I had set a tight departure schedule to give me time to return before I was 18 years and 41 days of age, which would break David Dicks's age record.

Somehow we did it. I bought *Lionheart*, an S&S 34, with money Mum lent me after re-mortgaging her house. Miraculously, Matthew Gerard, the head of electrical company Mistral, joined the effort as the major sponsor, providing $160,000 for equipment and labour to get the boat ready in time (it was a deal that would see Matthew eventually outlay $350,000 all up); Sandringham Yacht Club broke the shackles of yacht club stiffness to provide me with a launching pad; and the *Herald Sun* newspaper came on board with an offer for me to write a weekly diary for school kids so that they could follow my progress. All this happened in the space of a few months.

While that was going on, I was learning everything about solo sailing, navigation, weather and generally how to survive anything the sea would throw at me.

I set sail on Sunday 6 December 1998, from Sandringham, farewelled by about 350 people. I was 17 years and 100 days of age. Over the next 11 months I sailed around the bottom of New Zealand, around Cape Horn, up to the Azores, which was the antipodal point of my journey (the exact opposite point of the earth from my starting point), down to the Cape of Good Hope and across the Southern Ocean to home.

It seems odd describing my trip in one sentence, but that was basically it.

During the trip I suffered the boredom of becalming, the terror of *Lionheart* being knocked over, and the pure elation of rounding Cape Horn. I also suffered the agony of loneliness and the joy of nature at its finest. And I discovered exactly what I was capable of and what I wanted out of life, to the point where I could do anything I imagined.

The 27,000-mile journey was meant to take only eight months to complete, but calm weather blew it out considerably, to nearly 11 months. At 6.28 a.m. on 31 October 1999, at the Port Phillip Heads – 327 days, 12 hours and 52 minutes since I had last passed that point – I became the youngest person to sail solo, nonstop and unassisted around the world. I was older than Dicks, at 18 years and 66 days, but was able to claim the record for, unlike David, I hadn't received any assistance during the trip.

As I returned I knew deep down that my life was about to change dramatically. My suspicion was confirmed as I sat in my yacht off Sandringham Yacht Club and marvelled at the sight before me. The media reports said there were 25,000 people waiting for me that day. I don't doubt it.

Along the breakwater were more faces than I'd ever seen before – old people, young people, people I knew, but mainly people I'd never seen before. My first thought when I realised that all those tiny dots lining the shore were people was: 'what the hell are they doing here?' I knew there had been a lot of interest in my trip through the diaries I'd been writing in the newspaper, but to think that so many people would come to see me was beyond my comprehension.

The cheer from the crowd as I stepped from *Lionheart* was deaf-ening, a bit like you'd hear at a football match. I was really touched by the reception. It made me feel warm all over and tingling inside. In those rare few seconds I felt like letting out my own roar. I wanted to step outside myself and feel in awe of what I had achieved. I wanted to hug someone. No, I wanted to hug everyone. I wanted to be like them, watching a kid who had left Melbourne on a blustery day with little experience but with a plan to sail on his own, nonstop and unassisted around the world.

People wanted me to sign flags that had been handed out for my arrival and some hardy souls even wanted photos of me holding their babies. I felt like I was up for re-election.

I was shown to a room packed with cameras and reporters.

Everyone I knew looked so different, kind of grown up. I sat at a table with a microphone and a glass of water and answered questions.

'How does it feel to be back?' was the first question.

How could I explain that?

'It feels great,' I said.

'What was the hardest time?'

'The storm I had off South Africa.'

That was an easier question, for I'd had five knockdowns that night and didn't know if my mast would still be up by the morning.

'What are you going to do now?'

'You mean after drinking beer with my friends?'

I was being flippant, but I knew exactly what I was going to do. I was going back onto the waves, to sail the world again. But this time it would be different. I would take my mates and stop off at the most remote and unexplored places in the world. We would experience all types of adventures in the far-off lands I'd sailed past. We'd see cultures I'd read about in *National Geographic*. We'd ride across barren Easter Island on horseback and swat mosquitoes in Borneo.

As I sat there, being grilled by the media, I was raring to go. I'd spent the previous three months typing away on my laptop computer, putting down my vision for the trip. So I answered the question again.

'I want to go around again on a Polynesian catamaran with friends, navigating by the stars and living as they did a century ago.'

I didn't know how I was going to make it happen. I had no money. In fact, as I sat there, I was hopelessly in debt. But I felt like the richest man in the world because I had my dreams. I could have as many as I wanted and I knew I could live them all.

The next few months were crazy. I had 11 months of life to catch up on. While I was sitting aboard *Lionheart* all my mates were finishing school, getting their drivers licences and partying hard. It was a time of great change for any 18-year-old, let alone one who had missed out on so much.

Not long after I returned I was approached to see if I was interested in becoming involved with Reach, a youth organisation. I was invited to a breakfast Reach was holding to raise money at one of those swanky hotels in the city that no one I knew could possibly afford to stay at. And it was so early! Hell, if I knew it was going to be on that early my Reach involvement may never have happened. The mainly corporate audience had paid to hear about the work of Reach, eat breakfast, and be in the office by 9 a.m.

Any thoughts of feeling sorry for myself because of my lack of sleep quickly disappeared when some young people got up and began telling their stories about their violent families, school troubles, drug addictions and their dreams for the future. It was raw and honest and I was genuinely moved. I wanted to know more about these people and how Reach had helped them. I started attending the courses run by the young members of Reach for school kids.

Meanwhile, I was getting more and more requests to talk about my trip from organisations, ranging from primary schools that had followed *Lionheart*'s voyage, to companies who wanted their employees to hear an inspirational message.

I was terribly nervous standing up in front of an audience because I'm not someone who likes attention. And it showed. My words came out in some twisted form that barely made sense. I rambled on, spewing out whatever came into my mind. However, people encouraged me and I generally received a good response from my audiences. It was strange. I knew I was mumbling and was all over the place but people wanted to hear what I had to say. And some of them even paid me!

A few months after my return I was approached by a book publisher keen to publish the story of my trip. I'd never been much of a writer but I decided to give it a shot and a very tight four-month deadline was set. It wasn't the best fun I'd ever had but it was a good experience to read through my journal and churn out up to 2000 words a day. And after all the excitement of getting home, it rekindled my desire to get back out onto the water.

I also had a shoebox full of video tapes I had filmed on the trip. Filmmaker Paul Currie was enlisted to make a documentary of the trip and immediately set to work filming interviews with all the major players involved in the trip. My main role was to help Paul's assistant editor, Amelia, go through the tapes and log the most interesting bits. We had 60 hours to wade through, which took a couple of weeks to view before the editing even started. Sometimes I'd do it without Amelia and sometimes she'd do it without me.

One day I arrived at the studio expecting to be the only one there, only to find a young guy scrolling through my footage. He had long, dark, straight hair down his back and was looking through some of my most intimate moments. He quickly stood up and said hi.

I vaguely recognised him as the brother of one of the leaders from Reach. His name was Josh. He said Paul had invited him to help with the documentary because he had done some short films at school and was keen to get into filmmaking. We sat together for the rest of the day, not saying much, just going through the footage and commenting on it. It was a strange start to the strong friendship that would soon develop.

Josh was a year older than me and was also a Reach leader. The more I got know Josh and his friends, the more I got into Reach. I slowly learnt how this mixed group of people had been pulled together. What impressed me more than their stories was their attitude. Like me, they believed that they could do anything, so a lot of their work was aimed at showing people not much younger than themselves that their potential was limitless. These kids were inspired and the parents thought the leaders were saints. I liked these people too – a lot!

I was in a strange stage of my life. I found myself with two groups of friends – my old friends from school and the Reach friends I was getting to know.

One night was pivotal in me being accepted into my new group of friends.

It happened at my house at Sassafras, on a rare Saturday night when Mum was away. Nine of us – five guys and four girls – were having a great night, drinking and partying, when the challenge was laid out – everyone had to get nude. We'd dabbled in nudie runs a couple of times, but that was only ever a couple of guys larking about. This was a dare for each of us to bare all as friends, not as a sexual thing and without the silly carry-on of streaking.

Chocko, an extroverted Sri Lankan, was first, followed by another of the guys. They emerged from my bedroom totally starkers and casually walked to their seats in the circle. Mika, another Reach leader was the first girl and soon everyone had shed their clothes. Admittedly, the lights had been dimmed, and I think we were all slightly stunned by what was happening. But after the initial sneaked glances of curiosity, we forgot everyone was naked and the night went on. The music was cranked up and body parts not usually invited to public functions were flying about as the dancing continued.

To top off the night, we filed out the front door and ran about 300 metres down the road to a main intersection. Under a street lamp we danced around naked, revelling in our friendship and freedom and hoping for a passing car to scare.

From that night on I felt so much closer to these people.

Before we headed home to bed I took a moment to stand back and watch everyone. I loved being home, people liked me and I was having fun, heaps of fun, but deep down I yearned to be out on the sea again, living the adventure of a lifetime. I could think of little else but getting back out onto the water.

As I stood there on that cold August night, my naked friends dancing around me, I knew the time to move on had arrived. I'd done the planning, I'd dreamt the dreams, now it was time to make it all come to life. It was time for the Kijana adventure.

CHAPTER TWO
COMING TOGETHER

A YEAR AFTER I RETURNED FROM MY SOLO trip, my book, *Lionheart: A Journey of the Human Spirit*, hit the shelves. The initial prediction by the publisher was for sales of about 20,000 copies, a bestseller by any standards in Australia. By the time it came to publishing, they'd tapped a rich vein of publicity, so the print run was boosted to 50,000. Within 12 months, *Lionheart* had sold more than 100,000 copies, with editions in the United Kingdom, Germany, South Korea and Denmark.

Around the same time, my documentary of the same name was released. Paul had done a fantastic job and it was sold to an international distributor at a very good price. With money from the book and the documentaries, as well as my corporate talks, my appearance in an advertising campaign for a major telecommunications company and appearances at events for organisations, I was able to pay off my debt to Mum. Clearing that allowed me to turn my attention to my next trip.

I already knew the route I would take. I planned to leave Melbourne and sail up the east coast of Australia, heading straight for Papua New Guinea; then on to Indonesia, India and Africa, where the crew would leave the boat on the coast of Tanzania and cross the continent by land while another crew would sail our boat around to meet us on the other side. I wanted to ride camels across the Serengeti Plain, then raft down the Congo River to meet the boat on the Atlantic coast.

Whether all of this was possible, I wasn't sure. But there was no harm in aiming high. From Africa we would head to South America and venture up the Amazon River as far as possible, then through the Caribbean Ocean and Panama Canal to the Galapagos Islands. From there we would stop at Easter Island, then make our way though the Pacific back to Australia. It was the ultimate adventure, and would take up to three years to complete.

When asked by teachers to 'inspire' their students, I always found it difficult. I was inspired by adventure, but I found it hard to express in words what exactly it was about adventure that captured me. So I intended my next trip, in a way, to do the talking for me. I planned to do this through weekly email updates and documentaries that could be viewed around the world. I figured these would be more effective than me standing in front of a classroom umming and ahhing.

My choice of crew would be vital in inspiring young people. I didn't want to take a crew who already had fixed ideas on what to expect, and the last thing I wanted was to have a hardened sailor on my back. I wanted a crew of novices; people who could show others that such a trip was achievable for anyone. Therefore, highly trained sailors and adventurers were out of the question. The crew would have to be pretty raw, with the trip revealing the emotional ups and downs and the physical difficulties of sailing around the world. I certainly didn't want people to think that it was drinks at five every night after we had spent the day sunbaking on beautiful calm seas. Making your dreams come true would mean enduring some hardship.

But before I could select a crew I needed to turn my attention to other matters – such as a name for my adventure. I searched the web for a suitable moniker to reflect the intentions of the journey. I was drawn to the sounds of Swahili words. I came across several, including hashiki, meaning passion. I liked it, but decided 'passion' was a bit cheesy and it sounded too much like Contiki, those organised holidays for under 35s. The 'hash' bit was also a bit of a worry, for obvious reasons.

The only other word that really appealed to me was kijana. It means 'young people', which pretty much described my idea of the trip. I liked the sound of it, and so did everyone else, so Kijana it was.

I could almost buy the sort of boat I needed with my royalties from the book and documentary, but I still had to find money for food, computers for the office and boat, video cameras, a satellite phone to stream our updates to the website (which needed to be developed), insurance, outboard motors, tents, surfboards, snowboards, dive gear, medical equipment and training.

Some rough income projections showed that if we produced a 13-part television series of Kijana, the income would more than cover everything. But that was down the track. We needed cash now if anything was going to happen.

Our only practical option was to obtain the equipment and financial help through sponsorship. I didn't really want sponsorship and I was especially against having the boat plastered with logos. I wanted this to be an adventure, not an ad venture!

It wasn't that I was opposed to sponsorship, it was just that a group of friends would not normally head off on a journey with such heavy corporate backing. There had to be a balance between ideals and the reality of setting a boat up to be the ultimate adventure platform.

Over the next six months we raised nearly all of what we needed. One of our biggest contributions came from telecommunications giant Telstra, who gave us satellite equipment and agreed to pay our communication costs. In return, we would send Telstra a short, edited video update every week for their website.

Apple computers gave us some of their latest computers so we could start editing a promo tape to help us raise more funds, and insurance company NRMA agreed to cover all our insurance.

In return for the help of these companies, we agreed to display company logos on our website and in our documentaries. We worked overtime to ensure that the boat's hull remained clear of logos.

The schools program, which the *Herald Sun* had run for

Lionheart, was something we aimed to replicate. The newspaper had produced a map of the *Lionheart* route and an activity kit, which was sent to every primary school in Victoria. For Kijana we expanded this to include newspapers across Australia, with a weekly diary and activity kit that teachers could use in the classroom.

Reach let us use part of their warehouse in Collingwood as our headquarters. In our small corner we proudly stuck an A4 piece of paper on the front door bearing the name of the company that had been formed to run the trip – The Kijana Partnership Pty Ltd.

I was still living at home with Mum and Beau, an hour's drive from the office, where I was spending most of my time. I wanted – and needed – somewhere I could call my own that was closer to the Kijana office. I had some cash, which, combined with a bank loan, could get me a flat and some furniture.

I eventually found a one-bedroom apartment in St Kilda, an inner-city beachside suburb which has always had a fairly seedy reputation, particularly for drugs and prostitution. I was well aware of that, but I didn't realise it would actually take place in the stairwell leading to my flat. I started to recognise the prostitutes who stood by my driveway and, despite being pretty uncomfortable at first, I was soon saying g'day to the transvestites in flat three.

I was finally on my own, and loving it. I could have people over any night of the week without worrying about cramping Mum's style and St Kilda was a great launching pad from which to hit the pubs and clubs. If Beau and his friends didn't meet at my place on the weekends, we usually saw them at the Irish pub on Fitzroy St. Half the time they were refused entry because they were too rowdy, but Chocko, my Sri Lankan mate, often knew the bouncers and could get them in.

One night, not long after I moved in, Chocko, Beau, his friend Harley and I gatecrashed the birthday party of a girl I didn't know. I sat quietly in the corner enjoying the free beer and hoping my cover wasn't blown, when I looked up to see a tall, elegant girl heading our way. I only had time to mumble 'she's hot' to Chocko before she was onto us. I thought the gig was up, but it turned out Chocko knew her. Her name was Maya and she was the birthday girl.

Chocko introduced us and she thanked me for coming. I stupidly held up my glass as if I was toasting her. Here we go again, I thought. I always managed to act the goat every time I was around a pretty girl. Luckily she ignored me and kept talking to Chocko. My eyes wandered from her mouth to her shoulders and then to her eyes. She was beautiful and I felt myself starting to sway. I put my glass down and took a seat, like some pissed idiot.

More of her friends came through the door so she excused herself to go and greet them. As she turned and walked away, Chocko and I shot a glance at each other and covered our smiles by reaching for our near-empty pots of beer. The speeches began, but I was doing more staring than listening. My attention shifted only once, when Beau lost his balance and nearly landed on one of her family.

Near the end of the night Chocko suggested I ask her out to dinner or over to my place. Surely she had a boyfriend, I said. He didn't think so. Excellent!

* * *

Finding a suitable boat was proving a major challenge. My first preference was to build the Polynesian catamaran I'd dreamt of while aboard *Lionheart*. I had even commissioned some professional plans for a Tiki 46. It was, naturally, 46 feet long with two masts and gaff rigged wing sails. While most catamaran designers were building giant boats that look like a block of flats on the water and cost a bomb, the designer I'd chosen, James Wharram, was into tying the hulls and beams with rope in the traditional Polynesian way, so the vessel could flex with the ocean, rather than force its way through it. James also designed his craft so the layman could build the vessel in his backyard out of plywood, making the dream of sailing into the sunset much more attainable for the average Joe.

Alas, such a craft would take more than a year to build and I had a tentative departure date of only six months. If I were delayed I'd have to wait another nine months for the right season before I could leave. Yet, I still wanted to sail something that would reflect the timeless journey of Kijana. I had great admiration for the men and women who discovered new lands and embarked on epic adventures without modern technology – under sail on wooden boats, navigating by the stars with no electronic communication.

During a publicity tour to New Zealand for my book, I discovered a beautiful schooner at the Auckland museum. It seemed perfect, if a touch big, sporting a topsail on the forward mast which made it look like something Captain Cook would have sailed.

The curator of the museum told me it wasn't for sale and, if it were, it would be well out of my budget. It was occasionally used to take people out sailing and was a prized possession of the museum.

I must admit I was a bit ambitious hoping to buy a boat from a museum, so I turned to a more reliable source – *Trade-A-Boat* magazine.

Trade-A-Boat was my bible. I first turned to its thousands of advertisements when the idea of sailing around the world filled my head when I was 14. It was where I found *Lionheart* and, once again, its pages revealed what I was looking for – a 54-foot timber yacht that appeared to fit the bill perfectly. She was designed by Captain Pete Culler, an American fishing boat designer of the early 1900s.

She was a cutter-rigged ketch with beechwood decks and beautiful sweeping lines leading to a proud upright bow that gave the feeling she could take on any wave that Mother Nature would throw at her. She had a rear captain's cabin, engine room, main cabin and V-berth cabin up the very front. It was perfect for a crew of five. To top it off, she was built in New Zealand, which boasts some of the world's best boatbuilders.

I flew to Queensland, where the yacht was moored at Manly Boat Harbour in Waterloo Bay. The broker picked us up from the airport and took us straight to the boat. She was absolutely beautiful. (The boat, not the broker.) Her name was *Integrity 2*, and boy did the name suit her. The owner had taken 14 years to build her, and it was obvious he had put a lot of love and time into her. The broker said she was the best boat he'd ever seen and would have bought her himself if the timing were right. For once, I believed a salesperson.

I left the harbour convinced I'd seen the boat that could take me around the world. They wanted $295,000 for her, so I headed home to Melbourne to mull over the price.

It was time to turn my attention to the crew. There were three criteria for crew selection. First, and by far the most important, was the ability to live harmoniously together for up to three years. If the crew couldn't stand each other, Kijana would go nowhere.

Secondly, anyone who came on board had to be prepared to work. They had to be able to sail the boat, maintain watch in the middle of the night, and perform under the pressure of a storm. They also had to be able to take orders.

The third criterion was the specific skills needed to make Kijana work. I needed a cameraman, writer, mechanic, cook, photographer, dive master and first aid expert. However, if I took that many people the bloody boat would sink. So there needed to be a bit of multi-tasking on board. (I was learning something from hanging around businesspeople.)

The first person I turned to was Mika. She was a leader at Reach and had been over at my place in St Kilda lots of times. She was quiet, but confident, and I liked her a lot. I knew she was a good leader and wasn't shy in front of a group. There was something about her hard work and quiet confidence that reminded me of myself. But perhaps, above all, I was influenced by the fact that she was a girl. I felt the journey needed an even share of guys and girls. And she could write.

I invited her to dinner at a Vietnamese restaurant in Richmond, not because her dad was Vietnamese but because I loved the restaurant. I'd been there many times with my own dad. I didn't plan on asking her to join my crew that night. I wanted to know how good she was at writing, as I knew she had written plays for Reach and I hoped she could write the web updates during the voyage. Halfway through my noodle soup, as Mika balanced a shrimp on the end of her chopstick, I decided to broach the subject of her joining Kijana. I felt pretty confident she was the right person, so it all came out. I felt my face turn red as I asked her and she blushed too but acted quite calm about it. She said she was very interested and wanted me to talk more about it. She finished her meal while I kept chatting about my adventure dream. We walked back to our cars and I said I'd be in touch. She later told me that once she was in her car she let out a scream of excitement and sang at the top of her voice all the way home.

Josh was my next selection. Not long after I met him the pair of us joined another of his mates, Jules, and headed to Queensland in an attempt to make a documentary on Schoolies' Week, the annual migration of school leavers to the Gold Coast. He'd proven to be a capable cameraman, so when it came time to choose someone to do that job he was my first and only choice. Josh was over at my flat fiddling with the TV and I was putting some dishes away when I broached the subject.

'Hey Josh, you know how I need a cameraman for the trip? Well, would you like to come and be that person?'

He stuck his head around the corner with a petrified look on his face. 'What? Tell me you're joking. Are you joking?'

I smiled a huge grin and said no, I was serious. I wasn't sure if he was about to cry as he walked into the study and stuck his head near the window. 'I need some fresh air,' he said. There was no need for Josh to say anything else. I knew he'd signed on.

I now had a writer and a cameraman. The third crew position would be filled by my brother Beau.

At first glance, we didn't appear to be the closest of brothers, as we had very different personalities, but we had a deep respect for each other. We also carried the strong bond from the experiences we'd shared, having seen our parents separate when we were young. The separation affected Beau and me differently. I was shy and conservative and was too scared of confrontation to get into trouble at school, instead escaping into my head with dreams of adventures. Beau was the opposite, getting into all sorts of trouble as he dealt with his demons, being booted out of school for smoking marijuana and being caught stealing stuff.

This, of course, had caused considerable grief for Mum, and being the eldest son, I felt compelled to take him away from the distractions of home. I figured if I could get him away and give him some of the experiences I had had on *Lionheart*, at least he could then make his own life choices from there.

But there were also more practical reasons why I chose him. He knew how to take a great photo and cook a good meal, having trained as a chef. And after sailing the small catamaran with Dad along the Queensland coast when we were kids, as well as our sea kayak expedition together in Papua New Guinea, I knew he would perform when it mattered, that I could trust him in a crisis. He may have driven me mad at times, but I knew I could live with him.

To me, it was a young dream team – Mika was the oldest, at 23, Beau was 18, I had just turned 20 and Josh was nearly 21.

The four of us flew to Queensland to inspect the boat I was considering buying. I wanted to see their reaction to what could be our home for up to three years. Beau made a beeline for the kitchen, while Josh joked that we should change her name from *Integrity* to *No Integrity*. Mika spent her time quietly looking around, imagining what it was going to be like sailing the world on such a craft.

I boarded the plane home even more convinced that it was the boat for us. The others knew nothing about boats, so I went to great lengths to explain that she was sturdy and had a good layout compared to most boats I'd seen. I must have been convincing, for they were soon converts to the obvious merits of the boat.

As a 54-footer, she could easily accommodate five crew, so the search was on for our final member. The thinking on the role of the fifth member had started to change. What was becoming more important than finding a grease monkey was to find someone who could help get our message to a wider audience. That meant turning to the world's biggest market – the United States. If we could get an American on board it could really open some doors.

We advertised the crew position on our website, with applicants asked to answer questions and send in a video of themselves. The news that we were looking for a crew member spread, and applications began to pour in from around the globe.

Each time we received a little red ticket informing us a package had arrived someone would race to the post office; then we'd eagerly gather around to watch the applicant's video. Some people were totally wacky, others were shocking, even going so far as to leave some rather suggestive offers towards the captain, while others took a more conventional approach, talking directly to the camera. The advertisement on our website stipulated that applicants must be aged 18 to 23, but that didn't deter many applicants aged well into their forties from putting forward the case for experience.

We had a difficult decision ahead of us, for we were still not sure what we were looking for. We preferred a girl, but it wasn't a prerequisite; we wanted someone who acted normal in front of the camera, yet they had to have an interesting personality; they had to be easy to live with, but how the hell could we determine that from a three-minute tape; and they had to be willing to try new things, for which we could only take their word. We desperately hoped somewhere among those little red tickets would lie the perfect crew member.

One day, it appeared our hopes had come true.

Josh had grabbed the mail early and watched the tapes before the rest of us. When we arrived, he said there was a tape we should take a look at. It was sent by a girl called Nicolette, from Michigan in the United States. I was getting to know that if Josh was excited, it was a pretty good recommendation. As a female American, she'd already passed a couple of major hurdles.

We gathered together to watch her tape. She was driving in her car talking to her friend who held the camera. On the car radio was a song that I liked. She took us on a tour of her home town, which was called Hell. We all thought this was pretty funny. She had long brown hair and a great laugh. At the conclusion of the tape she sat on her couch with some soft music in the background. She looked into the lens as it zoomed in on her face and told us: 'I'm at a point in my life when I have to make decisions and, well, this just feels right for me'.

As a group we sat there, awestruck as the tape ended and the screen went to blue. We all believed her.

Things were really rolling by this stage. We successfully negotiated to buy *Integrity* for $285,000 in September 2001, immediately changing her name to *Kijana*. The excitement was palpable as Dad, Beau, Josh and I sailed her out of Brisbane, bound for Melbourne, where she would undergo her transformation to an around-the-world adventurer. It was the first time Josh had sailed and the first time Beau had been offshore. It was also my first time on the water since the solo trip, and it felt just right. I'd almost forgotten the sensation of a yacht leaning with a full sail of wind.

She sailed just as I had imagined – with direction and confidence. No wonder she'd been named *Integrity*. I remember being pleased at how little she pitched over the swell, due to her length. *Lionheart*, at only 34 feet, would have had us rocking up and down with every small wave. She definitely felt like a sturdy traveller, one that would easily carry a novice crew around the world.

Back in Melbourne, my days were busy but the nights were becoming increasingly lonely. I had the best group of friends, but on weeknights I would arrive home alone after a busy day feeling that something was missing. Of course, I'd spent many nights alone on *Lionheart*, but I'd never felt deprived of human contact because those were the rules of my record attempt. But since returning, something had changed. On one hand I deeply valued my own space, yet I craved to be close to someone just as much. I had never had a girlfriend before because I'd always felt so inadequate impressing the opposite sex. But now that I was 20 I had the sudden urge to bite the bullet and give the girlfriend thing at least a go.

I would never had thought to try my chances with Maya had it not been for Chocko's encouragement, so I asked him to track down her number from one of her friends. By the time she got my message on her phone asking her out to dinner, I assumed she knew I was chasing her. Luckily, she still said yes. I wanted her to say she was free the following evening, but the date was set for her to come over to dinner at my flat later in the week.

The day of our dinner-date finally arrived and I was as nervous as hell. I'd seen her a few times since her birthday, but always in the company of friends. I chopped the onions and had the oil warming in the pot while I waited for her to be dropped off by a friend. She was 15 minutes late, even though she lived just around the corner. God, those 15 minutes dragged on.

Finally the intercom rang, jolting me out of the 'she's not coming' routine. I turned up the heat on the stove, dumped the onions in the pot and casually opened the door as if I had forgotten she was coming. By the time she came up the stairs, a fantastic smell was wafting through my flat, giving her the impression that I was an accomplished chef instead of a nervous wreck.

The encounter was uncomfortable at first. In fact, it was uncomfortable for most of the night. Maya leaned up against the kitchen doorway while I busied myself with the cooking. Even through the smoke she was the most beautiful girl I had ever seen. I desperately wanted to watch her as she spoke but I couldn't bring myself to stare for very long. Instead, I had to settle with making a vegetarian sauce.

I wanted to tell her she was as beautiful as her namesake – Maya Bay in Thailand – one of the places I dreamed of visiting on *Kijana*, and the location of the Leonardo DiCaprio film *The Beach*. But that would have been a bit forward so early into our first date.

The next two hours were spent discovering more about each other. I prayed she hadn't discovered that I stare a lot. At the end of the evening there was no goodbye kiss, not that I expected it. In fact, I would have been embarrassed at not knowing what to do next if we had kissed. It was an awkward night but something about the nervousness made me feel alive and I couldn't wait to catch up again.

Early the next morning Mika, Josh, Beau and I gathered around the speaker phone as the international number for Michigan was dialled. It was late at night for Nicolette and she was more than a little shocked to hear from us, but she sounded very pleased. She said she liked playing guitar and singing. Mika asked if she would sing for us. She took a few moments and sang a bluesy song amid the heckling of her family in the background. I put my captain's hat on and explained that we expected to go through some hard times out on the water. We'd be covered in salt for days on end and have to live on a schedule of night watches and catnaps. We'd be seasick and homesick and there'd be storms and fights. She confidently told us she knew what such a trip would involve and she was still determined to join us. We all felt she was the perfect choice.

The following week we told her she'd been short-listed even though we knew she was the one.

I continued to eagerly pursue Maya. We were becoming more comfortable in each other's company, until we did what I had dreamt of for so long – we kissed each other. Not a goodbye peck, but a full-on kiss, just like in the movies.

· I was sitting on the couch at my place and the conversation about the movie we'd been watching had run dry. She was sitting on the carpet but I wanted her next to me. I didn't know what to do so I decided to go for it the only way I could think of – I grabbed the doona off the couch and pulled it over my head to form a tent.

I asked her, in a slightly muffled voice, if she'd like to join me.

'What for?' she asked.

'So we can kiss,' I replied. (You're embarrassed. How do you think I feel writing this!)

I stuck my head out from under the doona to see her blushing. She was sitting dead still, facing away from me. My eyes followed her line of sight, to the imaginary spot on the wall she was staring at. A few moments passed until I spoke again. 'Well, do you want to come under here or not?'

Thankfully she said yes, but I could tell she was embarrassed. She still refused to look at me, so I explained that was why I had the doona – so we couldn't see each other. I reached down and helped her onto the couch. With a flick of the doona we were in complete darkness. It was the first time I'd kissed a girl while sober. It was an amazing feeling and my embarrassment soon passed, allowing me to concentrate on the subtleties of the experience. It felt nice and warm and she tasted as pure as she looked.

After a few weeks I noticed how I became a different person when I spent time around her. Often I'd break into a stupid impromptu dance of excitement when I saw her. It was childish but I didn't care. I really looked forward to the simple things when I saw her – the sound of her voice, her expressions, her timidity, even the way she said my name. I loved everything about her.

Of course, overshadowing this feeling of euphoria was the fact that I would be leaving in three months on a three-year voyage around the world. Also, she was already locked into spending several months on a long-planned working holiday to Canada, departing in a little over a month.

The thought did cross my mind more than once that Maya could perhaps be our fifth crew member, despite the fact she'd never brought up the possibility of joining us. However, I didn't have the guts to front the crew and office team with the suggestion to bring my brand new girlfriend on board. And I knew we were promoting Kijana as an adventure trip, not a cruise aboard the Love Boat.

Two months after our first date, I saw Maya off at the airport and, for the first time, I saw her cry. She was trying hard not to let me see her tears, putting her head on my shoulder and holding me tight.

I didn't know what to say. If all went to plan she'd be back in a few months, by which time I'd be sailing the world.

I wished her well, then she turned and walked through those awful airport doors that seem to swallow people and break hearts.

I immediately threw myself into preparations for the trip. I sold my car and commandeered Dad's old Valiant, then listed my flat for sale. Everything I had was going towards my ultimate dream. Besides, I wouldn't need a car or a place to live – *Kijana* would soon be my new home. I also liked the idea of getting rid of my 'stuff', and streamlining my life.

The flat sold for a higher price than I'd paid, which was nice, and once the loan was paid back I had about $50,000 to further invest in Kijana – everything I owned.

Around the same time we informed Nicolette of her successful application. Within weeks she arrived, shuffling between Mum's house and my flat, which I was allowed to live in until *Kijana* departed.

Nicolette was everything we'd expected, and almost straightaway her presence began to pay dividends. Since we confirmed that Nicolette was on board we had heard from a large American publisher interested in discussing an advance on a possible book about the journey. If we could secure the deal it would give us more financial freedom and allow us to embark on some great adventures.

We had what seemed like a million things to organise as our departure date screamed towards us. Every aspect of the boat fit-out had to be decided on, then completed. And then there was stuff like medical training, undertaken by Mika, Beau and Josh at Melbourne's Alfred Hospital.

Kijana was looking a treat. Over the previous month dozens of people had swarmed over her as she sat in a cradle out of the water. The crew and friends had helped sand back the anti-fouling before she was repainted with five coats of toxic paint to stunt the growth of barnacles. All this was conducted under the expert eye of Dad, who had assumed the role of boat manager, as he had with *Lionheart*. He organised tradespeople to oversee the electrics, the welding that would support the solar panels and wind generators, and an overhaul of the engine. The mast came out and the rigging wire was replaced, thanks to some friends who supplied wire cable. She even had new red sails that complemented her traditional design. And of course, she had a brand new name across her stern – *Kijana*.

On board was a full inventory of new equipment – dinghies, scuba diving gear, computers, cameras, a fold-out satellite phone, even a PlayStation 2 with heaps of games. The boat had been kept free of sponsor logos thanks to the hard work of our team and the understanding of sponsors.

Once she hit the water our intention was to learn to sail our new boat as a team, but the organising, sponsor meetings, media interviews and equipment installation left us with only a few weekends to head out on the bay and get familiar with our new home. However, I wasn't too worried. I'd only sailed *Lionheart* a couple of times before I embarked on my solo trip. I knew that once we got the trip underway we could take it slowly and learn as we went.

Getting to the starting line on time, however, was something I was less confident of.

We worked every waking hour to get ready for our launch. It had become such a big production that there was no way we could delay the start because of the level of media interest in the trip.

As the departure date loomed, the work increased and one day melted into the next. It was exciting, especially working on the boat, where a carnival-type atmosphere had developed among the crew and helpers. But with the excitement came stress, particularly for the office crew, who were juggling sponsors, the media, organising the launch event and keeping an eye on a crew of young novices.

On the business side of things, the sea crew looked to the office team for direction. They were older and experienced with business and public relations. For the boat preparations and logistics everyone looked to me. I assigned each crew member certain tasks and responsibilities. Beau decked out the galley, Mika wrote presentations and Josh took care of the production equipment. Nicolette had, unfortunately, arrived at the last minute and didn't have the experience to tackle any tasks on her own. To make matters worse, no one had the time to explain anything to her, so she was just expected to fit in and help out where she could.

The day before our departure we headed to the yacht club to pack our equipment and personal belongings into the tight spaces below decks. All the crew was there except Nicolette and no one knew where she was for the entire day.

Aboard *Kijana* I was relieved to find we had more room than I'd expected, but it still took well into the evening to get everything in place.

I returned home to my flat for the last time, still unsure where Nicolette was and mildly concerned that none of her stuff had been packed or that she wouldn't know where everything had been placed on board.

My concern turned to anger when she arrived at my flat later that night having spent the entire day shopping. With less than 12 hours until departure, I had neither the time nor the inclination to raise my concerns with her. She was, after all, the least experienced, so I was willing to forgive a one-off indiscretion. As it was, I didn't get much sleep that night as I wrestled with last-minute problems.

In the meantime, Maya had decided to come home from her Canadian trip. She was scheduled to arrive in Melbourne the morning *Kijana* departed. I was over the moon when she told me, but came down to earth with a thud when she said she wasn't sure if she wanted to come to the marina to see me, for she feared she'd be too upset. Her flight was arriving early in the morning so I offered to meet her at the airport, as I wasn't due to leave until late morning. She said she'd prefer I did what I had to do and not worry about her. That was easier said than done.

Departure day, 10 March 2002, finally arrived. For months it had felt such a long way off, and now it was here. But there was no fanfare as the sun rose, just a bloody lot of hard work ahead of us.

I said a quick goodbye to my flat as Nicolette and I packed the last few boxes into Dad's car and drove to Sandringham Yacht Club where *Kijana* sat silently by the dock. I wondered if she knew what lay ahead.

Unfortunately, it wasn't a simple matter of jumping on the boat and leaving, as I had done on *Lionheart*, a little over three years before. This was a slicker affair, with freebies and music, and a crowd of thousands. There was a formal function for everyone who had helped us get out on the water and a video presentation highlighting what we hoped lay ahead. The Victorian Government even sent along the Deputy Premier to say a few words.

One by one, each of the crew, adorned in our uniform – T-shirts bearing the names of our biggest sponsors – was presented to the audience and asked to say a few words. There were plenty of tears and laughs, particularly from Josh, and then it was my turn. I'd given little thought to what I was going to say, but I knew that whatever I said I needed to thank those who had helped get us to that point.

I directed most of my appreciation to Mum, Dad and the office team who'd done so much for me and the crew to get us to this point. Then, out of the corner of my eye, I spied Maya. She had slipped in unnoticed and unannounced. Her face flushed red when our eyes met. I'd been thinking about her all morning and suddenly she was there. I hadn't seen her for nearly three months and suddenly, in a crowded room swimming with emotion and television cameras, she just appeared. My lips started to shake and my mind began to swim. I was about to break down in front of everyone. So I quickly finished with: 'I just do what I want and I get all this help.'

Reading those words on a cold page makes it appear like the jabbering of a spoilt brat. But I honestly felt I was the luckiest person in the world – I was able to actually follow my dreams, and all these wonderful people were willing to help me. I felt as though I had everything in the world – everything.

I stepped off the stage and began to battle my way through the crush of well-wishers. It seemed to take forever, but I was finally able to touch Maya. I wished we were alone, not surrounded by hundreds of people. Holding her hand as if it were my lifeline, we slowly made our way down to the water.

The jetty was crammed with family, friends and everyone from the Kijana office, while thousands more lined the shore. Outside the marina lay dozens of spectator craft waiting to escort us down the bay. It was chaos.

Beau, Mika, Josh and Nicolette slowly made their way to the boat, wishing their loved ones goodbye. The media was clamouring to get their best shots and the TV crews staged a mini press conference with the crew on board. Josh had brought along his fake teeth and put them in for the photographs. We had a group photo of the land and sea crews together at the front of the boat, then Maya and I sat on the deck talking and smiling at each other.

Suddenly it was 11 a.m., the scheduled time of departure – an around-the-world odyssey had to start sometime. I said goodbye to Mum and Dad and started the engine. Maya was trying not to look at me as she wiped tears from her face. I told her she was beautiful but she said she thought she looked horrid.

I wasn't the only one being torn from a loved one – Mika was leaving her boyfriend of seven years.

People started to step off the boat until only the crew remained. Beau and Nicolette undid the lines tying us to the jetty and pushed the bow out. I gave it a bit of throttle and *Kijana* began to move.

We rounded the breakwater of the marina, where the water was covered in streaks of wakes as yachts, motorboats and windsurfers followed us towards the heads of Port Phillip Bay.

Gradually they dropped away as we sailed the four hours to the heads. By the time we got that far there were only three boats left – Dad on his small catamaran, the office crew on a power boat and Mum and Maya with our friends, Steve and Julie O'Sullivan. Eventually they could hang on no longer, lest they end up on their own around-the-world voyage, and were forced to turn back.

With the boats disappearing from view, the only thing left to do was what we had all dreamt of doing for so long. We raised the sails and hit the big blue ocean. The Kijana adventure had begun.

CHAPTER THREE
FINDING OUR SEA LEGS

THE MILE-WIDE OPENING INTO PORT PHILLIP Bay from Bass Strait may be one of the most treacherous port entrances in the world, but it is a special place for me. Each time I've passed through it I've felt something new, as if being reborn by Mother Nature. Today was no different. The sunlight splashed across the coastline and a stiff wind sent spray flying over the cockpit, giving us our first taste of what was to come as we turned east. We were finally on our way.

Aboard *Lionheart* I had felt like a small dot in the middle of the ocean. Now, on *Kijana*, I felt like the captain of a real ship. While not exactly the size of Captain Cook's *Endeavour*, *Kijana* was much bigger than *Lionheart*, and was also much more sturdy and took on the waves like an experienced traveller. The conditions *Kijana* faced as we entered Bass Strait were far from dangerous but still uncomfortable enough for us to realise we were on an adventure, not a pleasure cruise.

I stood in the cockpit holding the wheel, every shudder of the wooden hull being relayed to my fingers. The crew was positioned across the deck, up the side ladders and on the bowsprit. I had an overwhelming feeling that my crew would prove just as sturdy as the wooden planks we were standing on. It was this feeling of adventure that I loved. With the salty spray hitting my face, the realisation of something that was once only a dream was satisfying beyond words. I wondered if the rest of the trip would continue in the same vein.

Dusk fell, revealing a starry sky that marked our first night together. The excitement of the day had finally passed through our system as we took time out to gather our thoughts and explore our new surroundings. The rocking sensation as we headed into the waves had finally quelled the enthusiasm of Mika and Nicolette, and they were officially feeling seasick. They had both taken the seasickness drug dramamine to quell their impulses to throw up, which, in turn, spaced them out, making the stars even more pretty.

Beau and Josh were in better shape. Their experience in sailing *Kijana* from Brisbane to Melbourne had given their bodies a taste for the movement.

As the sun disappeared, Beau swung into action to prepare our first meal. He immediately discovered that the bike pump required to pressurise the kerosene tank for the stove was missing, forcing him to prepare a cold meal of dry biscuits and guacamole with tinned oysters mixed into it.

He handed the girls their meal (you can imagine being served that while feeling seasick – they were less than impressed), then hit the sack at 8 p.m. after drawing the fourth watch in the early hours of the morning.

I wanted to make sure we got far enough away from land before I also went to bed, so Josh stayed on deck to keep me company. We sat at the rear of the boat, the glow of the compass lighting the cockpit as we talked about the day.

At one stage we were looking out into the darkness at the black water when Josh broke the silence by thanking me for asking him to come on the trip. I was taken aback, but I didn't think it was the right time to thank him for accepting my invitation. I knew he appreciated being aboard. I saw it in the way he did things. While Beau was the muscles of the crew, doing the hard jobs and committing his all to any task at hand, I considered Josh to be the apprentice captain. Even before we hit the water he was eager to learn everything about sailing, including all the theory, as if he thought I was going to fall overboard one day.

Josh may have thought I was doing him a favour, but, as I saw it, he was repaying me tenfold with his enthusiasm. We sat and talked about what he should do with the sails if the wind changed or a gust came through unexpectedly. His questioning gave me a sense of support that was invaluable. I knew *Kijana* was in good hands.

When I woke the next morning we were well on our way to Wilsons Promontory, the southernmost tip of mainland Australia. The conditions were overcast and the wind had died down a little. I was glad to hear that Mika and Nicolette had completed their watches. Each crew member had completed a four-hour watch overnight. Josh and Mika had kept watch after I went to bed, then Beau took over Josh's role, then three hours later, Nicolette took over Mika's role. I shared the last watch with Nicolette.

During those first few nights there were always two people awake in case any problems arose. Having two people on watch also meant you could keep each other company and prevented anyone from drifting off to sleep.

A keen eye had to be kept for any other ships, and every hour our position was plotted on the chart and course adjustments made depending on our progress and position.

Even though the girls were seasick, they appeared to enjoy life out on the water. The scenery was always changing, whether it was overcast or a blue sky, and we appreciated having finally left the hectic schedule of organising and the crowds. It was the first time in months that any of us had been able to sit down and chat without the pressure of having things to do.

It was great to relax and just enjoy each other's company. But there was plenty to do on board. For instance, in the months leading up to our departure, each of us had completed a navigation course. However, we'd finished it before Nicolette arrived, so she had missed out. We spent the first few days teaching her how to plot our position using the GPS (global positioning system).

It took us four days to round the south-east corner of the Australian mainland and start on our northward course. Although the wind was becoming increasingly fickle, I estimated we were only four days' sailing from Sydney, where we had an appointment with the National Maritime Museum for another media launch to drum up more publicity for our sponsors. Josh was also having problems linking the computer to the satellite phone, which was preventing us from emailing, so we were keen to get to shore so that Telstra could help Josh work it out.

The wind continued to die, forcing us to fire up the motor so we could make Sydney on time. The day before we arrived, *Kijana* was visited by its first pod of dolphins. Aboard *Lionheart* I'd got so used to dolphins that I forgot what a thrill it was to see them. In a mad rush, and amid screams of delight, everyone rushed to the bow to see them playing in front of the boat. Josh headed in the opposite direction, grabbing the camera, like a good cameraman should, before joining us.

We got to Sydney in time for a series of public engagements and got the email system working. Beau got his hands on a bike pump for the stove, while Dad drove up to help with more last-minute jobs on the boat. Most of the office crew were also on hand to organise interviews with the Sydney media.

After two weeks in port, we were ready to set sail again. Our departure felt even more crazy than when we had left Melbourne. As we were heading direct to Papua New Guinea from Sydney, Customs came down to the boat and stamped everyone's passport amid a frenzy of further media interviews. The call had gone out to yacht clubs to escort us out of Port Jackson. I counted at least 30 boats as we motored to the heads.

It was all a bit overpowering and confusing. We'd already said goodbye in Melbourne and there we were doing it all over again, complete with all the emotions. It affected Nicolette the most. With so many people swarming around her, all the attention took its toll as we sailed towards the open sea.

She sobbed as she spoke to her mother over the satellite phone with helicopters buzzing overhead and foghorns blasting in the background. Despite her discomfort, we knew it needed to be filmed. If we were going to make documentaries they had to show the truth of what happened on *Kijana*. That meant capturing the intimate moments we would not normally share with the outside world.

Within an hour we were at the heads, accompanied by only one boat. As soon as we entered the Pacific Ocean, the wind died down until it seemed we weren't even moving. Our solitary companion bid us farewell and turned back, revving its motors and leaving a trail of white water away from us.

On board *Kijana* the only signs of movement came from the clang of the rigging against the mast and the smallest of ripples that showed we were making some progress. What we needed was a strong wind to get us out of there.

The mood on board was one of melancholy. Beau read some letters from friends, Mika sat at the wheel with headphones on listening to music, Nicolette leant up against the mizzen (rear sail) mast staring out to the cliffs along the coast. Quiet tears rolled down her bright red cheeks.

But Josh's reaction shocked me the most. He was the one we could rely on to make a silly comment and snap us out of our mood. Yet, he too sat uncharacteristically quietly, mulling over his thoughts. I walked along the deck to where Josh was lying with his T-shirt covering his face. When he saw me with the camera he gave a look as if to say 'please, not now'. But he knew the rules and smiled reluctantly.

'What's going on?' I asked.

He took a few moments, his eyes red from tears, and looked straight ahead at the bright blue sky, as if it would provide the answer. 'I dunno,' he said. 'It's just … just … sad.'

I knew exactly what he meant, but I couldn't explain it in any better way.

There we were, on the threshold of an amazing adventure, free to go wherever we wanted and do anything we wanted, yet all we could feel was – sad?

Being the lucky ones about to sail the world hadn't made us immune to being sad. In fact, I suspect it had made us more susceptible to every emotion. It was as though we had been on a high for weeks, and now that we were finally on our way we were hit by an amazing downer as the reality of actually being out there and doing it dawned on us. With so much freedom at the tips of our fingers it scared us a little.

Josh dried his watering eyes and continued. 'I just don't want to let everyone down – the office and all the time they've spent away from their families. All the hard work we and everyone else have put in. I just hope it's worth it, that people can say they're glad we did it.'

The wind picked up slightly that night, but over the next four days our slow progress did little to lift our mood. One night we actually drifted backwards.

On one of these calm days Beau cooked a breakfast of bacon and eggs to everyone's delight except Josh's. As our resident vegetarian, Josh was the butt of jokes by Beau and I over what he could expect to be served up in Papua New Guinea.

'What are you going to do when they serve you up a slice of wild pig from a wedding ceremony?' we'd ask. 'You can't say no 'cos it'll be an insult.'

However, he had a good answer: 'If it's part of a cultural experience then I'll try it.' It soon became his mantra.

On the fifth day out of Sydney the wind returned and filled our sails and lifted our spirits.

The crew looked to me as their sailing teacher, but as much as I told them about how I did things on *Lionheart*, I was learning just as much from them. I discovered some of the crew were better at doing tasks than others. I found that I had to make a conscious decision not to always ask Beau and Josh to do the work. They'd spent more time on the boat, so had more sailing knowledge, and they also attacked each job with more enthusiasm. My major concern was that if one crew member began to dominate a particular job, the others would leave them to do that job all the time. I wanted everyone to be competent in all tasks, just as I had been forced to be on *Lionheart*. In an emergency, whoever was on watch had to be able to fix the situation.

It didn't take long before I noticed Mika and Nicolette were beginning to drop behind in the number of tasks they performed, relative to Beau and Josh. They were seasick again as soon as we hit some swell, taking comfort in dramamine and spending a lot of time in their cabin.

On the sixth day out of Sydney I woke to shouts of distress. Nicolette was on watch and I dashed up the steps to find her leaning over the stern. The inflatable dinghy had come loose and was dragging behind us, held to *Kijana* by only one hook. The other hook had straightened out under the weight of the dingy as it bashed about in the messy sea.

Soon everyone was up on deck to check out the commotion, Josh with the camera rolling. The sea was very messy, tossing *Kijana* about and damaging the inflatable dinghy as it bashed against the hull. I grabbed a rope and gave one end to Mika while the others unhooked the dinghy until it dropped freely into the water. We weren't moving quickly enough to worry about losing it, but there wasn't enough time to sit and think about it either.

I grabbed the other end of the rope and jumped onto the upturned dinghy. I was in my underwear and the water was freezing. I tied the rope to the dinghy before *Kijana* travelled too far away, while Beau tied the other end to *Kijana*. We dragged the inflatable dinghy alongside *Kijana* and tried to lift it onto the deck, but in the choppy sea the dinghy proved too heavy. Our only option was to tow the dinghy to land so we could lift it back on board and fix some of the damaged ropes that secured it to the boat.

We reluctantly turned on the engine and headed towards the coast for Shoal Bay on Port Stephens, the closest major centre settlement, which lay 15 miles to the north-west. I was aware we'd officially left the country, according to Customs, but maritime law states that vessels in distress must be able to land irrespective of their custom and quarantine status.

It was our first minor emergency and it was annoying having to head back to land. But what concerned me more was the obvious difference between the guys and the girls during the crisis. We had needed to act fast and with gusto to rescue the dinghy, and whether it was strength or commitment, the girls had taken a back-seat approach throughout the whole ordeal.

We were determined to make our stop in Port Stephens as brief as possible, which we managed with just an overnight stay while the hook was bent back into shape and the dinghy lifted out of the water and secured tightly to the davits, the steel arms used to hoist the dinghy on and off the boat.

We were not only sick of the delay in getting clear of mainland Australia, we wanted to avoid the melancholy feeling of yet another farewell. We slipped out of the harbour quietly without alerting the authorities, and headed directly into a north-easterly wind.

Once more Mika and Nicolette were sick, although not to the point of vomiting. It was an uncomfortable part of the trip for everyone, with an overcast sky and constant showers.

During the second night out of Port Stephens the wind eventually swung around and came from the south-east. This tamed the waves we were bashing into and gave us some good sailing. Travelling at a good speed, safely away from shore, allowed me to finally get a decent sleep. But on what should have been my first uninterrupted night I was jolted awake by the sound of Josh yelling.

Without thinking, I leapt out of bed and dashed up the stairs in survival mode. I was slightly annoyed when I realised Josh, who was on watch, had yelled out my name so I could see some dolphins. For crying out loud, I thought, I nearly knocked myself out on the hatch slide to look at some bloody dolphins. All I could see was complete darkness, with the lights of a few fishing boats dotting the horizon. What the hell was he on about?

'You know that sparkly stuff, what's it called?' Josh asked.

'Phosphorescence,' I replied, spying the familiar glow spreading across the bow wave, like angel wings.

'Yeah, well there's dolphins or something covered in it.'

I'd seen dolphins and phosphorescence while aboard *Lionheart*. When they broke the water's surface to breathe, the microscopic animals on the surface would whip themselves into a frenzy to form a fluorescent greeny-white glow, much like a firefly.

'Where'd they go?' I asked, still only mildly interested.

'Dunno. They were just here.' A few seconds later he pointed into the darkness. 'Yeah, just there.'

I immediately saw what he was so excited about. Gliding beside us below the water's surface was the outline of a dolphin in almost perfect detail. The bright glow surrounding its entire body made it appear as if we were being shadowed by a digital dolphin. Each flick of the tail sent fluorescent lines darting over its body, before they trailed off into a cloud of glowing water. It was so clear we could see the point at which its nose pushed against the water.

I was blown away and immediately forgave Josh his excitement.

'Wow,' I said, 'they don't usually look like this.'

Josh darted below deck and grabbed the camera. By the time I reached the bow he had returned and was behind me. There were four dolphins, perfectly illuminated as they played with each other against a perfect black background. I suspected the camera wouldn't pick up the phosphorescence, which Josh confirmed, much to our disappointment and they disappeared soon after.

The following days the wind picked up until it was blowing a strong 40 knots downwind. *Kijana* carried very little sail and was handling the long swell beautifully. But the sides of the boat were dipping low, to the point where water was constantly pouring onto the decks, and occasionally making its way down the companionways. Below deck it was akin to being in a washing machine, which was putting the girls through living hell.

The girls' sickness had been a constant since departing Melbourne 32 days earlier. Their inability to do little more than lie in bed and eat chips and chocolate meant we weren't running at full crew capacity, and with several weeks before our arrival in Papua New Guinea, the idea of pulling into Coffs Harbour, to our west, until the weather calmed and we dried our clothes and bedding, was greeted enthusiastically by all.

We changed course and willed *Kijana* along the remaining 23 miles so we could arrive before dark.

The sun was dipping behind the mountains by the time we

spotted the town. The harbour entrance was tricky and, as I never expected to pull in there, we didn't have the necessary charts, having to rely on one that didn't have much detailed information. Nevertheless, it was either stay out in the weather or get into the marina before dark.

As we entered the harbour a rain squall hit, making it difficult to see the rocks we knew were on either side of us. We made it into the small harbour as the light vanished behind the hills.

It was a nightmare trying to locate the marina, then, once inside, it was chaos trying to manoeuvre the boat in the small space amid the driving wind and rain. After half an hour of me screaming orders to secure the mooring lines to one side, then the other, then back again, we had one shot at coming alongside a large steel-hulled fishing boat, which was the only mooring space available.

It was extremely difficult to pull off without damaging our wooden hull, for the wind was pushing us into the fishing boat. *Kijana* had to be slowly steered sidewards, then reversed at the right time so the wind would push us into position. A few scratches here and there and a hoarse voice, and we were safely tied up, albeit soaking wet and hungry.

I apologised for my yelling and I knew I was forgiven by the relieved grins on everyone's faces. It was time to relax and get some food.

The trip so far had been uncomfortable for all of us. I was on a downer because I wanted to get to the tropics, away from the cold, wet weather. Most cruising yachts choose to stay in a marina until the season is right for travelling, then leave when the weather forecast looks good for a week. But we were in such a rush to get to Papua New Guinea to start our adventure that we were enduring appalling conditions. I decided to hang tight in Coffs Harbour until the weather eased.

The rain had stopped by the morning but the wind was still strong. Everyone had managed to get a good night's sleep so we decided to get stuck into the mountain of jobs that needed doing. I compiled a list of everything I thought needed doing, then asked everyone to choose a few jobs to do during the day. These included wiping the salt streaks from the wood in the cabin, washing the dishes, drying the carpet outside, tidying the sail lines, putting the binoculars and charts away, washing the deck and hull with fresh water, checking the diesel, drying the bathroom, retying and covering the sails and buying supplies.

Josh took his list of jobs and headed into town. Back home he didn't have a car, choosing to walk everywhere. I think he was glad to get off the boat and move his legs again after being cramped up for five days since we had left Port Stephens. The rest of us decided to get our jobs on board out of the way so we could go ashore too.

Some jobs needed two or three people to tackle them, but most were individual efforts. Mika and Nicolette seemed to work at a slower pace than Beau and I, and often asked annoying questions. Not sailing-type questions, but commonsense stuff that I thought everyone should know.

'I dunno, just make sure it's clean,' was my typical response. Any more effort on my behalf to answer a query on how to put things away from the table and I figured I may as well do the job myself.

About an hour later, I saw Beau grab his dirty clothes and I looked around to see that all his jobs were done. That's what I liked about him, he just did things.

He said he was going to do his washing, so I asked if he could wait a few seconds while I grabbed mine as well. I wanted to get off the boat as much as anyone, and I'd just finished what I had to do.

We had a bit of trouble finding the marina washing machines, then we had to get change for the machines. We had just put our washing in and started the machines when Nicolette and Mika stormed into the laundry and dumped their clothes on the machines next to us. They looked extremely pissed off and Nicolette had a go at us for not offering to do their washing. The thought had crossed my mind but I knew from experience that when either of them asked for a few seconds to get something it would take five or ten minutes. All I had wanted was to get away and do my own thing.

I could see that both were genuinely disappointed and angry, yet

I couldn't understand why. Nicolette reminded us how she and Mika had done everyone's washing at Port Stephens. With that, they put their money in their machines, pressed the button and stormed off.

I was dumbfounded. It was as if I'd been reprimanded by a school teacher for doing something I didn't know was wrong. It didn't take long for a seething anger to rise in me. My head was full of ammunition to hit back with. I began thinking of everything I wished I'd said. I wanted to cut them down and let them know how I felt about their performance, that so far on the trip Josh, Beau and I had done all the sailing, while we waited for them to stop being sick and start pulling their weight on board.

One half of me was saying I should be understanding because they didn't yet have the confidence to take the initiative on board, while the other half wanted to have a go at them for personally attacking Beau and me. I wanted to remind them that they did the washing in Port Stephens because they weren't doing anything else, while Beau was cooking a meal and Josh and I were trying to send our update on the satellite phone. Beau and I sat in silence as we waited for our washing to finish.

That night Josh was lying on his bed while Beau and I played cards in the main cabin. Nicolette announced she wanted to call her mum from the phone on the fishing wharf but didn't have enough change. None of us did, so I suggested she hitch a ride into town to change a note. It hadn't been dark long and the shops would still be open.

She disappeared and I went to bed, leaving Beau to clean up the kitchen. A few minutes later, from under my sleeping bag, I heard her ask Beau if he would go into town for her to get the change because she didn't know how to get there. It made my blood boil and I hoped he'd say no. After the laundry incident, my patience was quickly running out.

I was wondering what Beau would say, when I heard him say 'OK' in a tone I knew so well. It was the one he used when Mum asked him to do something he didn't want to do.

As he left the boat, I pictured him taking the note and walking in the dark to find a passing car, arriving in town, changing the note and arriving home a couple of hours later, all so Nicolette could call her mum.

The next morning he told me how the guy he got a lift with was smoking a joint and Beau had been concerned at the speed he was driving on the winding road to town.

By the third day in port the wind was still strong with no change in the forecast for the next two days. I was becoming more frustrated at the time we were wasting. I wanted to get everyone into the tropics where the winds were lighter, the climate warmer and we could catch fish for dinner. So far we hadn't caught one fish!

We were only 140 miles from Byron Bay, the easternmost point of the Australian continent. At that point we planned to veer away from mainland Australia into the Coral Sea en route to Papua New Guinea. I was becoming increasingly concerned about this leg. It could take us several weeks to complete and there was no land on the way that we could call into to rest if this poor run of weather continued. I was also aware of a growing dark mood among the crew and was not keen to embark on a long leg until the mood had lightened.

The option was to continue along the Queensland coast, around to Darwin, then on to Indonesia. There was no reason why we couldn't change plans – we'd simply visit Papua New Guinea on our way home. The only problem would be explaining to those back home why our course was changing. I really had nothing solid upon which to base my growing doubts about the performance of the girls, so it would be difficult to use that as an excuse. And to change merely because of the bad weather would seem a cop-out.

I spent all day wrestling with my dilemma. It was all so complicated. I had the office back in Melbourne to answer to, and then there was the media, who were eagerly following our progress, sponsors and, of course, the crew themselves.

I was wandering around deep in thought when I stumbled across a Wharram Tiki, a Polynesian catamaran, at one of the marina berths. It was the exact boat design I'd originally planned to use for my trip, except much smaller. I inspected its construction and admired its beautiful shape. A part of me couldn't help wishing I was aboard this small 24-foot boat, rather than the huge ship I was in charge of, with all its associated baggage. I sat there for the best part of an hour with all my thoughts.

I spent most of the day away from the boat and crew. As darkness fell there was nowhere else to go but back to the boat. Beau had cooked us a great meal of dhal – my favourite, especially when it's cold and miserable. It was the kind of meal I needed and it meant all the more coming from Beau.

It was another subdued evening. I hung out on the couch in the main cabin (my bed!) and casually talked with Josh. He'd done much the same as me that day, wandering around, thinking and listening to music. While we talked, Mika was off somewhere, and Nicolette and Beau were in their respective cabins – Beau at the front of the boat, Nicolette at the rear. It may have been a large yacht, but you could hear almost every movement of the crew, no matter where they were.

I heard Nicolette open the slide to her cabin and go out onto the deck. It was quickly followed by a loud thud. Josh and I looked at each other and I said 'Nicolette'. Moments later she stuck her head down the companionway to tell us she'd twisted her ankle. That was no surprise. Nicolette was a self-confessed klutz, which was made worse by being aboard a moving boat. She would knock into stays, hit her knees against the stairway and scrape her shins against the winches. Her clumsiness was becoming one of those silly issues that was starting to bug me. Every time she bashed into something I winced because it usually looked like it hurt.

The boat wasn't even moving this time. Josh and I climbed on deck and inspected her foot. She seemed to be in a lot of pain. It made me cringe as I imagined how she felt. 'Do you think it's broken?' I asked. She wasn't sure.

We did some prodding and worked out where it hurt the most, which indicated to me it was probably a sprain, not a break. Within a few minutes she was feeling better and able to clamber over the railings onto the neighbouring boat and hobble to the marina toilets. Josh and I went back downstairs and started to play cards. About

20 minutes later Mika charged into the cabin to announce that Nicolette had broken her ankle.

'Yeah we know, but it's not broken, she just fell over on deck,' I said

She disappeared as quickly as she arrived, so we continued playing Uno.

A few minutes later, Mika returned and shouted down the steps to us: 'She needs help getting back to the boat, she's really hurt!'

Her tone carried the heavy hint of accusation that we were a pair of heartless bastards. I think she expected us to follow her out when she came in the first time.

'For God's sake,' I felt like saying, 'get your story right, Mika. She was OK to walk over the fishing boats on the way to the toilet and now, all of a sudden, she needs help to get back.' But I held my tongue.

Mika's tone annoyed me as much as Nicolette's seeming need for attention. Josh and I climbed the stairs and followed Mika over the boats to the marina car park where Nicolette sat in tears. We helped her to her feet and Mika got under one arm while Josh got under the other to help her limp back to the boat. There was no room for me to help so I stood there like an idiot, trying to hide my suspicion by looking sympathetic. Her red cheeks shone from her tears and through the strands of hair hanging over her face she gave me a look of total disappointment.

The next morning I called the crew together. I broached the idea of changing course to continue along the Queensland coast. I explained my concerns about such a long stretch at sea in possible bad weather and that the proposed route would mean we could call into land as required. I didn't say it, but I also believed that while we were still sorting out teething problems our home country was probably the best place to be.

I explained to the office how seasickness had been a major issue for the crew and how the rough weather was to blame. Once we got to the calmer water of the tropics hopefully the problem would disappear, but I needed to stay close to the mainland in case further problems arose.

There was unanimous agreement that the change of course was a good idea, so we officially re-entered Australia by notifying Customs. A weather window opened up two days later, so after seven days in port, we departed Coffs Harbour bound for Mooloolaba, on the Queensland coast north of Brisbane. It had been 39 days since we left Melbourne.

At sea, rather than leaving the troubles of what happened behind, I couldn't help feeling a growing divide in how I viewed Beau and Josh compared to the girls. It was not a question of experience. I knew none of them had sailed before so it was my responsibility to pass on what I knew. Nor was it a question of physical strength – Nicolette was probably stronger than Josh and me. Sailing around the world was a matter of attitude and approach, not skill, experience or muscle. I was able to sail around the world on *Lionheart* because no one was there to do it for me and I wanted the girls to approach Kijana the same way. I didn't think I'd made a mistake choosing the crew, I just desperately wanted Mika and Nicolette to start doing what I still thought they were capable of.

Our course was taking us nearly due north and, as expected, the weather became warmer. It didn't feel tropical but it felt like a good summer's day and the rain all but disappeared.

Five days after leaving Coffs Harbour we reached Mooloolaba to send our updates and take on fresh fruit and vegetables.

By the time we arrived, my mind was spinning. I didn't know what to do. The trip was not going how I had imagined it, and every time I searched for a reason I would always come back to the girls.

As soon as we docked we cleaned up the boat, then each of us headed off in our own direction. I desperately needed to get away from the frustration I felt when I was with the girls. Even the sight of them conjured up suppressed anger. I knew it wasn't healthy but I just couldn't quell the strong feelings I had.

I stood at an intersection on the main road and spotted Josh down the road. I caught up with him and we decided to get a beer. We tried one pub but weren't allowed in because of our bare feet. We decided to try further along the beach. Along the way we came across Beau, who was more than keen for a beer to accompany the fresh pack of rolling tobacco he'd just bought. We finally found a bar that would serve us, and sat down with our Coronas. It was nice to be off the boat, but it was nicer for the three of us to be on our own. We enjoyed each other's company and talked easily.

By the second beer I felt the need to share some of my troubles. I wanted to offload what I was feeling, and particularly wanted to know if they were as frustrated as I was. Josh was always brushing off the little incidents with a joke here and there, so I wasn't sure where he stood. I suspected Beau was feeling the same as me, as I could sense his mood on the boat.

I broached the subject by asking if they knew where the girls were.

'Probably back at the boat,' Josh said, with a slight, almost undetectable, tone of sarcasm.

Before I could say any more, Beau brought up the washing machine incident. Oh boy, it felt good hearing him talk about it. Not because he was getting stuck into the girls, but because I finally knew I wasn't being an unreasonable bastard.

Slowly, one by one, the three of us offered a little more. 'Did you see when she did this?' or 'I can't believe this happened', and so on.

I knew deep down that what we were doing was wrong. In a small crew, having one side gang up against another is not healthy, but it shared some of my burden, and that was a huge relief. Beau and Josh were thinking *exactly* the same things as me.

We discussed how best to handle the situation. All were adamant we wanted the girls to stay. I loved Mika, and she and Josh had been friends for years. We wanted them to flick a magic switch and tackle their tasks with gusto, without anyone asking them to do so.

The decision was made to confront the girls that afternoon. We went through our options. Neither Josh nor I wanted to be the one to initiate it. Beau was probably the best at confrontation but he claimed he couldn't think of the comeback lines quick enough to hold a good argument. Josh's friendship with Mika pretty much excluded him. And, he argued, he needed to be behind the camera to record the confrontation. I knew, as captain, it was always going to come down to me.

We walked back along the beach in a mood we hadn't felt for the previous three weeks. I felt close to the guys and I liked the fact that Beau and I were on the same team. At least one aspect of the trip was turning out the way I'd hoped.

We arrived back at the boat as darkness fell. It was empty. We set up the cameras and microphones ready for the girls' return, but the night wore on with still no sign of Mika or Nicolette. As we sobered up our bravado began to disappear, until we decided to put it off until the morning. The girls arrived back at the boat after we'd gone to bed but I remained awake for hours dreading what was to come in the morning.

It was unusual for us to have formal meetings, so after breakfast when I called everyone together I sensed that Mika and Nicolette already knew what was coming. I wanted to approach the issue as diplomatically as possible but, in hindsight, my style was probably too direct and accusing. I can't remember how it started but it only degenerated into a slanging match.

I told the girls that I was upset at how they were behaving on the boat. I said they needed to pick up their game, show more initiative and not rely on Beau, Josh and I to do everything. I was happy for them to make mistakes, as long as they were having a go. At first they were shocked and asked for examples. I asked Beau and Josh to help me out and the girls listened as they detailed a few minor examples. But it was hard to give examples when they weren't actually doing anything wrong. The point we were trying to make was that they weren't doing much at all.

They pushed for more examples and, regrettably, I reached deeper into my ammunition bag to make my point. That was a mistake because things started to get personal. In my frustration I started to accuse their personality types and things became pretty ugly as they threw their own mud back at me over my poor leadership. They were angry, confused and upset, and the tears began to flow. I was way out of my depth.

Gradually things clamed down and we concluded with the agreement that I would take more time to explain things to them, while they would try to help more with the work.

We left Mooloolaba the following day in good weather and favourable wind bound for Cairns, about 700 miles north. It was the start of the pleasant sailing that I had yearned for. We caught the first fish of the trip, a yellowfin tuna, by trailing a lure behind the boat. Beau prepared it as sashimi to mix with wasabi and soy sauce, as well as steaks for dinner that night.

The atmosphere was much lighter than during the previous leg, with the crew getting on well. Josh was integral to breaking down any barriers between the guys and the girls. His forgiving nature and will to make people feel comfortable proved a godsend. Everyone was pitching in. We rotated shifts each night and everyone did a two-and-a-half-hour stint on their own. The first shift usually started around 8 p.m., the second at 10.30 p.m., the third at 1 a.m., the fourth at 3.30 a.m. and the last shift at 6 a.m., which lasted until everyone had woken for the day.

The best shifts were the first and last. I hated the second shift because it meant being woken just as you entered a deep sleep. I reckoned third and fourth watch were better than second because at least you could get a good few hours of solid sleep. However, Josh liked second watch better than third. The final shift was fantastic because you could sit watching the sunrise as if you were the only person on the boat.

Most of the work during that leg involved plotting our position, reefing the sails as the wind picked up, or putting away books and dishes. Mika and Nicolette were doing more work, which was obvious – perhaps a little too obvious. I often felt they were putting on a show for my benefit, doing things so I could see what they were doing. They tidied ropes that were already tidy and suggested making sail changes when I was already in the process of setting up the lines. I felt like I was seeing straight through them, so my answers when they asked questions weren't as encouraging as they would have been if I'd felt their enquiries were genuine.

I was beginning to understand why I had such a beef with the girls. Once we hit the Third World countries, a lot of bad stuff could go down. In those times we'd need a crew that would take action for the good of the team, not so they were noticed.

However, I couldn't deny they were trying hard, even if they weren't doing things the way I wanted. And I had to admit I hadn't given them a clean slate from which to start again. I still held a grudge I couldn't shake. One part of me said if my heart was open and forgiving, they'd sense it and feel they didn't need to prove themselves to me. But my other side couldn't help but ask why they couldn't act with good intentions like Josh and Beau. If they did that *then* I'd lose my attitude towards them.

I spoke to Beau and Josh about the new approach of the girls. Once again, they felt the same way I did. I wasn't convinced that saying anything would result in any changes. I still had strong memories of Nicolette in the laundry and I didn't fancy another outburst directed at me. I figured I should just stay calm and continue as usual in the hope that time and better weather would change things.

As we got closer to Cairns I resigned myself to the fact that it simply wasn't working with the girls. Beau and Josh agreed. We concluded that there must be something in our personalities that didn't gel when we were on the boat, so I decided I would tell the office as soon as we arrived that we wanted the girls to leave. There seemed little use in having another meeting with them for they hadn't responded to our first discussion in the way I wanted.

We arrived the following morning and spent the rest of the day checking the boat into the marina. That afternoon I phoned the office and told them of my decision. It came as a shock to them as I'd kept a pretty tight lid on the situation until then. Also, we were only two months into the trip.

The office took what I was saying very seriously, with a couple of the office staff immediately jumping on a plane to come up and see if they could help us work through the problems.

Not long after they arrived, we sat on a remote beach out of town for a crew meeting. The main rule was that only one person could talk at a time and it had to be directed at someone. The person it was directed to then had to repeat how they understood what was said and if it wasn't understood then the person who spoke first had to explain it again until everyone was clear on it.

It began with Mika saying she respected everyone but that didn't translate into trusting everyone. That was not hard to understand considering Josh, Beau and I had been talking behind her back. Nicolette felt totally out of the loop and accused us of lacking compassion. She, like Mika, had been struggling with seasickness the entire trip and felt she owed everyone so much. She'd been flown over two weeks before we left, hadn't had to do any of the organising and was suddenly on a trip of a lifetime funded by someone else. She also felt like the token American, there only to provide an accent. She missed her family and friends and felt alone. She hadn't known any of us until two months prior, while the rest of us had known each other for at least two years.

I could understand her point.

After they gave their side of things I actually felt for the girls by looking at things from their perspective.

We talked for most of the afternoon, each taking it in turns to speak. Nicolette was getting upset and Josh was getting frustrated at the rules of repeating what had been said. He was finding it hard to explain the problem until it got to the stage where he felt he had to blurt out how he felt. He interrupted Nicolette, then summed up in a few words what I'd been wrestling with for the past few weeks.

'OK, it's like this Nicolette,' he started. 'Why should Beau get in a car with a stoned guy to get change for you? We're going to Third World countries where we'll be doing much worse stuff than hitching a ride. You have to be independent. Jesse wants it to be like this and that's the way it should be. It's his trip and it's his idea and we're on this adventure because of him. This is Jesse's dream and I'm more than happy for him to be the captain. This is where I think it comes down to – we could die on this trip. Are you willing to do that? I definitely think we could die on this trip, you know!'

My body quivered at how raw the conversation was.

Josh couldn't have explained it better. I was thrilled that he had backed me so much. He was closer to the girls than Beau and I, and was the one who hadn't wanted to come down so hard on them. Afterwards he told us how bad he felt saying it.

It had been such a weird day we decided to stay on land that night, at a backpackers' hostel. The next day, despite the meeting the day before, Beau, Josh and I still wanted the girls to leave. However, the office staunchly opposed any move to expel them, fearing the damage it may cause to Kijana's image.

We walked to the beach for another meeting. On the way I felt as though I had the weight of the world on my shoulders. I wanted to set a good example for the kids following the trip. I wanted to do the right thing by our sponsors. I wanted everyone's financial sacrifices and hard work to be worthwhile.

By the time I got to the beach I'd started to crumble. There was too much weighing on this trip to not at least try to forgive the girls. Nicolette and I spoke in private and I swallowed my pride and apologised for the way I'd ignored her feelings. It felt good to have a laugh together and the depressing feeling of the past few weeks shifted from one of my shoulders. Then Mika and I had the same chat. I felt I was taking the elusive first step. I hoped from all we'd been through that the girls would change themselves.

It was a total 180-degree turn on my behalf and it took everyone by surprise when I announced that I wanted the girls to stay. We all felt as though we were starting afresh.

Everyone except Josh, that is. He was disheartened at how I'd changed my position so suddenly. I'd gone back on everything Beau, Josh and I had agreed upon.

I could tell he was disappointed in me, especially after putting his neck out and defending me the previous night. But Josh being Josh, I was soon forgiven. He even made up with Nicolette so there were no hard feelings between them.

CHAPTER FOUR
MIRACLE

OUR NEW SENSE OF UNITY, TOGETHER WITH the fact that we'd hit the tropics, made it feel like the adventure was only just beginning. We left Cairns under beautiful sunny skies for the day's sail to Low Isles – our first tropical island. Three hours into the trip we hooked a decent sized mackerel. We were now sailing the coastline that Beau, Dad and I had sailed when I was 14, which made my memories of that trip even more vivid. Nicolette played her guitar on deck and, for the first time in ages, I liked the sound of her singing. We felt like we had the whole world at our feet.

We approached Low Isles just after dark and dropped anchor in the lagoon between two small islands. Beau filleted the mackerel and, combined with the fresh food we'd stocked up on in Cairns, he cooked a sensational meal. We went to bed that night feeling pretty pleased with ourselves.

The next day we woke to a tropical paradise. Everyone donned snorkelling gear and swam to the nearby coral reef. We explored the mangroves and considered setting pots for mud crabs. The water was crystal-clear and small fish were darting everywhere. We chased a turtle in the dinghy, then went back to the boat for lunch. Low Isles was great but I knew a better spot nearby. Snapper Island was one of Dad's favourite haunts when he used to live in the area. It was eight miles on the chart, so we left that afternoon, arriving in time for a spot of fishing.

Not long after casting my line I hooked a red emperor, but Josh made me put it back in the water so he could film me reeling it in. All this mucking about caused the bloody thing to come off the hook and disappear. We accused Josh of plotting its escape because he was a vegetarian. The mood aboard was great. I was getting on with Mika and Nicolette better than ever.

We hung around the area for a few days, getting up when the sun rose and going ashore to explore the rugged beauty of the island. I started to become convinced our previous problems had stemmed from the bad weather during the first stretch of the trip.

We departed Snapper Island and continued north towards Lizard Island, a distance of about 100 miles, with the intention of doing some diving on the nearby reefs. The wind was blowing from the south-east, giving us a good run at a comfortable seven knots. If we kept up our speed we would arrive the following evening. I couldn't wait.

The mere mention of Lizard Island brought back such good memories. The island lies 20 miles off the Queensland coast, which means it is well clear of any muddy river water that affects underwater visibility. This makes the island one of the world's best diving destinations. The waters are packed with marine life, and minke whales make their annual migration past the island, providing a spectacular sight.

As the sun dropped below the horizon and the night sky began to spread out, we followed the shipping channel to pass between two small reefs about a mile apart. The reef closest to land could be seen by the flashing lighthouse on it, which made me confident we were on course to go straight between the reefs.

As we got closer I could make out the exposed reef at least half a mile to our right. Directly ahead was the flashing light on the left reef, which was strange, I thought, for it appeared that the reefs had shifted. Either that or we were heading on a wrong course. I decided to play it safe, asking Nicolette, who was standing near the autopilot, to change course a further 15 degrees to the right, in case we were caught in some current, which was pushing us closer to the left reef.

We were moving fast, so I rushed down to the chart table to check our position. I had a feeling there was some current, but how long we'd been in it unnoticed I was about to find out. The GPS took a little more than a minute to provide our coordinates, which showed we were close to the left-hand side of the channel, which was a little too close for comfort.

I was calculating all this in my head as quickly as I could, but as it turned out, not fast enough. As I headed up the companionway to change the course further to starboard I felt a subtle vibration that could have been mistaken for a normal creak or groan of a wooden boat. But it was enough to force my body into complete shock.

My heart and limbs snapped into action. It took only seconds for me to clear the stairs and realise we hadn't turned enough to the right and were skidding up onto the left-hand reef. Had Nicolette changed the course in the right direction, I wondered.

'Get the sails down!' I yelled. Everyone looked at me, momentarily stunned by my shouting.

'Just get the FUCKING sails down as quick as you can!' I screamed. 'We're in serious fucking trouble.'

The crew sprang into action. They still hadn't realised what I was on about until moments later the inevitable crunching of reef meeting keel got louder and *Kijana* ground to a halt.

'We're on a reef,' I announced, for the benefit of anyone who didn't know by that point. The boat felt very strange. All around us was water, but the usual movement of sailing over the waves was no longer there.

'Someone check the bilge. Make sure we're not taking on water,' I barked.

The sails, which were still up, were forcing the boat forward but she was obviously stuck. Each wave that approached from behind lifted up the stern slowly then dropped it onto the reef, sending a shudder through the rigging. The wave would continue its path along the boat, lifting the bow as it passed. I knew that the water ahead became shallower as the reef slanted upwards towards the surface of the water, while behind us lay the deep water. The seesaw action caused by each passing wave slowly edged *Kijana* further onto the reef, decreasing our chances of ever getting off.

Josh was torn between getting the camera to film the disaster unfolding, and helping to get the sails down. I'd always told him whatever happened, he had to film it. Even if someone got hurt, I'd told him, the others could help them. His job was to film.

He faced a difficult split-second decision. Every second the sails were up we were losing hope of ever getting off. When the tide went down *Kijana* would be smashed to pieces as she lay on her side on the exposed reef. If the boat was going to go down we needed to film it, but was the footage worth losing the boat over?

Despite what I'd always told him, I was glad to see him unwrapping the mizzen halyard to drop the sail. He knew how to take orders but he also knew when to break them. Beau and Nicolette were desperately trying to pull down the mainsail, while Mika was in the cockpit letting the yankee sheet free.

I started the engine and, without giving it time to warm up, slammed it into reverse at full revs. The motor screamed and sent white water streaming all around us, but *Kijana* wouldn't budge. I tried again, to no avail. I left the wheel and grabbed a radio in each hand to send out a pan pan on HF and VHF. In the marine world this is the emergency call one step below a mayday. A mayday means 'grave and imminent danger' and can only be used if a boat is sinking. For all other distress, the pan pan must be used. No one answered the call, so I handed the radios to Beau for him to continue.

'Try the higher frequencies,' was all I could suggest.

Darkness had descended and we were struggling to see anything. To add to the chaos, Nicolette saw one of our dinghies floating past. Its rope had got caught in the propeller when I'd rammed it into reverse, and snapped.

'Someone get in the other dinghy and go and get it,' I yelled. 'Everybody else, start dumping anything heavy over the side.' I figured that if we lightened the boat, maybe it would be enough to lift us off the reef.

Nicolette climbed over the safety lines to get into the small dinghy. This dinghy only had oars because, of course, the one drifting away had the motor.

The dinghy began to disappear into the night. 'Someone keep their eye on it,' I said, as if we had a crew of 20 sitting around doing nothing. Nicolette began rowing into the darkness while Mika strained her eyes to see where the dinghy was.

Josh had by now grabbed the camera and was pointing it at me. 'Has anyone answered Beau?' I asked.

'Yeah there's some guy, but the radio's fucking up and keeps going to channel 16 every time he replies and Beau misses what he says,' Josh replied.

'It's an emergency. Tell Beau to talk on 16 and plot our position to exactly where we are.'

I was frantically getting the chain ready to throw the stern anchor out to stop us from moving further up the reef when another idea struck me. I thought if we could get enough power by going forward I might be able to steer the boat around and at least point it in the direction of safety. My reasoning was that the motor was not as power-ful in reverse as it was in forward, so the only movement I was going to get would be forward. It was risky, and could rip the guts out of the boat, but it was our only realistic option. It would take only 20 metres to turn around and if we weren't fully stuck by then there was a chance we could get off the reef.

I couldn't wait any longer for Beau to plot our escape route, so I opened the throttle and pulled the steering wheel hard right, hoping the channel wasn't too far away.

The next wave picked us up and I sensed some slight movement forward. I hoped I hadn't imagined it. The next wave definitely lifted us, with the bow starting to swing to the right.

'Come on,' I urged, sounding like Lleyton Hewitt. 'Keep going.'

With the whine of the motor rising and dropping with each wave, we slowly ground a path over the reef, until we were facing east and the waves were side on.

'We're moving!' I yelled with excitement, but it proved premature.

We kept turning until we were facing the open water, but I couldn't straighten the steering because the rudder was dragging hard against the reef. With the steering on its hard right course we kept turning through south, then west, and all the way through until we were pointing north-west again, in almost the same direction we'd started from. It was painful. Not to mention the damage I knew we must have been causing by dragging the hull over the coral.

The wind and waves were growing bigger and the shallow reef was making them very messy. Mika was up the ladder trying to find not only the lost dinghy but, more importantly, Nicolette, who had drifted from sight.

'Can you see her?' I asked.

'I thought I did but now I can't,' she yelled back.

'Does she know how to start the outboard?'

'No, I doubt it.'

I suddenly realised I had a bigger problem on my hands than a boat stuck on a reef. There was no way anyone could row both dinghies very far, especially into those rising waves. Unless she started the outboard she would be blown either onto the crashing reef at its shallowest or past it altogether and out into the Coral Sea. And that was if she had caught the bigger dinghy at all!

With all the bad luck stacking up against us, I resigned myself to the fact that a search plane would hopefully spot her drifting up the coast and, apart from being scared and sunburnt, she'd probably still be alive.

'Just keep trying to find her,' I yelled towards the front of the boat, hoping Mika could hear me above the engine.

'Josh,' I shouted, 'turn every light on.' Even though we couldn't see her, I knew that somewhere out there she could see us.

'What's going on with the radio?' I demanded.

No one answered. I was clinging to the hope that someone would arrive to throw us a line and drag us off. I knew it was wishful thinking, as we were about 15 miles from Cooktown, the closest settlement, and few boats would be near the reefs at night.

'Josh, what's bloody going on with the radio?'

Josh stuck his head out of the cabin and announced that a fishing trawler was heading towards us. At last, something was going our way.

Mika jumped into the cockpit, still searching for Nicolette. Beau was manning the radio and constantly talking while Josh passed the updates on to me. Beau had also plotted our most recent position but the reefs were so small that the charts gave no indication if there were any channels nearby for us to escape through. I really thought this was going to end in disaster.

Amid the absolute frenzy of activity, I couldn't help thinking of everyone back home, especially those at the office who'd put the last two years of their lives into preparing our trip. I had let them down.

There was no sign of the trawler so my only option was to go forward again and try once more to turn around. All it would take would be for us to land on one sharp reef outcrop and jam the keel, and we'd be stuck forever.

This time I decided to turn left instead of right. I had no alternative. I swore and cried as I revved the motor and yanked the steering wheel to the left. I didn't care that I was losing it. I would do anything to get off that reef in one piece. I asked Mika if she believed in God. She thought about it for a moment, and slowly replied, 'Yes'. I yelled out to Josh: 'I'm gonna pray Josh, and whoever or whatever it is you believe in, please pray as well.'

I grabbed Mika's hand despite our recent turbulent history. She stood up while I revved the motor, and looked up at the starry sky. If it hadn't been so serious, I might have been disgusted at how corny the scene looked. But I didn't care. I was resigned to the fact that our only hope was out of our hands.

The next wave lifted the keel slightly off the reef. The furiously spinning propeller began to move us forward while I fought the wheel to continue turning us left. The more we moved, the more the wheel moved, until we had some momentum, passing west, then south-west, then south. I could feel the entire keel dragging on the reef as each wave moved us forward.

I battled the wheel to straighten up our course until I could feel the rudder turn. We were facing south, directly into the wind, and on course for open water. I quietly said to Mika that this could be it. I didn't want to raise my hopes again. All I had to do was keep the boat facing into the weather. If I veered too far to the left or right the wind would want to push the boat side on and we didn't have enough speed to correct it. It was akin to walking a tightrope.

I steered dead into the weather so the bow broke the waves right down the middle. I feared that any second I would feel the keel snag and stop us dead. But it never came.

'I think we're picking up speed,' I yelled to anyone who was listening. We hobbled about 30 metres until the bumps and scrapes petered out. It was the most amazing feeling to be back in deep water. I wanted to stretch out and feel the space around us.

'We're off, Mika!' I shouted, almost laughing. 'We're fucking off ... Tell Beau to get on the radio and let the trawler know.'

It was a miracle all right. We'd been marooned for 40 minutes. We could have been smashed to pieces on the reef, or waited for the tide to go out and our lovely ship to die a slow, painful death. Someone was on our side, for we'd been given a second chance that we definitely didn't deserve.

Beau and Josh looked like they were about to collapse with relief, but we couldn't relax just yet. *Kijana* was heading south but Nicolette was still somewhere out there being blown north. She'd be able to see our lights getting further away and either she was motoring towards us or rowing into the weather and being beaten backwards.

I dropped the revs so we wouldn't get too far away and began to think what to do. Beau told the trawler that *Kijana* was safe but we had a crew member missing and could they look for her. We had to stay in the area so she could see and catch us, but there were bits of reef lurking all around us. I didn't fancy going through that whole ordeal again. The other option was to anchor. But I feared that if the wind got stronger and the anchor dragged, we could find ourselves back on the reef.

As I mulled over what to do, Mika yelled out: 'I think I can hear something'. It was hard to hear anything above the motor, wind and waves. I strained to hear if Mika was right. She was!

'Get up the ladder and try to see her,' I ordered. Josh and Beau were also peering into the dark behind us.

'Yeah, it's her,' Mika yelled.

'Is she motoring?'

'I can't see,' she answered, but by that stage I could hear the unmistakable sound of an outboard motor. I couldn't believe it.

She came into view and I could see her struggling as the dinghy she was towing tugged violently with each passing wave.

'Well done!' I thought. She finally got to *Kijana* and coolly handed the dinghy lines to Beau.

'We got off, you might have noticed,' I said casually.

She had a beaming smile. 'Yeah, I guessed that.'

I had no idea how she managed to start the motor in those conditions, but she deserved the highest praise. She was so proud that she'd actually pulled it off. In fact, we all were.

We were all safe, the boat was safe and everything was almost back to normal. Except for the keel. Who knew what damage had been done. There was water in the bilge, but not enough to indicate whether we'd split a plank and were in danger of sinking. But the kind of crunching and shuddering we'd been through could not have been good. We urgently needed to know what damage we were faced with and how much it would cost to fix.

We motored through the dark for an hour before anchoring on the protected side of a small island. The wind was much stronger by then so Josh stayed up to make sure we weren't dragging. The rest of us went to bed, exhausted from the evening's ordeal. If it was adventure we were after, we'd just been served a big fat slice of it.

The following morning, Beau, Josh and I got the underwater camera and snorkel gear and plunged over the side to inspect the damage. The lead along the bottom of the keel had been gouged and scraped, but it was nothing that couldn't be fixed at the next major port. There was no obvious damage to the hull, which was another miracle. I remembered how many times I'd cringed as the boat came off a wave and slammed onto the reef. I knew she was a sturdy vessel, but she'd proven herself well beyond my expectations.

We got out of the water and had something to eat in the cockpit. The sun was beginning to peek through the clouds and everyone began to recount the previous night's events. Beau told how he was so full of adrenaline from talking on the radio that when he realised we were off the reef and the panic was over he felt as if he'd been out at an all-night rave.

Josh told Nicolette we had been praying for her. I glanced at Mika but didn't say anything. Holding her hand and praying out loud had been an experience we shared but would probably never talk about. Still, it was a special moment, and whatever we'd said together it had worked.

After breakfast we weighed anchor and continued on to Lizard Island.

Lizard Island is a complete contradiction. It is uninhabited and virtually untouched for much of the island, but tucked away in one small bay is one of the most exclusive five-star resorts in the world. Few Australians have heard of this small patch of paradise that caters to the world's biggest celebrities. The rumour sweeping the resort when we arrived was that film stars Brad Pitt and Jennifer Aniston were due in a couple of months. It's the sort of place that offers private beaches and the best in fine dining and service.

After we arrived, alas not at the resort but anchored in a nearby bay, Josh compiled an audio grab from the footage he had shot the previous night. We emailed the file to the office as soon as possible so school kids and the public could hear about our near disaster. But the office didn't want to release it. They argued that we should keep the good stuff for the documentary at the end of the trip. Plus, they were also concerned about the impact on current and potential sponsors if we showed how close we had come to going belly-up.

I understood the reasons, but nevertheless it cheapened what I had always felt was the very point of the journey. Also, it was annoying, considering how Josh had risked plenty to film what had happened so we could show those following us the most interesting parts of the journey. We ended up writing an update for the web, which sorely lacked the impact of the audio and our moment of drama passed by unnoticed.

The office then delivered a bolt from the blue. For a long time we'd been trying to get American interest in our journey. And our efforts had paid off beyond our wildest dreams. *The Late Show with David Letterman*, America's highest rating variety show, wanted me to be a guest on the show. It meant I had to leave the boat and fly to the United States for a week. It seemed a bit strange to leave the trip for the sake of publicity, but it was an opportunity we couldn't afford to pass up. We desperately needed money to pay for our expenses and we were certain we could clinch the book deal with the American publisher if they saw we could attract that sort of publicity.

As a bonus, I would have to fly to Melbourne for a night before flying on to New York, which meant I could spend time with Maya. The bad news was that the airstrip on Lizard Island was the only one for miles. With my appearance on the show not due for another two weeks, it meant *Kijana* would have to stay anchored at the island for a further few weeks – just as we were getting some momentum.

The effect this delay had on us was devastating. The disharmony among the crew soon returned. Somehow there seemed to be an association between being held back from getting on with the adventure and the guys' unhappiness with the girls. Maybe it was frustration at having to wait around.

We got to know some of the younger resort employees, and began to frequent the Marlin Bar, the watering hole for Lizard Island employees. These evenings were the only times the crew spent much time together, and even then we struggled to get on. For example, when it came time to head ashore, Beau, Josh and I would find ourselves sitting in the dinghy having already shaved, put on some clean shorts and sprayed on some Calvin Klein aftershave. As we waited, small waves would splash over the side of the dinghy, wetting us as every minute passed, while we waited for the girls to appear. Five minutes of this, with our shorts soaking wet, and our patience was worn out. One of us would be forced to jump back on board to investigate the delay and hurry the girls along. Josh, the diplomat, was best at this. He'd politely remind them that they could tidy their cabin during any number of spare hours we had during the day.

It was the same story during the day. Any spur-of-the-moment idea we had to liven up those weeks was rejected by the girls. It was as though they didn't want any adventure.

The two weeks felt like two months. Finally, it came time for me to leave for the United States. It was such bad timing. I knew the crew needed to keep moving, but instead they would end up staying at Lizard Island for a month.

I arrived in Melbourne late at night and was over the moon to see Maya waiting at the airport to greet me. It was such a bizarre feeling standing in a modern airport. My hair was salt-encrusted and I felt so dirty. I hugged her for a long time, then we drove back to her house and talked late into the night.

I was up early the next morning, had a warm shower and left for the office. I felt like such a cheat. I was meant to be on the adventure of a lifetime and here I was back in Melbourne. I met the team at the office for a quick chat about the publicity, before our publicist Flip, who was accompanying me, and I left for the airport for the 20-hour flight to New York.

On the plane I studied my surroundings. Everywhere was plastic – plastic walls, plastic doors, plastic seats, plastic wrapping. It felt cleaner than the brown wooden walls of *Kijana* but it also felt too uniform and perfect. There was no charm, no character. I knew how I'd rather make my way around the world.

I was served a small portion of fish squashed up against steamed eggplant. It seemed impossible to think that the fish I was eating had once been swimming in the same water that *Kijana*'s bow had been pushing through. I knew it was fish, but something about it was unfamiliar and didn't feel right.

It was dark when we arrived in New York and after 20 hours in the air I was totally spaced out. The cab drove at lightning speed in and out of the traffic. I was mesmerised by so much concrete and swerving highways. It made the place look like a futuristic city. The cab felt like a prop in a movie and there was steam pouring out of the sewers, like something from the *Teenage Mutant Ninja Turtles*. It was weird!

Since *The Late Show* had invited me over, other American media had become interested in our story, so the first three days were spent doing interviews. Flip and I dashed all over the city, catching cabs from one place to the next, then back to the hotel for another phone interview. We visited the Letterman studio with one of the producers to get a feel for what it was like before the actual night. From a publicity point of view it was a great catch to get on the show, but they were mainly interested in my solo trip on *Lionheart*. It was my mission to give Kijana a plug and try to turn the interview to discussing the current trip.

Despite the excitement, a few things were getting me down, besides the jet lag. Since seeing Maya in Melbourne I had become convinced that she should join Kijana. I got angry as I thought about it. Nicolette and Mika were clearly not working out, and I now knew Maya wanted to come. The issue of our reef collision was also eating away at me. There I was, on the verge of our greatest publicity opportunity, and I wasn't able to talk about the one incident that encapsulated the adventure and team spirit of Kijana. I felt like a bit of a fraud, as if I was hiding something.

The day of the show, 21 May, arrived. The producer took me through the questions Letterman was going to ask. I got the sense this wasn't for my benefit but because he wanted to hear my answers to make sure they were OK. I must have passed the test, for he made me promise I would give the same responses on the show. I said sure, I'd try.

Flip and I sat in the waiting room an hour and a half before a woman called me to the studio because I was due to go on. It was freezing and I was getting jittery at the thought of going on live TV in front of such a big audience. It was all up to me. I could make or break the success of Kijana in the United States, not only by the words I uttered, but by how I said them and how I acted. If I was too keen to push my point, I'd stuff it up. But if I failed to mention Kijana, then a lot of effort had been wasted.

The commercial break finished and Letterman started to introduce me. I walked out to applause and we started to chat. It went well.

He made a lot of jokes, mainly about sailing solo around the world at such a young age. He showed some footage from my documentary, and we talked until the next commercial break. At the end I managed to get a few words in about Kijana. It wasn't much, but they got on air. The cameras stopped rolling and Letterman checked his sheet for what was up next. A sound guy removed my microphone and showed me back out. And that was it – a month's standstill in the trip for a few minutes on TV.

On my final night in New York I received an email from Josh.

Jesse

Just found out you're not back 'til Wednesday. What the fuck? I miss my Martin and Lizard Island is starting to kill me. Supplies came in – only a little mix-up has it that we are right for Weet-Bix and precious little else.

Jesse, when you're here I can block out the other problems and just enjoy us hanging out. Without you this journey of five friends turns to shit. Pretty apt Kijana is in a language I don't understand because this 'Journey of young people' crap is beyond me.

The girls have edited a bullshit problems segment that is beautifully done to make them look like angels and us like heartless pricks. If only I'd filmed more of them, but how can you capture annoying questions, the times we worked at port and they shopped or the moments when the weather turns bad and we're the only ones left on deck?

Whatever happened to being on Jesse's next trip? Fuck, the media understand it, if only the crew could catch on. When did it turn from Jesse asking me on this trip to – 'I deserve to be here'?

They were asked on this journey. Get into it or leave and let someone else enjoy it.

Hope you don't feel the same. Hope when you return you'll smile and I'll forget this feeling. Somehow you being here makes me feel it'll all be OK. I miss you not being on the boat. Email me time of arrival back at Lizard so I can meet you at the airport and count down the hours 'til we leave this island. Sorry for burdening you with my crap. I just want this to be the dream we talked about in your apartment. The dream in the last page of your book about five friends sailing the world. I love that page. I miss that dream.

Josh

Josh didn't need to be sorry. It felt good to know he felt the same. I desperately wanted to get that dream back as well. My fear of being bossy and controlling paled in comparison to the fear of doing nothing and watching the dream disappear. I had to return and take back my dream. I needed to show some leadership, if not for myself then for Josh and Beau and the young people who were following our journey for the *adventure* part of our dream.

CHAPTER FIVE
HUNTING

WE RETURNED TO MELBOURNE, WHERE I spent one last night with Maya. Lying in her bed was the only place where I could forget about everything. Her soft voice reassured me that everything was going to be OK. She was so gentle that all I had to do was watch her and be in love. She never swore, even when she got cross at her dogs and told them off in an angry tone. Her voice gave the impression she was trying to be angry but she didn't have an ounce of anger in her. She was so much more pure than I would ever be.

For the first time we talked about her joining *Kijana*. She admitted she would be keen, but wasn't sure whether I wanted her aboard. I reassured her there would be no opposition from me.

I arrived back at Lizard Island at the end of May. The crew was happy to see me, because my arrival meant *Kijana* could finally set sail. The light plane touched down at midday and we weighed anchor that afternoon.

We sailed through the night and it felt so good to be back on the boat. We paid special attention to the surrounding reefs, keeping as far away from them as possible. I felt relaxed back on the boat. Despite all the crap that had gone down, I really felt I was home when I set foot on *Kijana*. But if it were truly my home, Maya would be on board. My desire to have her join me had grown stronger since I had seen her again. And Josh's email had convinced me we needed a crew change, for things just weren't working out. The divide between the guys and the girls had grown even bigger.

Expelling Mika and Nicolette would be complicated. The journey had grown into something much bigger than a group of friends sailing around the world. It had become a corporate thing, with many people having a vested interest in the trip, not least the sponsors and investors. My actions not only affected myself and the crew, but a long list of other people. The study kits distributed to schools, for instance, were already printed with crew names on them. Book contracts were being negotiated and TV pitches were circulating.

My preferred option was for the girls to leave of their own accord. I wasn't sure if this was going to happen, for I'd wanted them to leave in Cairns. To test their resolve, and to get my mind back on track, I decided to stop letting the girls affect me. I would focus on the adventures and if the girls fell behind or didn't want to become involved, then that was their bad luck.

The girls had the rear cabin to themselves, so they could talk freely to each other, but the boys had no such area, which made things difficult. So I decided us guys should have some time away on our own. After dropping anchor at Forbes Island, where we had decided to stop for a few days until Josh recovered from a nasty accident involving his hand and one of the spinning generator blades, I quietly suggested to Josh and Beau that we head ashore to camp for a night – just us guys.

'The girls will crack it,' was Josh's immediate response.

'I know. But if we want to go and have time to ourselves, then why shouldn't we?' The decision was unanimous to leave when the girls got back from the island, so we quickly got ready to load the dinghy when they arrived.

Nicolette questioned us first. 'Why do you want to go camping?'

''Cos we're bored.' Josh casually replied. Well, he was telling the truth.

As a parting gesture, Beau offered the girls some dip and crackers he'd just made, then we loaded the dinghy and waved a polite goodbye. We motored to a nearby island, relishing our newfound freedom.

We put our blankets and mosquito nets under a tree, then went exploring. The island was as beautiful as Lizard Island, but it felt much wilder. We ate oysters and clambered to the top of a hill where we saw crashing waves on the windy side of the island. It felt like paradise.

Back at camp we cooked dinner over the fire and felt free to make rude jokes without having to look over our shoulders. Then we played our favourite songs on the guitar late into the night.

The next morning I woke to find the fire was still smouldering. I was covered in sandfly bites and the smoke had infiltrated every part of our bodies and sleeping gear. Needless to say, I felt pretty ordinary as I blew a combination of sand and snot from my nose. It made us appreciate our nice clean boat more than ever.

Before heading back to *Kijana*, we vowed to remember that night forever. I even convinced the others to join hands and raise them in memory of the night.

Then we motored back to the boat anticipating a frosty reception. It never came. Instead, the girls were eager to tell us how much fun they'd had in our absence, staying up until 4 a.m. talking and having a grand old time.

We set sail almost immediately, bound for Cape York, the northernmost tip of mainland Australia. From the cape would be a three- to four-day crossing of the Gulf of Carpentaria to the town of Nhulunbuy on the Gove Peninsula, in Arnhem Land. This was the traditional land of the Yolngu people, where we hoped to spend a week living with the locals.

After two days of good winds we found ourselves one day away from Cape York. Josh woke early, as he usually did, to find *Kijana* sailing along with no one at the helm. Although the sun had risen, Nicolette, who had been rostered on the final shift, was slumped behind the wheel fast asleep. Josh told no one else but me and, despite the obvious danger of the mishap, I was perversely pleased. It was evidence too good to be true, made even stronger by the fact that Josh had pressed record on the camera when he found her.

We rounded Cape York and arrived at a river simply known as Number Two River. We'd passed Number One River and further down the coast was, naturally enough, Number Three River.

It was a part of the world relatively unexplored by white man and the perfect location to get up close and personal with the notorious saltwater crocodile. We headed ashore, where we found plenty of animal tracks along the riverbank. However, none of us knew what a crocodile track looked like.

'Everyone try to stay away from the water,' I ordered. 'This looks like prime crocodile territory.' At least I sounded like I knew what I was talking about.

The water was teeming with critters. Sand crabs ran into the deep water when our long shadows passed over them and shovel-nose rays stopped swimming and tried to blend into the sandy bottom when they sensed us approaching. We grabbed the cast net and fishing lines to see if we could catch some dinner, but the sun was going down, leaving the water too dark and dangerous to hang around.

We decided to call it a day and return the following day to try to catch some fish. As we began walking back to the dinghy I spotted what I thought was a small crocodile hiding in the water under a fallen tree. Everyone stopped. It was definitely a baby crocodile, probably about one metre long and almost totally submerged with just its nose and tail breaking the surface.

I asked Mika for the cast net, then slowly headed for the tree. I'd taken no more than five steps when, in a flick of a tail, it was gone. There was no way I was going to wade into the water to chase it. I didn't fancy meeting its mother.

Nevertheless I was pretty stoked to have come so close to a crocodile in the wild. 'How cool was that!' I said to no one in particular, as I watched the ripples disappear.

I could tell Nicolette didn't share my excitement by the expression on her face.

'Why would you want to catch a crocodile anyway?' she asked in a way that suggested I was being childish.

I couldn't handle her. Did I need to explain my every action to her? I was well aware how conservation-oriented she was. We all were concerned about the environment, but obviously in different ways. Netting a small crocodile wasn't going to hurt anyone and I couldn't be bothered skirting around the issue, as I would have previously.

'So I can wreck the environment as much as possible,' I shot back sarcastically, surprising myself at the outburst. But I was glad I'd returned fire.

She took off in a huff, storming to the dinghy, cursing my answer as she went.

Josh woke me early the following morning. He wanted to go ashore to catch some fish for breakfast. Beau joined us and we started loading the dinghy. We tried to do it quietly but the girls woke up, so all five of us headed ashore in silence. The events of the previous day hung heavily over us. I actually felt sorry for Mika. I knew she would have been happy to catch a crocodile, have a look at it then let it go, but she was pretty much bound by Nicolette's stance.

We motored to shore with our gear, including a rifle, one of two we had on board for safety's sake. I didn't want to kill a crocodile but if it was a choice between its life or one of ours, the decision was fairly obvious. We dragged the dinghy onto the sand and secured the anchor above the tide line. Five minutes later we crossed a ridge and came across a great fishing spot. But before any of us had time to set up our fishing gear, Mika urgently whispered 'pig'. We ran to where she was standing and looked in the direction she was pointing. A few hundred metres further along the riverbank stood some wild black pigs, feeding on weeds. They hadn't spotted us yet. 'Pig for lunch,' was the first thought to enter my mind.

Adrenaline began to surge through my body as I picked up the rifle. Josh followed with the camera and we left the others behind. We crossed over to the other side of the ridge, planning to sneak up behind them. I was surprised the pigs hadn't seen us yet. And I was excited at having the chance to actually shoot one for lunch. I had no qualms about knocking off a wild pig. In this part of Australia they are considered the worst vermin, with the Government making many attempts to control and eradicate them.

We crouched down and ran as fast as possible through the scrub. It took five minutes until we got to the spot where we figured we would have to cross the ridge again. If our calculation was out, we risked the pigs spotting us and running away.

I'd never shot a pig before, although the experience somehow felt familiar. It may have been the stories I'd heard about Mum and Dad living in a humpy in the far north Queensland rainforest. Dad would shoot a pig and share the meat with neighbouring families. I couldn't remember ever being with him when he shot a pig, but my mind had created images and false memories of being there by his side. When my parents separated, and Beau and I moved to Melbourne with Mum, I often imagined Dad, rifle in hand, providing meat for the community. As I grew up it was really the only picture I had. Now I felt like him.

My heart was pounding and I could feel it twitching in the veins of my neck. 'Keep low,' I whispered to Josh as we approached the top of the ridge.

I slowly loaded a bullet into the breach and flicked the safety button off. I raised the butt of the rifle to my shoulder with one eye scouring the scene ahead through the rifle's sights. Josh was behind me, virtually replicating me, his eyes firmly fixed on the viewfinder of the camera. I heard what sounded like snorting and glanced back at Josh, who raised his eyes from the screen to confirm he'd also heard it. It had come from behind a rise in the sand. I knelt down and braced myself. My heart was pounding harder than ever. I knew I could cover both sides of the mound at a moment's notice, so I decided to wait until one of the pigs wandered out. I could clearly hear them snorting and digging no more than 30 metres from where we crouched. A sandfly bit my ankle, but even that wasn't enough to make my concentration waiver.

Suddenly, something black appeared from behind the rise of sand. 'We're close enough. Let's just look at them,' Josh whispered. There was a hint of fear and desperation in his voice.

A second pig appeared, walking directly behind the first. Everything was dead quiet except for the grunts coming from our target.

At the target range where I learnt to shoot, the heavy calibre ammunition made such a thunderclap it would make me jump. It was the scariest part of shooting. The instructor told me I had to relax. If I anticipated the noise, I would jolt and my aim would be askew. Still, I never got used to the noise. But as I squeezed the trigger this time, I knew I was going to hit my target.

The moment I did all hell broke loose. One of the pigs began squealing and trying to hold itself up. Two more adults sprang out from behind the rise, with half a dozen piglets close behind. A large male boar with tusks ran straight for Josh. I stood my ground thanks to the confidence of a loaded gun but when Josh started running I wondered if I should as well.

Thankfully, the pig changed its mind and detoured into the scrub, followed by the trail of piglets. I moved closer to the wounded animal and fired another shot to complete the exercise. The squealing stopped abruptly.

The echo rang out up and down the river course until all that remained was a high-pitched ring in my ears. The sweet smell of gun-smoke filled the air as Josh and I stared silently at the body.

Suddenly I felt bad. I dragged the body under a tree and covered the blood-stained ground with sand. I was shaking – partly because I couldn't believe my success and partly because I'd just killed a wild animal and stopped its life. The sudden realisation that it could no longer rummage through the bush happily eating roots, started to eat at me.

I inspected its snout and glazed eyes. It looked cute in a funny way, which made me feel sadder. It looked like a mother. Those were probably her babies scampering for cover. I wondered what Dad would have thought.

Beau arrived with a bag slung over his shoulder and a fishing rod in his hand. He punched the air in victory. I was glad to see his smile. I wanted to know I'd done the right thing.

Josh swung the camera around into my face. I didn't know what to say.

'Are you ready to butcher it?' I asked Beau. He smiled and said he'd cooked pig before, but never cut one up.

Josh stopped recording and lowered the camera. I asked how he felt. 'Strange,' he said. I didn't pursue it.

'Let's clean this mess up before the girls get here.'

Beau baked the pig in an underground oven with peeled potatoes and garlic. Mika was keen to see what it tasted like, while Nicolette withheld any comment about the whole event and opted instead to eat the fish we'd caught. As I was not Aboriginal, Josh didn't feel he could classify the meal as a cultural event and break his vow of vegetarianism, so he got off on a technicality.

We left a few days later in brilliant sunshine. The Gulf of Carpentaria lay between Number Two River and Nhulunbuy, a distance of roughly 300 miles. We made good progress through the night and the following day. However, by the second night the wind had picked up and swung to the south-west, causing the waves to approach us from the forward quarter. The wind continued to strengthen, making the ride more and more uncomfortable.

The day we arrived at Nhulunbuy was miserable. Rain drenched us and *Kijana* was leaning heavily to starboard, fighting hard against the wind to sail around the Gove Peninsula and anchor in the safety of Melville Bay.

We arrived in Nhulunbuy early the following morning. It was the only township on the Gove Peninsula, with a population of 4000 people. Despite its remoteness, it had a supermarket, post office, video store and facilities you'd expect in a larger centre. Its relative prosperity came from mining. In the early 1970s the mining and processing of a 250-million tonne bauxite deposit began in the area, despite staunch opposition from the local Yolngu landowners. Their concerns were relayed to the Commonwealth Government via the now famous 'Bark Petition'. But they were no match for mining royalties, and the Yolngu case was lost.

I was nervous about what we were doing there. We wanted to spend some time with the local Aborigines, to experience something of their lives. But it couldn't be a token thing. I couldn't just rock up to a family and say: 'Yeah, me and my friends are from Melbourne. We're on a huge expensive yacht anchored out there, sailing around the world with thousands of school kids following our adventures. We want to hang out, you know, get off the beaten track with you guys. Be seen to be multicultural and all that. Maybe you could show us some kangaroos and stuff. We'll take some pictures and put 'em up on the web. Maybe I'll buy a painted boomerang …'

That wouldn't work – for the locals or me. They needed to respect us and we needed to show respect for them. I didn't want to do the usual tourist thing. I really wanted to get an understanding of their lives, how they lived and, possibly, the issues they faced. We really needed to go bush and live off the land with them. I was particularly determined to see what it would be like to survive only on what we caught.

The office had made a few enquiries on our behalf, so by the time we arrived in Nhulunbuy, I had the name and phone number of a bloke called Noel in my pocket. I gave him a call and we met in town. He was a white Australian who ran tourist and fishing tours out of Nhulunbuy, but he had a close Aboriginal friend who he thought might accommodate our request to do something 'different'. Her name was Gayili and she lived on the edge of town. He gave me directions to Gayili's settlement, and told me he'd let her know to expect me.

The next day I hitched a ride in the back of a ute to the Aboriginal community, which was basically a cleared area along a beach, with dwellings haphazardly placed in odd locations. About 150 metres along the beach a huge pipeline jutted 100 metres out into the sea, with a service road built upon it. Apparently it sucked cold seawater to the mine and shot out the used hot water back into the bay. Children ran along the beach towards me as I headed to the closest shack, keeping a safe distance from the sick-looking dog that stood in my path. An elderly woman sat outside the shack, oblivious to my presence.

'Hi there,' I said nervously, hoping she would understand me, 'I'm looking for Gayili.' A loud stream of aggressive language erupted from the old lady, scaring the hell out of me. Thankfully, her abuse was intended for a man sitting beside a tree, who I didn't see until he responded with a similar onslaught. The lady then pointed to the next shack along the beach. I nodded in thanks and continued walking.

As I got closer to the next hut, I noticed a little girl sitting out the front fiddling with colouring pencils. She looked at me for a second, before looking back at her pencils. I asked if Gayili was there. Without saying a word, she went inside, then came back out. A minute later a heavy-set woman aged in her 40s stepped from the house, shielding her eyes as she squinted at the brilliant sun. She had strong Yolngu features and glistening dark skin. I immediately realised I'd woken her from a siesta, which, I figured, was not the best start to a relationship.

'Hi, um, Noel told me your name because I'm looking for some help,' I said, becoming very conscious of what I was saying.

She said very little and was extremely vague, but she did acknowledge that Noel had mentioned me to her. I went into detail about Kijana, and what we were doing. All the time she appeared to be totally uninterested in what I was saying. I told her how we wanted to include her culture in our adventure, that we wanted to live off the land with her and her family so we could tell others what life in these remote communities was like. I couldn't help feeling she regarded me as just another tourist chasing some novel experience before heading back to suburbia. I probably would have if I were in her sandals.

She told me to come back in two days, with no indication if that meant yes or no to my request.

Back at *Kijana* I told the others we had no choice but to wait while, I presumed, Gayili was getting tribal approval. While we waited we all kept out of each other's way as much as we could, with Beau and Josh heading into town a few times, everyone calling home and Mika writing an update for the web.

At the appointed time, Josh and I returned to the settlement. Gayili was her same old understated self as she told us she would grant our request. She then, in her firm but friendly manner, told us what we would do. She wanted us to collect her and her family the following morning, then we would sail to the opposite side of Melville Bay for a week of camping.

'No problems,' we said. 'How many people will there be?'

She said she didn't know, but come the morning whoever didn't make it on the boat wouldn't be coming. I'd liked her way of thinking, but it didn't necessarily instil any confidence in me.

We organised to head back to town with Angela, a young girl in her early teens, and bought supplies for the camping trip.

We came back with flour, tea, noodles and salt and sugar. I tried my best to reassure Gayili that we'd like to attempt to live off the land, to make it a challenge and an experience as close to how her ancestors had lived as was possible. The food would be for the children, she explained. Then we headed off back to the boat to tell the others.

The following morning we brought *Kijana* around and anchored off the beach in front of the settlement. Josh and I took the dinghy to pick up Gayili and her family. Under a tree lay a heap of camping gear, while all around us energetic little dark bodies bounced about watching us move their gear. It was unclear who was actually coming with us, so we began loading children and equipment into the dinghy. Gayili, who was sitting under a tree, would occasionally yell: 'Not that one, she's staying here.' It was very confusing.

'Are you meant to be coming?' I asked one little girl who had perched herself in the very front of the dinghy. Her beautiful eyes stared straight back at me with no hint of reply. I looked around at the other children who appeared to be slightly older.

'Is she coming?' I asked. This appeared to be the funniest thing they'd ever heard, and they fell about squealing. The laughter eventually died down, so I searched for a response from anyone. The oldest looking boy, who's name I later learnt was Cedric, gave me what appeared to be half a nod before fixing his eyes on the sand. I took that as a yes.

'I'll see you back here for the second load,' I said to Josh as I helped him push the dinghy, which was loaded to capacity, towards the water.

Four trips later and everybody was aboard *Kijana* – two adults, four teenagers, four children and a dog named Cindy who was the only one to get seasick, spewing litres of liquid across the deck.

Once we were underway the introductions began. Due to the language barrier, the introductions between our ten guests and the crew were long and complex. We were shocked to discover that none of the eight children with us belonged to Gayili. As we began to understand the complex structure of Yolngu culture, this became clearer. In this tribe, as soon as a child was born it was given over to its 'aunty'. It never again lived with its blood mother. But there was a more practical reason for this in Gayili's case. The influences of mining and an abundance of money had corrupted many of the local Aborigines, leading her two adult sons and most of their friends to become alcoholics and drug users. This left Gayili with the responsibility of raising her many grandchildren and plenty of others.

The three youngest girls were gorgeous. Keesha was still a baby, at only two years of age, and the other two, who were not much older, played with her endlessly. Salomi was the next oldest, at nine. She constantly hung around Angela, who she obviously looked up to. Angela, at 14, was old enough to act as a mother for the younger girls. Cedric was also about 14, but displayed none of the maturity of Angela. Instead, he leapt about with the enthusiasm and cheekiness of a teenager.

Ian and David were the eldest boys. They were closer to our age, yet were perhaps the most distant. They didn't get involved in the games we played with the younger ones, preferring to go off on their own.

The final introduction was to Banduwa, Gayili's husband. He appeared to be aged in his forties and wore a navy blue singlet the entire time we were with him. We found him a difficult person to get to know. When he spoke (which was rarely) it was a slow and steady process. A sentence would be left incomplete and I often assumed he'd given up trying to find the English word to answer my question. What felt like two minutes later a random mumbling would finish off the communication. I was left to desperately search my memory to fit the comment into our previous conversation.

We raised *Kijana*'s sails and headed to a point of land on the opposite side of Melville Bay. After about an hour we anchored off a sand spit leading from the mouth of a nearby river. By the time we'd unloaded all the equipment onto the beach, David, Ian and Cedric had returned from the mangroves with a bounty of mud crabs. There were about half a dozen of them, and they were huge, about 25 centimetres across the carapace. The boys dumped them on the beach, where they began wandering around. Their claws had been broken off so the younger children wouldn't get bitten.

The high-tide mark was about 100 metres up the beach, so we carried everything to the top of the beach and began to set up camp under a weeping tree.

By the time our tipi was set up, it was late afternoon. Gayili sat under the tree with the children and started a fire. Banduwa sat away from the group, chiselling a tree branch he'd found, slowly shaping what appeared to be a didgeridoo – or yakala, as he later told us.

The sky was turning a beautiful orange colour, similar to the colour of the crabs sitting in a big pot of water. Gayili's eyes alternated between watching our every movement and monitoring the progress of the crabs. There was no doubt she was not only the mother figure, but also the boss. She also spoke English very well and was forthcoming enough to initiate conversation.

'OK, they're ready,' Gayili suddenly announced as she leant over the fire to pluck out a crab by the leg. We each took a branch from what appeared to be a pine tree, placed it on the sand and used it as a plate for the crab. The crab was split down the middle and the meat around the legs was torn off. The taste was unbelievably good. I looked over to Josh, who nodded in agreement. Mika and Nicolette were up to their elbows in sticky crab juice, wiping splashes from their cheeks with their forearms.

I looked to Gayili, who had a leg sticking out of her mouth.

'So this is traditional land?' I asked.

'Yo,' she said, pulling another leg out. 'Where we are sitting right now, under this tree, is all my people's land.'

'And Josh said this is the first time you have brought whities here.'

'Yo, this is the first time us Yolngu have camped here with Balanda.'

Balanda, we had learnt, was the word for white person.

I nodded to David and Ian, who were sitting next to each other, then directed my question to Gayili.

'Can the guys show us how to catch crabs tomorrow?'

She smiled and said yes. Then, one by one, we headed off for bed, exhausted but very happy at how the day had turned out.

I woke next morning before the others. My stomach was a bit sore, having eaten nothing the previous day except for the rich crab meat. I wandered over to the fire where Gayili was sitting in the same position as the day before, stirring a pot of tea over the fire.

Not long after, Mika and Nicolette emerged from the tent together, closely followed by Josh, who walked towards Gayili and me. The girls, however, veered off in another direction. He sat down and looked at me.

'They're going to the boat for breakfast!' he said.

I was astonished. 'Really?' I said

He gave me one of his looks and I responded by shaking my head. We didn't want to say too much in front of Gayili. I was furious. It had only been one night, for God's sake. Did they even want to be on an adventure or not? I thought the intention was to only live on what we caught or harvested.

Beau, Josh and I decided to continue with our agreement to stick with that promise.

Beau walked over, clearing the sleep from his eyes.

'Where are they going?' he asked.

'Breakfast,' I spat out. 'Let's go and catch some crabs.'

Josh, Beau, David, Ian and I set off with the drag net and three spears. We walked to the river that led to the sea a short distance from our camp. Mangroves lined either side of the river and the water was shallow enough that we could easily cross to the other side. Sitting in pockets of mud were big fat mud crabs. Spotting them among the mangrove roots was tricky, but if a crab was in the mud it was easy. It would dig its body into the mud and stick its claws into the air, threatening to grab any fingers that came its way. One snap of a claw and a finger would be turned to pulp. Not that it was a concern for Ian. He'd slam his spear through the body of the crab, hauling it into the air in victory.

If, however, the crab was in clear water it could move a lot faster and the spear throw had to be more precise. My first attempt at spearing a crab ended in failure. As I threw the spear, my hand knocked a mangrove, sending the spear off-course. By the second try I had the hang of things.

At one stage Ian stopped abruptly, pointing to the sandy sea bottom about 10 metres away. 'Stingray, you see.' He launched his spear into the sand and pulled it out of the water to reveal a flapping baby ray. 'It's too small,' he declared.

A little later he bent down and swept something up in his hand.

'These shells here we use to make necklace. We boil them, then put them onto fishing line. Then we sell them.'

I inspected the shells. Each was the size of a corn kernel and covered in the most intricate patterns, with colours ranging from purple to yellow and black. I grabbed a handful and pocketed them.

After we'd collected half a dozen good sized mud crabs it was time to turn our hand to netting some fish. Our drag net was 40 metres long by 1.5 metres wide. At each end of the net was a pole. Two people would each grab a pole and drag the net through the water until it made a D-shape. It worked a treat, but was bloody hard work. We took it in turns dragging it through the water. The water ahead of the net teemed with fish desperately trying to swim away from the approaching trap. Many would leap into the air, some making it to freedom, but most were trapped. The net was angled towards the sand and pulled up onto the beach, where everyone pounced on the fish. The small ones were thrown back and the big ones kept. Most were mullet or garfish, which are good eating fish.

By the afternoon we were hungry and exhausted, so we gathered our catch of fish and crabs and headed back to camp. I couldn't wait to show the girls what we'd caught. I was sunburnt, hungry and exhausted, but a lot happier than I'd been that morning. The girls had no idea what they'd missed!

Our return to camp was met with cries of delight from the young ones. We passed the catch to Gayili, who immediately put them on the fire. Mika and Nicolette were sitting by the fire with Gayili. They asked what our day was like, so we enthusiastically recalled our conquests, as all good fishermen do.

The catch was shared among everyone, which meant the equivalent of one crab claw and half a handful of fish flesh. Nonetheless, the thought of having provided the catch for dinner was enough to satisfy me.

The next day, as I sat watching Mika and Nicolette weaving with Gayili, I remembered the shells I'd collected. Gayili admired my collection, then explained how to boil them for a few minutes, pick out the little creature within, puncture a hole, then thread them onto fishing line to make a necklace.

Banduwa was making progress with the yakala. He'd transformed the sawn-off branch into a smooth and rich-sounding yakala, or didgeridoo. The time, effort and care he put into making it was astonishing. Every swing of the machete seemed perfectly controlled to leave the desired rounded effect over the natural burls in the branch.

'What do you do with them once they're finished?' Beau asked.

'We sell them,' he answered, glancing warily at Beau.

'How many yakalas have you made?' Beau asked.

'Maybe ...'

I waited.

'One ...'

I waited again. I presumed he was going to say one hundred once he'd thought of the word. It couldn't be one *thousand*, surely. That would be one a week for 20 years. Then again, at his age, it was possible. I stared at him, willing him to answer. But it didn't come.

'One *hundred*?' Beau asked expectantly.

He was nodding his head as reassuringly as he could, but still no answer. I followed Beau's gaze back to Gayili.

'One,' she said.

Later that day we decided to go in search of yams – a type of native potato – and mangrove worms, and also took the opportunity to have a wash at a freshwater swimming hole. To keep in the spirit of our experience, we would have ideally walked to find yams. But I hadn't seen Gayili move from her sitting position near the fire unless absolutely necessary, so I doubted she was about to embark on a trek. Secretly, I didn't have the energy either.

Instead, everyone piled into a trailer hitched to a tractor which seemed to have appeared from nowhere, driven by Banduwa. I had no idea where this bit of rusting machinery came from, but I was damn glad to see it.

We followed a small track for more than an hour, ducking our heads to prevent the tree branches that swept across the trailer from slapping us in the face. Despite the bumpy ride, the younger girls fell asleep until, without notice, Gayili barked a command and we rolled to a stop. Angela and Salomi jumped off and followed the direction of Gayili's out-stretched arm. A few minutes later they returned with a bunch of leaves.

'These we use as medicine for sore eyes or skin,' Gayili said. The girls threw a few branches in the trailer, then the tractor started again and we continued on our way. Shortly after, we arrived at a beach and everyone jumped off the trailer to explore.

For the rest of the afternoon we followed Gayili in search of the heart-shaped leaves of the yams, then into the mangroves for the mangrove worms. While it seemed the yams required eagle eyes to spot, and a fair bit of effort to dig up, the mangrove worms required little skill at all. All one had to do was grab a branch of a mangrove tree and hack into it, until you reached the centre, where hopefully a mangrove worm sat waiting to be pulled out.

Most were as thick as my little finger, but the big ones were the thickness of a thumb and up to half a metre long. And they were disgusting. Despite my extreme hunger, I couldn't come at a slimy sheath filled with crunchy dirt. I mean, I ate one for the experience, but it tasted like mud. And it was as about as satisfying as picking my nose and eating it.

We came to a beach, where we lit a fire and Salomi showed Mika how to cook the sea snails that we had gathered from the sand. After they had sizzled on the coals the meat was picked out with a small twig and the chewy morsel popped into the mouth. They were good, but the three I got were the equivalent of a taste test at a supermarket. I needed a trolley full of them.

With a total of two yams, 30-odd sea snails and a dozen mangrove worms, we called it a day and headed for a swim in a nearby waterhole. Three days of salt, mud and sand were washed away, leaving our skin fresh and covered in goose bumps as we wallowed in the shade of the waterhole. Of course, the return trip on the tractor stirred up enough dust to cover us again.

Back at camp Gayili crushed the leaves we'd collected earlier, then mixed them with water in a bucket. After half an hour the mixture had turned thick, like papier-mâché glue, and we were instructed to smear any sandfly bites or abrasions with the goop.

We cooked the two yams, which amounted to little between the adults, while the kids happily gobbled down the mangrove worms. I was bloody starving.

Before it got dark, Gayili set to work making a damper for the kids, so I grabbed the net and asked who wanted to help trap some fish. Josh filmed while Beau and I dragged the net through the shallows. We were getting desperate and most of the fish we caught weren't big enough to eat. My body had no energy left to continue. Each time we dragged the net slower and slower, which meant we caught less fish. With a handful of barely edible fish, we returned to camp as an orange moon rose from behind the clouds which sat low on the horizon. Everyone had finished eating the damper and the few fish we had to show for our efforts weren't worth the energy to cook them. We left them with Gayili for the morning and crawled off to bed.

As we prepared to retire, the burning logs began to hiss with the onset of rain.

We offered Gayili and Banduwa a spot with us in our tipi so they wouldn't have to sleep outside by the fire, as they'd done every night since we had arrived. They never took up our offer. Within five minutes I was sound asleep, but outside our tent, sitting by the fire in the drizzle, Gayili felt uneasy. After Banduwa had nodded off, Angela, who was sitting with Gayili, pointed out a cloud in the sky that was in the shape of a crocodile. Then, a short while later, on the other side of the sky, another cloud formed, this time in the shape of a snake. For Gayili, these were obvious signs of bad news, compelling her to remain awake all night.

The next morning, the fourth day on the beach, I got up feeling more energised than I had been the previous afternoon. I discovered Gayili at her usual position with Banduwa asleep beside her.

'Did you get very wet last night?' I asked, as she slowly lifted her eyes from the fire.

'No. It only rained for the first couple of hours,' she told me in a weary tone.

She then informed me that David had fallen ill and she wanted me to take him back to Nhulunbuy. Also, we were running low on supplies, so Angela would return with us to buy more flour and tobacco. It was implicit that I would take them back.

Beau helped me sail David and Angela back. I watched David during the trip and he looked all right to me. There was obviously a reason to head back, a reason I'd only understand once we returned.

We arrived in Nhulunbuy midmorning. David didn't seem in a hurry to race off for medical attention, choosing instead to hang around under a tree. Beau and I followed Angela to a ute where an old man waited. He drove us to the supermarket for the supplies.

After living off nothing for four days, the supermarket was a fantasy world. The temptation was incredible. I knew I could pocket a chocolate bar without anyone knowing. I sure as hell could do with it. But I couldn't go back and face poor Josh knowing I'd stuffed my face while he continued to starve. Besides, I couldn't face the girls if I indulged.

I decided to get away from all that wicked food and head across the road to the post office. I had five minutes to write a note to Maya and post her the shell necklace I'd made.

Beau and I then made our way back to the beach where *Kijana* was anchored. We were waiting by the dinghy for Angela to show up, when a man with a lazy eye suddenly appeared and confidently strode toward us. He had a menacing and creepy look about him. I'll admit I was actually scared as he bore down on us. Such was his presence, I failed to see Angela and a younger man following him until they were virtually standing in front of me. The crazy-eyed man explained that he was Gayili's uncle and the owner of the land we were staying on. He said that he and Ricky, the younger man, wanted to come across with us.

'Sure,' I said, knowing that I really had no choice. 'Are you ready to go now?'

The two men carried nothing but a plastic bag full of frozen reef fish, and a pair of clapping sticks. They were ready!

It was a fairly quiet return trip. Few words were exchanged as we motored along. I could sense a heavy mood hanging over Ricky and the crazy-eyed uncle.

When we arrived, I secured the anchor while Beau dropped Angela and the two men on the beach. By the time he returned to collect me and we'd hauled the dinghy above the high-tide mark, the men were already sitting with the group around the fire.

I casually strolled up the beach and slumped down in the circle where everyone sat. There was little conversation, and certainly no explanation as to why they were there, except perhaps to check out their real estate. I suddenly felt uneasy. Maybe the uncle was upset that we'd eaten so many of his mud crabs.

My imagination was getting out of control when Gayili abruptly ordered everyone to be quiet. Ricky grabbed the sticks he'd been carrying when I first saw him and began to clap them together to a constant beat. Josh reached for the camera but Gayili shook her head.

Uncle, as he was known, then began to sing. It was a wailing, haunting melody, made even more sinister by the accompanying clacking of the sticks. His singing rose and dropped, following none of the musical rules I was used to hearing on the radio. He sang how you'd expect a 70-year-old man with no musical training to sing. It was croaky and rugged but in a beautiful, soulful way.

Uncle sang for several minutes, then put his head down to signal he had finished. His task was done. It was only then that Gayili felt relieved enough to offer us an insight into what had begun the previous night as an omen, and had now been completed. The two men had come to the camp to fulfil a role bestowed on them as relations to Gayili. During the singing Uncle had told her the bad news and she was almost visibly relieved. A distant uncle had died the previous night. The relief came from the fact that she had feared for her sons' wellbeing the moment she'd seen the strange clouds.

That night Gayili enthralled us with stories of the sacred land we were sitting on. She pointed out the natural ochre mines further along the coast, where her ancestors had collected their painting materials from, and even treated us to a poem she'd written, describing the shimmer of moonlight dancing across the sea.

With the crabbing experience still fresh in my mind, I asked if there were any saltwater crocodiles around. Yes, lots she said. She knew of a big croc who lived at the next point along, right where we had collected the mangrove worms. The local word for crocodile was 'baru'.

I asked if many people were ever attacked by baru. She told us the story of a local boy who had disappeared not long ago. She explained that when something tragic like that happened, the bad spirits were blamed. There was always a reason for the bad spirits to do such an awful deed. Maybe a family member had ignored a taboo and the young boy's death was the spirit's revenge. I shivered as I thought about it. It was bad karma of the worst type.

Despite the abundance of crocodiles in northern Australia, many Yolngu children still swim in the rivers where crocodiles are often seen. I wondered how safe we had been following the kids through the mangroves.

'Is there any danger when we fossick in the mangroves?' I asked her.

'Just do not think on it,' she answered. 'Do not think of anything bad. Only think of what you are looking for. When I am collecting in long grass I only think of the yam I am looking for. It is the same with the baru. What you think about will happen.'

Our last full day on the beach dawned a beauty. Gayili suggested we make our final night one of celebration. Her mood was decidedly more buoyant since Uncle had performed his ceremony.

Beau and Josh were clearly struggling for energy. Josh found it difficult to even pick up the camera. They both needed food and decided they had to break our promise and eat some damper. It was no good living off the land if the land could not provide for them.

We watched Gayili intently as she made damper, flattening it like a pizza and covering it in the hot sand by the fire to bake. Josh decided he'd give it a go, so Gayili showed him how. Josh proudly offered Banduwa the first taste of his damper.

'Taste like lady,' he said slowly, as if he was unsure of the wording. 'Ahhh ... lady-*damper*!' he said again, this time more confidently. We burst into laughter. Even Gayili was able to raise a giggle.

'I'll take that as a compliment,' declared Josh as he shared it around. I desperately wanted some but I couldn't. We had one day to go, so I picked up the drag net and mustered some support to help me go netting.

That afternoon saw us back at camp with a catch of fish in readiness for the feast.

The meal was to be cooked in an underground oven, so a pit was dug in the sand and lined with rocks. A fire was started in the pit, which eventually died, leaving bright red coals and hot stones. Meanwhile, what had once been Uncle's frozen fish, were now thoroughly thawed and combined with our recent catch of mullet and chunks of potato and pumpkin. The coals were covered with green leaves that would not burn with the heat. The food was placed on top of the leaves, then more leaves, a length of stiff bark, and finally a heap of sand was pushed on top to form our underground oven.

David and Ian lit another fire on the beach and sat with Ricky, who cradled the yakala that Banduwa had made. Ricky, we discovered, was reputedly the best yakala player there was. Earlier in the day he'd taken the yakala and cut 25 centimetres off it. He blew a few tunes and seemed satisfied. Now it sounded right! And Banduwa didn't seem to mind.

Mika helped Banduwa paint the children's faces before it was time to begin. After Ricky had warmed up, half a dozen sets of clap sticks began their beat, through which Ricky wove the deep drone of the yakala.

The boys and younger girls then began to dance. It was a magical time, helped along by the bright pink sun setting behind the dancers. Cedric led the dancers. He had transformed from the larrikin of the first day to a serious performer. His rigid knees and stern face reflected the seriousness of the spirit world he was imitating. Sand flicked from his feet as the performance climaxed. Cedric's body relaxed as he looked to Gayili for approval. It seemed Cedric the boy was dancing like a man.

Our time with Gayili and her family was drawing to a close. The thought of it made me sad. We'd made some good friends during the week. We'd told stories from our different worlds and shared common jokes.

But it was not only the end of our time with the Yolngu people that made me feel so melancholy. Our time with Gayili had cemented the end of the *Kijana* crew as it currently stood. I recalled an Aboriginal custom where it was necessary to leave the elderly or sick behind, when the tribe had to move on to fresher hunting grounds. I felt almost the same. *Kijana* would be leaving the safe waters of Australia and entering the Spice Islands of Indonesia. The girls were holding us back and they had to be left behind.

My decision was made – the girls had to go. The incidents of falling asleep on watch and going back to the boat for food provided enough hard evidence to convince the office it wasn't working. I would call them as soon as we got back to town.

The dance finished and the underground oven was opened. Steam rose from the pit and carried with it a smell that made the mouth water. Everyone scrambled around the feast and selected pieces of fish and vegetables to put on their bark plate. I reached for a piece of fish and put it in my mouth. It was superb. I went to get more but stopped when I saw the colour of the fish I'd just tasted. It was red, not the grey of the mullet we'd caught. I was eating one of the frozen reef fish brought over by Uncle. All that discipline and I'd stumbled at the final hurdle. It didn't matter any more, I didn't have anything to prove to anyone. I hesitated for a couple of seconds then skewered the biggest supermarket potato I could see.

That night I slept well for the first time in a week. We'd been living on the beach for six days and it was only now that we were faced with the prospect of leaving that it felt like our home.

We left the following morning, and sailed everyone back to Nhulunbuy, where we thanked our friends and said our goodbyes. Then I headed to town to make the call to the office to tell them of my decision.

I hesitantly dialled the office number and my voice was soon being broadcast on the speakerphone to those in the office. I told them how the bond among the guys was getting stronger, but the relationship between the guys and the girls was getting worse. I could not keep going this way, I told them, for I was at my wits' end.

They simply told me to hold on.

'Don't say anything just yet' until there is a clear plan, they said. A plan for *what*? I suppose they needed time to let it sink in. Meanwhile, I had to keep my mouth shut and not mention my conversation to the others, least of all the girls.

Back at the boat, as we prepared to leave Nhulunbuy the following morning, Mika asked if she could talk to me – alone. She asked me straight out whether I wanted her on the boat. I answered truthfully – no. She didn't respond, instead heading up on deck to sit on her own in the dark. Fifteen minutes later she came into the cabin and announced to everyone that she would be leaving the boat in Darwin. So much for the office's plan! The following morning we weighed anchor and began the five-day leg to Darwin.

It was the most miserable leg of the entire trip. The weather was overcast and no one spoke. Beau, Josh and I spent most days on deck huddled behind the steering wheel, while Mika and Nicolette rarely came out of their cabin. There was no 'dinner' together, as previously.

Nicolette didn't say much at all. I wondered what she was thinking. Josh made an effort to make things less miserable, spending time sitting with Nicolette and joking with her as best he could.

The fourth of July came and nearly went. Late in the evening I remembered the significance of the date. Not because it was American Independence Day, which may have been significant to Nicolette, but because it was Josh's birthday. I double-checked with him if it was the right date, then wished him a happy twenty-second birthday. He glumly told me it was the worst birthday of his life.

As we sailed past Melville Island, a few hours out from Darwin, I checked the emails, hoping for some word from the office. Suddenly, Nicolette swept into the cabin and demanded to know if I wanted her to stay on the boat. I couldn't lie to her, so I said no. She said she would leave with Mika once we arrived in Darwin.

A heavy mood hung over the boat as we entered Darwin's Fanny Bay. Mika and Nicolette had gathered their stuff and were ready to leave. We entered Cullen Bay Marina and tied up to a floating pontoon. Mika and Nicolette loaded their possessions into the dinghy and Josh took them ashore. There was no farewell between Beau, myself and the girls, just relief that they were off and that maybe we would be free to find and film paradise.

Forget the plan, my email to the office said, both the girls were already off. The office immediately organised their flights back to Melbourne and Flip, the publicist, was called back from holidays that day to work out a strategy to let the public know. The aim, of course, was to keep it as low-key as possible.

The interest in what had happened was high. All the daily newspapers across Australia covered the story, and I did quite a few radio interviews. I was honest in what I told them. Things hadn't worked out with the girls, so they had decided to leave. I didn't reveal how they'd driven me crazy and that I'd discovered that I certainly wasn't the best captain to have ever sailed the seven seas when it came to people management.

The one question most people wanted to know was who would replace Mika and Nicolette? The guys knew we could sail the boat on our own, as that's what we had virtually done since day one. So we didn't necessarily need people with sailing experience. In fact, we didn't really want to take a 'sailor' with us. We liked our routine and most sailors we'd met were the cliquey type who used sailing terms way too often for our liking. The three of us were relaxed and we wanted people who could fit into that groove. Attitude was the most important attribute. But how could we judge that until we were out sailing with them? It was a case of once bitten, twice shy.

I wanted Maya to come on board but I hadn't mentioned that to the others. How could I, especially with the problems we'd had with Mika and Nicolette. It would look like I wanted them off so Maya could come on board. That wasn't the case and I certainly didn't want anyone thinking it was. Josh asked me about her joining and I said, yes, of course I wanted her to join. As far as Beau and Josh were concerned, she had as good a chance as anyone of fitting into our groove.

Sure, she didn't fit any of the roles we had designed in the Kijana mission statement, such as extreme sports coordinator, mechanic, etc. But we'd discovered they were just words anyway. An adventurous attitude was more important than any specialist skills.

So, we had one girl and needed someone else. Or did we? We thought about it and came up with an idea. Why not leave the fifth position open for people we met along the way to come with us for short stints. After a couple of months if things weren't working out we could say their time was up. If we got on well, we could ask them to stay for the rest of the trip. It was a great idea.

We stood at three consecutive payphones in Darwin, each dialling the number for the conference call with the office to discuss our plans. We stood and listened as the job description for new crew members was read out to us. We were told we needed someone who could write the web updates, be a mechanic, sailor, researcher, female and preferably someone who wasn't Australian.

We were digesting the impossibilities of finding such people in Darwin, when they delivered a bombshell. The deal with the American book publisher, worth $100,000, had fallen through. The fact that we no longer had an American on board was being blamed. It was a huge blow. We'd been counting on that money to pay for virtually everything. We basically now had nothing in the bank. It meant the documentary series had to be sold immediately to cover food, fuel and the wages of the office staff.

As we digested this news, Josh suggested Maya as a crew replacement. I looked over at him as he listed the reasons. We didn't need a sailor, we needed someone we could get along with. He explained that he and I could write the web updates and we had plenty of time while sailing to read about the interesting places to visit, so we didn't need a researcher. Beau was doing great with the cooking and together we were a strong team.

But the office were firm. No way, we were told. Imagine what people would think. As soon as Mika and Nicolette get booted off then

Jesse's girlfriend comes on board. We had to think about our image for the sake of our sponsors.

But they offered one small concession. If we kept going, filmed more and got the documentary series sold to secure our finances, then maybe Maya could be considered. I was not surprised by what they said, and I had no choice but to accept it.

We had two weeks in which to find a crew member who could quickly join us, so most likely they would already be travelling. The fifth position could be left open for someone we met while in Indonesia, our next destination.

Losing the publishing deal was a big blow, but at least we heard some good news during the call. We'd received more than two million hits on the web page – people logging on to see the video clips and read the updates. A lot of those, we were told, were from school children. It was the first feedback we'd had about how the updates were going. It was just the tonic we needed as we set about finding a new crew member and getting the Kijana adventure back on track.

I had to call Maya and tell her she would not be joining us. It was difficult, because I couldn't even tell her who was. It was a bit like saying anyone was better than her. 'Someone with a foreign accent,' I said in passing as I tried to play it down.

I wondered what Josh and Beau thought about our conversation with the office. Most times I spoke to the office on my own and filtered what I was told to the crew. I was, after all, a part-owner of the business, captain of the ship and director of the filming, so I had to keep some stuff to myself. But after the conference call with the office I wondered what Beau and Josh were thinking about the workings of the trip. The trip was never designed to be so political, but they were now very much caught up in it. I wasn't surprised when a few days later it came out.

Kijana had been hauled out of the water in Darwin to repair the damage to the keel. Beau and I were under the keel ripping off a plank with screwdrivers, while Josh climbed about the place trying to find the best angle to shoot some footage of us at work. Like so many times before, Josh asked Beau to hide his cigarette. Beau reluctantly butted it out, then took out his frustration on the keel.

'It doesn't look natural,' Josh said referring to the angry scowl on Beau's face.

'Well, what do you want me to do?' Beau asked. I could see he was getting pretty steamed up.

'Just do what you were doing before, as if I wasn't here.'

'This is what I mean,' Beau said, in a huff. 'This is what I hate about the trip. We're meant to be making honest docos out here, but it's not honest. It's not real. When Jesse first told me about this trip what I loved about it was that we were real people going on a real adventure without make-up or any of that stuff. But this is fake. We're meant to be inspiring young people by being ourselves but I have to hide a stupid cigarette. It's bullshit.' He settled down a bit and started working again.

'Do you know what I mean?' he asked Josh.

Josh had lowered the camera. 'Yeah, it's kind of fake but in the docos you can't make everything absolutely real. We're aiming this trip at students and young people. How do you expect a school to endorse our study kits when there's footage of one of the "role models" smoking?'

I interrupted before Beau could answer.

'I know what you mean Beau, but no documentary or film can be totally real. Robert McKee (a world-renowned scriptwriter) even says it's only an interpretation of real life. So if that means we have to hide a smoke so we can get the good message out about young people achieving dreams, then surely that's not a big deal.'

I was relieved when Josh put the camera away. I knew Beau had to be handled gently.

Josh picked up a screwdriver and joined us under the keel. It was two against one. I knew in any other circumstance Beau would have stuck to his guns, but my opinion held sway with him. I knew what he was saying and I even agreed with him. It was just that I needed support from both guys and didn't want the argument to escalate. With the girls gone I had a much better chance of making the trip 'real' for all of our sakes.

We got the keel prepared for the shipwright to fix the damage, then gave her a few extra coats of anti-fouling. While I supervised the work at the dry dock, Josh and Beau distributed an advertisement for a crew member at every backpacker hostel in Darwin. They even hung around bars handing out leaflets to anyone who looked like a traveller.

Over the next week we interviewed a few people, but there was only one who filled our main criteria – a foreign female. Her name was Maria, and she was a backpacker from Denmark. She was working at a pub when Josh and Beau met her. Josh shouted over the bar above the noise as he handed her a leaflet. She read it, then came back to their table with a free jug of beer and her phone number.

I met her two days later and, knowing Beau, was not surprised to discover that she was good looking. She was 22 years old and had been travelling in Australia for several months. She had blonde hair and tanned skin with a slim figure. She also had a heavy accent, which would prove very entertaining as we got to know her better. She'd finished her studies and was travelling before working out what she wanted to do with her life.

At the outset I stressed that we were considering her for a two- to three-month stint only, which I made sure I told her a number of times so there would be no confusion later.

But it was not a one-way interview. She had to be convinced we were legitimate – not just three guys trying to pick up a pretty girl. She wanted to know exactly what type of filming we were doing. 'Our travels,' we told her, which must have sounded suitably suspicious. We gave her the Kijana web address for added assurance.

She must have been convinced, for she accepted our offer on the spot. She had to return to Darwin to meet her brother in about three months, so the timing was perfect. She seemed pretty laid back and we all had a good feeling about her. She also told us she was a hard worker, which was all we could hope for. We made plans to leave in three days' time, despite the fact that she hadn't even seen the boat.

I phoned the office and told them of our choice. They had a short chat with her and seemed satisfied with our decision. Not that there was much they could argue with. She was Danish and a girl. Two of their wishes had been granted.

Over the next few days Maria gave notice at the pub and packed the bulk of her belongings into storage. She updated her immunisations and Customs officially checked us out of the country.

Finally, we were off. After more than a month in Darwin, and five months after beginning our journey, we were leaving our home shores in search of adventure.

Being on *Kijana* as she heaved up and over a swell had become an unfamiliar feeling. The guys even commented that they'd forgotten how to sail. We had to make a conscious effort to remember our sail-raising routine. But it was good to be home.

Our destination, the city of Kupang, lay 600 miles north-west across the Timor Sea. Kupang is the capital of the West Timor province of East Nusa Tenggara. West Timor, in turn, is part of Indonesia. We chose Kupang as our first port as it was the closest place to Australia we could get our papers stamped by Indonesian Customs. From Kupang we planned to cruise along the hundreds of Indonesian islands, stopping in to check out the notorious komodo dragons as we headed towards Sulawesi on our way to Thailand. There, in the southern islands of Phuket, we planned to hang out at Maya Bay, the location of *The Beach*, before we began the long haul towards India and onward to Africa.

Maria felt a little queasy as we got underway, but she hid it well. We showed her over the boat and she practised raising the jib and unfurling the foresail.

The wind died down on the second day out of Darwin and we were forced to motor. By the third day the water was oily calm. We motored through big patches of fish breaking the surface of the water on either side of the boat. Beau and Josh unpacked the fishing rods and tried casting a lure to the place where the most recent fish had disrupted the surface. They tried for half an hour with no luck.

The lack of wind made it very hot. The book I was reading was dotted with wet patches where sweat was landing on the page, so we rigged an awning over the cockpit to enable us to read in the shade. Josh was reading about a man who lived with a tribe of Indians in the Amazon Basin. Every now and then he'd read out a passage, then relate it to us.

Beau was reading the Buddhism book *Zen and the Art of Living with Fearlessness and Grace*. He'd already clocked up four Buddhism books since leaving Melbourne. He was trying to work out which strain of Buddhism he wanted to follow. Maria recommended her Stephen King novel to us, while I found relief reading about an Arctic dog-sledding adventure.

The searing heat of the tropics made night the best part of the day. The soft glow of a hurricane lantern reflected off the canvas awning, lighting our little cocoon of a cockpit. The moon was nearly full in those first days and sent a searchlight-like beam across the water. It was beautiful and warm and everything was under control. I couldn't remember being on the ocean on more beautiful nights.

Josh put on the George CD for about the twentieth time since leaving Darwin.

'Who is this?' Maria asked.

'George,' we told her, as if the band was an old friend.

'I like this one,' she declared.

We took it as a compliment. We told her George had played at the St Kilda festival back home and reminisced about what it would be like sitting on the grass with friends listening to George play live. Maria produced her selection of CDs and shared her favourite songs with us. *No Woman No Cry* by Erykah Badu and Jimmy Cliff was a favourite, as well as The Cranberries. She explained that her brother had made a CD for her before she left for Australia, which she constantly played as it reminded her of him. We liked her music and she liked ours. It was a good sign.

I'd taken over the back cabin since the girls had departed, which allowed me to stretch out for the first time on the trip. I wasn't too keen on heading back to the main cabin when Maria arrived, but I graciously offered her the back cabin. She insisted we share, which I was happy to accept, as it was a damn sight more comfortable than the couch I'd been sleeping on, and at least I now had a spot to store my own gear.

The next day the wind picked up enough for us to raise the sails. Maria was delighted when a pod of dolphins swam beside our bow for a while. In the afternoon Beau noticed the fishing line was tight and Maria pulled in a small tuna for dinner. It was our fourth day at sea. At our current sailing speed we expected to arrive in Timor the next day.

We had a competition as to who would be the first to sight land. The winner would get a whole can of Coke at dinnertime. Before lunch on the fifth day Beau claimed the prize.

We were all excited, but Josh displayed it the best. Whenever he got excited he made us all feel good.

'More tea!' he exclaimed in his best taking-the-mickey tone.

Beau, Maria and I looked at him. I didn't get the joke, but the way he said it was funny enough.

'*More* tea,' he said again. This time I wondered what the hell he was on about.

Then, in his loudest voice, he pointed to the land on our left and shouted: 'TEA MORE.'

We fell about laughing. (You probably had to be there.)

It was a great feeling. We were finally in another country, we were a strong team and the journey of Kijana was heading in the direction I had always hoped it would.

CHAPTER SIX
CELEBRATION

KUPANG WAS LIKE ANOTHER WORLD. SITTING on the western tip of Timor, it is the major trading centre for the region, with a population of 148,300 people.

We anchored off the main beach, which we were surprised to discover was covered in ratty piles of junk. On either side of the beach were tall cliffs that contained what appeared, from a distance, to be termite apartments burrowed into each face, their small windows facing the sea. As we got closer, we realised they were significantly bigger than we had first thought, and there was washing flapping in the breeze from the windows.

Nestled into the left-hand corner of the beach was a shack made of rubbish. Driftwood was combined with faded plastic sheets and rusted corrugated iron to make something that I could only describe as a chookhouse. Where the sand of the beach finished, concrete steps led up to street level where hawkers gathered and buses and bikes flew past.

We arrived late in the afternoon and there was only one other sailing boat anchored off the beach. We decided to say hello and ask how we should check in with Customs. It was a large steel vessel with a dark blue hull, owned by two Australian men aged in their forties.

As soon as we arrived on board they took one look at *Kijana* and told us to take our quarantine flag down immediately. This flag indicates that a vessel has arrived in the country and requires Customs to check the crew's papers. We'd raised the flag to abide by maritime law but our new friends gave us a quick lesson in the Indonesian way of things. The local authorities, they told us, didn't like to do any work and if we flew the flag, they were obliged to come out and see us. And this would make them angry. 'Just check in over the next few days,' they told us.

We chatted some more about the local nuances, then bade our farewell. Our departure came with one final warning.

'Your boat will be safe here. Just make sure you lock it every time you go to shore.'

We rushed back to *Kijana* to lower the yellow flag, then made our way to the beach.

A few kids gathered to watch us arrive. We jumped out of the dinghy and began pulling it up the sand. The children stood around watching us strain to lift the heavy outboard until a small, old man pushed them aside to help us up the beach. Following his lead, the children swarmed around the dinghy and together we hauled it above the high-tide mark.

We asked the small man if it was safe to leave the dinghy there, but he didn't speak English. He looked around at the kids, but it seemed neither did they. Using a few hand gestures, I pointed to the man, then at the dinghy and joined them together, then pointed to us and did a walking signal with my fingers. He said something and nodded his head. I smiled at him and he smiled a big toothless grin back. We had to trust him and his friendly demeanour.

We said goodbye to the small man and climbed up the steps onto the street. The sun was quickly disappearing and the traffic headlights had already been turned on.

There was no point in trying to locate Customs so we found a small eating place and ordered dinner. Maria came back from the bathroom with a puzzled look on her face. She was unsure if she'd 'gone' in the right place, for all she'd found was a floorboard missing in the corner with a bucket of water and a scoop next to it.

Josh and Maria didn't eat much of their meal. It was all weird stuff, and most of it contained meat, which automatically put Josh off. The guidebooks recommended eating only well-cooked meals and to steer clear of meat if we weren't sure where it came from. Of course, how can you be sure of where any meat has come from unless you have caught it and killed it yourself? Beau and I, on the other hand, ate every morsel on our plate. Asian food has always been a favourite for both of us, and the Kupang offering was no exception.

As we returned to the beach I was relieved to see our dinghy still on the beach. The small man was nowhere to be seen but a sheet of plastic had been wrapped around the motor for protection.

The next morning we woke to the sounds of loud engines roaring past *Kijana*. The new boat in town was attracting quite a bit of attention. Small Indonesian fishing boats were scattered from the shore out to sea, laying fishing nets and pulling in their catches. While they waited, they would dash past our boat, their motors screaming as they waved madly at us.

After a breakfast of cereal, Beau checked the emails. There was one from the office reminding us of the need to find something interesting to film for the first episode of the documentaries.

But before that could happen, we needed to get ourselves organised. We needed to replenish our fresh food stores, then find Customs to stamp our passports. Only then could we explore and find some adventures.

One of the blokes from the other yacht came over to check how we'd managed since we last spoke. We told him about the small man who'd covered our motor for us.

'He lives on the beach,' he told us. 'That shack made of rubbish is his home.'

He gave us directions to get to Customs, then wished us well.

On the beach we were again greeted by the small man. He smiled broadly, revealing what appeared to be a mouth full of blood. We later discovered it was actually stained from chewing the betel nut, a form of stimulant chewed like tobacco.

The only Indonesian word any of us could remember from the

travel books was 'nama', which means name. Josh introduced us, saying 'Nama Josh, Beau, Maria, Jesse'.

His name, he told us, was Wadu. He helped us pull the dinghy up the beach, insisting we drag it closer to his hut. I pointed to the ramshackle construction and tried to ask if he lived there. His face lit up with another smile that again revealed the extent of his stained gums. He proudly turned and showed us through his home. He swept open a sheet of plastic to reveal his humble abode, looking back at us proudly. A rooster, tethered by a thin cord tied to its foot, was pecking through some ashes in the corner, searching for food. The place was definitely a work-in-progress. Additions were made by adding whatever the tide chose to leave at Wadu's doorstep. Outside lay two derelict canoes with outriggers. A mess of netting was dumped on top of one of them.

I wondered what Wadu did for a living, how he fed himself. He looked too old to work and a rooster and two leaky canoes looked to be all he owned. Still, his wrinkly face looked like that of a cheeky boy showing off his cubbyhouse kingdom. I gave him some money for looking after our dinghy the previous night, which he humbly accepted.

We entered the main street to search for Customs. We walked past stall after stall on what could loosely be described as a footpath. Each stall sold almost exactly the same as the last – large bundles of dark tobacco, ancient weights, padlocks, knives, watches, calculators, small bottles of whisky and brightly coloured plastic buckets. It was an odd combination of goods for sale. It seemed to me that a few random trucks had been hijacked by thieves, who then offered every stallholder in town the same hot goods. Who knows, I might have been right.

Beau decided we needed some green vegetables, bananas and eggs. We could have got all three at the first stall but, instead, we walked to the end of the stalls only to realise that each vegetable store stocked the same thing for the same price. The mixture of second-guessing traffic rules that seemed nonexistent, extreme humidity, and bargaining in a foreign language left us exhausted.

We decided to stop at a small eatery for lunch. Josh and Maria asked if they had sandwiches, but no one understood what they meant.

We were handed a plate with rice and pointed in the direction of the dishes displayed in the window. They were mainly curries, with chicken, beef, eggs and quail, as well as vegetable dishes that had the unappetising appearance of steamed gum leaves. Each bowl looked like it had been stewing in the sun for days.

As Maria returned to the table with some food, a man approached and asked if he could sit down. He was the first person we had met who spoke understandable English. We said yes, of course he could.

He introduced himself as Eric and asked where we were from and what we were doing. After we told him, he revealed he was a clearance broker. Nothing about his appearance gave the impression that he was telling the truth. His worn-out thongs and raggedy jeans certainly didn't give him an air of being a businessperson. But he was pleasant enough.

We told him we were on our way to Customs but he insisted it would take too much time. Sometimes the officials weren't in the office and we had to get paperwork signed by three different authorities, he told us. He said it was his job to help all yachts checking into the country to get clearance.

'How much?' we asked.

'200,000 rupiah,' he replied.

At only $30 Australian, it seemed fair enough, so we said yes.

'What do you need from us?' I asked.

Passports, boat registration, cruising permit and some other thing I didn't understand, came the reply. He seemed to know what he was talking about. He said he had some other business to attend to and asked that we meet him the following afternoon at the steps to the beach.

Before he left, Josh asked him a favour. He explained that he was vegetarian and wanted to know the Indonesian sentence for ordering food without meat. He happily wrote the sentence down on paper – 'Tidak daging ayam'. 'No beef chicken' it meant.

The following day we decided to explore our surrounds. We found someone who owned two motorbikes and hired them for the day. Beau was the only one with any experience riding a motorbike. I'd ridden a friend's Pee-Wee 50 in Grade 6, but that had ended in tears when

I crashed into a hanging pot plant and jammed my finger against the clutch.

Maria sat behind Beau, and Josh sat behind me with the camera at the ready.

The rest of the day was spent roaring around the streets, down little dirt tracks into the countryside, then back into town again. We were constantly lost but that didn't matter. As long as there was an open road ahead of us, and we knew in which direction the sea lay, we were happy. It was an incredible feeling of freedom, very different to sailing on the ocean. The speed was the main difference, and best of all, there were no rules. People waved as we rode past. We whizzed past goats grazing at the side of the road and a family of monkeys scrambled into the bushes before we ran over them.

Beau rode much faster than me, so he and Maria led most of the way. They were often forced to pull over while Josh and I caught up. One time I slowed down and came to a wobbly halt behind them, only to notice we'd stopped outside a sign that read 'Polisi'.

Outside the building sat four men in brown police uniforms looking rather bored. I gave a quick wave and whispered to Beau to keep going. 'It's the police,' I said.

Not only did we not have international drivers licences, but we hadn't even checked into the country yet. Beau was well versed at flitting away from the cops, so he sped off while I haplessly prodded the levers in an attempt to get it into first gear. One of the police stood up and said something in Indonesian.

'He's coming over,' Josh said in a panic.

'Just pretend you can't hear him,' I said as I continued to kick the gears. I finally got it into first gear, nonchalantly looked up at the approaching policeman and smiled as I took off.

Once we felt confident that we weren't being chased, we pulled into a shop for a drink where a couple of men told us about some caves that served as the local swimming spot. We agreed to follow them off the road and down a track to some boulders, where they pointed towards a small opening that headed underground. It looked like a good place to hide a dead body.

We followed them into the hole, the darkness temporarily blinding us. As our eyes adapted we could make out stalactites hanging from the roof. The sound of water dripping was punctuated by a loud splash somewhere further down.

We followed the two men along a worn path until we came to the swimming hole. A splash of sunlight made its way through a peephole above us, making the water an amazing deep blue colour. A few teenage boys were jumping off a ledge into the water. We paid the men some money for their troubles and spent the afternoon swimming. The cave provided welcome relief from the heat of the sun, and the water was a perfect temperature.

The following morning was dedicated to maintenance of *Kijana*. Josh and I continued our daily ritual of throwing seawater over the decks to keep the timber wet. In the tropical sun it could easily dry out and shrink, leaving cracks that would let water leak into the cabin. Maria polished the stainless steel with a rag and Beau cleaned the galley of fallen food scraps and kero leaks from the pressurised fuel tank at the back of the stove. Our small outboard motor had developed a nasty cough so we mechanically minded creatures opened the lid and cleaned whatever looked dirty. It seemed to fix the problem.

We had a video and a web update due so we decided to film our friend Wadu. We got some shots of his house, trying to frame in as much junk as possible, then left our dinghy with him and waited for Eric, the Customs broker.

While we waited I started to think about what we had just done. I couldn't help feeling we had used Wadu as some sort of prop, without really treating him properly. If he was not such a poor man, would we have treated him with more respect?

I was deep in thought when Eric arrived. We'd seen about as much as there was to see in Kupang, so we asked when we would be cleared to keep going. Hopefully by the next day, he told us. He would meet us there the following day at the same time.

We waited all next day, hoping we would soon be sailing. While passing time, we visited our Australian friends on the neighbouring yacht. Over a cup of tea they shared some of their stories of cruising

Indonesia. The men were business partners, who bought seafood from the local fishermen and shipped it back to Australia. They employed a couple of young locals to maintain the boat while they flew between Kupang and Australia.

They were currently exploring the local seaweed market. Many Indonesians around Kupang are into seaweed harvesting. They use old softdrink bottles they find washed up on the beach, attaching them to the shallow coral reefs with fishing line. When the seaweed grows on the bottle they scrape it off, dry it out and sell it to businesspeople throughout the nearby islands.

The demand for sushi rolls must have been strong around that part of the world. I couldn't think what else they'd use it for. The two guys noticed the surfboards tied to *Kijana*'s safety lines and asked if we were surfers. We admitted we were novices who wanted to learn. Did they know of any good places we could visit, we asked.

Beau went back to *Kijana* to get our chart of the area, while the two men quizzed their Indonesian crew about where some good waves could be found. There was a village near a few well-known breaks at the end of Pulau Roti, an island further south, the crew replied. Beau came back with the chart, which revealed it was two days' sailing away. We thanked the men and their crew and headed back to shore to meet Eric.

We waited on the beach for ages. As each minute ticked past the arranged meeting time, I became more worried. If he had done a runner with our documents we were stuffed. Not to mention what he would end up doing with them. Then, without acknowledging his lateness, Eric arrived and handed over our papers. Boy, I was relieved. I checked all our passports and paid him. They appeared to have the official stamps. We thanked him and decided to spend the rest of the afternoon on the beach.

I imagined the waves at Roti as we watched a soccer match that had started on the beach outside Wadu's shack. There were no boundaries and the goals looked uneven to me. But no one seemed to care. I saw Wadu pottering around his shack, gathering rubbish. It may have been an extremely dirty place but now that the sun was setting behind *Kijana*, the place was beautiful. This was Wadu's million-dollar view.

As we sat enjoying the sea breeze, I wondered about Wadu. What had happened in his life to lead him to where he was? We hadn't really captured much about Wadu when we were filming – just a funny old man and a derelict house. How could we portray a man based on that? Next week we had to have a new update and that meant a new story at a new place. There was so much about Wadu that we would never know.

Before we headed back to the boat to get ready to leave in the morning, I gave him some money for his help. We said goodbye and motored back to the boat. He stood on the shore waving. Did he think we'd be there in the morning to give him more business or did he know we were leaving?

Josh was the first to wake in the morning. He roused the rest of us and soon we had weighed anchor and were sailing south-west towards Roti. We initially made good progress on a stiff breeze, but as the day wore on the wind dropped and our progress stalled. We stayed a night in a small bay before continuing the next day in a light breeze. As we sat on deck hoping for the breeze to pick up, Beau got out the surfboards and waxed them to provide some grip for when we eventually hopped aboard.

A few 'wax on, wax off' jokes later and we were again wondering how to pass the time. Then I had an idea. I climbed over the safety lines onto the outside of the gunwhale. Beau reached through the safety lines and held the front of the surfboard so the fins trailed in the water.

I gave him the signal and he dropped the board as I jumped and landed on top of it. Still holding onto the side of *Kijana*, I found myself surfing.

'It's just like a skateboard,' I yelled. I did a few swerves, then jumped back on board and Beau had a go, practising for when we would take on the real waves in a day or so.

It was late afternoon when we arrived at the southern tip of Roti. *Kijana* rose up and down on the swell that wrapped around the point of the island and broke on the reefs lining the shore. To the south, we could see a four-metre left-hander rolling over the reef. To our north was a smaller right-hand break. Through the binoculars we spotted four boats – a small catamaran, two monohulls and a large power boat.

When we got close enough we dropped the sails and motored between two surf breaks to where the other boats were moored. We dropped anchor 200 metres from the northern break, cutting the motor as soon as the anchor dug into the seabed. The noise of the motor was immediately replaced by the sound of waves crashing on reefs.

The scene was in stark contrast to the grime and bustle of Kupang. Instead of the rush of traffic and crowded streets, we could see only small huts between the tall coconut trees that lined the beach. Closer to shore was a maze of floating objects, which I concluded was a seaweed farm.

'Gnarly,' Josh said behind my shoulder. He was right, but it wasn't a word I'd heard from him before. Beau and I turned our heads to see him smiling. It'd only taken a few seconds of hearing the roar of near-perfect waves on a remote Indonesian break to turn him into a surfer-lingo-speaking dude.

Beau dragged out an awful American accent in an attempt to add a line from the movie *Point Break*: 'And your balls man, they are *this* big'. It wasn't what he said but how he laughed at his own joke that cracked us up.

Maria didn't have to put on an American accent, as she already had an accent of her own. 'Go back to the valley, man.'

What a great feeling it was to hear her getting into our cabin-fever humour. It was a further sign that she'd become one of us.

All eyes turned to me, the only one not to have said anything surfy. The pressure was on. I knew the movie but couldn't think of any lines so I said, 'Totally wicked'.

No one really laughed, not even me. Josh was able to muster one of his nervous giggles at how lame my effort was.

'Let's go ashore,' I quickly added to cover the silence.

The village was called Nembrala. Its location seemed to be a closely guarded secret in the surfing community, only shared by the surfers who frequented the village.

Over the next couple of days we became familiar with the layout of the village. It was small and basic. The streets were gravel and the houses neatly arranged, with the border of each property marked by fences of wood and blocks of coral placed on top of each other. There was no mains electricity and only the wealthiest families could afford to run a generator for lights.

At night we could pick out the few privileged homes by the intensity of light coming from their windows. The rest of the houses were lit by the dim glow of hanging lanterns.

The village centre was marked by a dusty soccer field that doubled as a market square twice a week. Beside this field sat a church and a small school. Most of the townsfolk walked everywhere, with the occasional motorbike sending up a cloud of dust. These bikes always appeared to be hooning along, but I think the fact that they were so rare accentuated their loudness and speed.

The landscape was very dry. Were it not for the coconuts that fell from the tall palms shading the village, the pigs, chickens and goats may have starved. The covering of palms fronds 20 metres above the ground provided a type of air conditioning for the village. The ocean breeze blew under the palms making the heat more bearable, rustling the leaves to create a cooling effect.

The only place with a television was a home-stay close to the beach. The family that operated it had built extra living quarters and provided clean sheets and meals to the band of surfers who lived with them for a few weeks or even months.

It was a peculiar little community, where local Indonesians and sun-bleached surfers lived in harmony. Many of the surfers had been visiting Nembrala for years and spoke fluent Indonesian, while many locals had, in turn, picked up the art of surfing from these visitors.

On our second day we eyed the nearby waves with a mixture of desire and fear. We'd watched a constant stream of surfers disappear into the thunderous surf of the southern reef. Wave after wave would pass by with no sign of life until a rider would suddenly appear, carving out a ride with apparent ease. It looked so easy and heaps of fun. But, at the same time, really treacherous. The waves were twice the size of the surfers, and were breaking over a razor-sharp reef. Also, these guys looked like they knew what they were doing. This was not a case of going for a day at the beach with Dad on a boogie board. These guys were doing all the moves I'd seen in surfer magazines.

We decided we should tackle the northern break first, as its waves were half the size.

As we discussed which break to try, a launch approached *Kijana* and pulled up alongside. It was the skipper from the big power boat, which we soon discovered was a charter vessel. He admired *Kijana* and told us he'd heard of us leaving Melbourne. Did we want to come over for an ice-cold beer? Of course!

The charter boat looked even bigger once we were inside. Steve, the skipper and owner of the charter business, introduced us to his five crew and eight passengers. The youngest on board was his eight-year-old daughter who had her own full-time nanny, who also doubled as a school teacher. Each week they picked up new passengers from Kupang and cruised around the best surf breaks offering first-class food, accommodation and, of course, surfing.

His clients were a different breed of surfer to the ones living in the village. They were generally older men with business backgrounds, who probably had once lived the surfing life on the beaches of California. But after university their busy corporate lives swallowed every spare moment, so instead of bumming around the beaches and hanging out, they would embark on this annual 'surfari' in search of the ultimate wave. If that meant flying to the other side of the world and paying big bucks to get to the best waves, well, so be it. They could afford it. For them, time was more valuable than money.

It had taken us two days to sail from Kupang to Roti. The big power cat could get them from the Kupang airport to those same breaks in six hours. On the rare day when the surf was not performing, DVDs, air-conditioned cabins and a full galley complete with microwave oven kept the edgy surfers in comfort until they could hit the waves again.

We were each handed a beer as we sat at a table littered with surfer paraphernalia – digital cameras, surf magazines, you-beaut board wax and fashionably expensive polarised sunglasses.

The passengers were intrigued by our trip. We told them where we'd sailed so far and where we were headed – Africa, South America, then through the Pacific back home. We explained how we were filming and updating our website, and about the schools that were studying our trip.

I could see the dreamy look in their eyes, the look many people got when I told them about the trip. To those blokes it would no doubt be the ultimate surfari.

'If you ever need crew …' one of the older men said, 'I'll drop my job in a heartbeat.'

Steve invited me up to the helm to look at the navigation station, which had every navigational device known to man. He checked the latest weather fax.

'Wind should die off to 5–10 knots tomorrow – nothing!' he said. No wind meant no waves, which was bad for business. We discussed the route of *Kijana* and, upon hearing that we didn't have any detailed local charts, he lent me his to plan our route through the rest of Indonesia.

Back at the table, the inevitable the topic of surfing came up.

'How do you like the waves?' we were asked.

We looked sheepishly at the other. We were about to be exposed as posers.

'Yeah, they look great don't they,' I answered. It was a pretty safe answer. I hadn't seen waves like them anywhere. Out at sea they never curved over in such a perfect oval shape.

'Poetry in motion,' I added, this time more confidently, thinking I was tapping into the surfer mindset.

'So you don't surf?' The question sat there like an ice-cold can of beer. They were on to me. I thought about mentioning the 'practice' we'd had hanging off *Kijana* the previous day, but I decided to cut my losses, and 'fess up.

'Well, not actually on a wave … that's moving. We're thinking that northern break is looking pretty good.' I nodded to the pathetic waves that had died down since the morning.

Steve stepped in to save us.

'Would you like to go out with some of my guys?' he offered. 'When the swell dies down – possibly tomorrow.' Two of the men eagerly volunteered their services.

We gladly accepted the offer, on the proviso that the swell was not too big. Steve agreed to collect us in his launch when he was ready. We thanked our hosts for the drinks, then headed for the dinghy and spent the rest of the day cleaning *Kijana*.

The morning brought with it three great reasons to get up and enjoy the day. Firstly, the wind had died off and the sun was spectacular; secondly, we were going to learn how to surf some gnarly Indo waves, and finally it was 26 August 2002 – my twenty-first birthday.

Maria and Josh each gave me a homemade card decorated with drawings and photos from home. I wondered when they'd made them – I thought I knew everything that went on aboard *Kijana*! Beau handed me a plastic bag that contained a jar of dill cucumbers – my favourite.

'Sorry your birthday wasn't like this,' I said to Josh as I offered around the cucumbers.

Josh didn't look like he'd slept too well, for something more important than organising my birthday presents had occurred during the wee hours. Josh and Beau battled each other to tell their story. Their cabin, they blurted out, was infested with 'bed bugs'!

After we'd all headed to bed, Josh tossed and turned as he was attacked by what he thought were mosquitoes. About midnight he let out a frustrated sigh that woke Beau.

'Can't sleep, hey?' Beau asked.

Josh then switched on the light, sending Beau immediately scurrying under the covers of his bunk.

'What the hell are these?' Josh cried.

Beau got up and immediately saw what he was talking about. Josh's bed was crawling with little bugs, about one-third the size of a ladybird. They were everywhere, darting into any dark crevice they could find. However, some of the spots weren't moving. On closer inspection, Josh realised they were blotches of blood on his sheet.

'That's my blood!' he cried, as he began to slap every bug he could see, leaving even more red marks.

Despite Josh yelling 'kill 'em all!' Beau decided on a more humane approach. He ran to the galley and grabbed a cup from the top shelf.

By the time he got back, Josh's tally was five. The rest had managed to scramble away. Beau trapped one under the cup.

'Kill it,' Josh demanded. Beau had other ideas. He was becoming a Buddhist and had to respect all life.

'He's done nothing to me. I'll let him go up on deck.'

'Yeah, but it's been biting me,' an exasperated Josh declared. 'If you don't kill it, it'll climb back down and bite me again. Let me do it.'

They argued about whether to kill it or save it. Finally, they agreed to leave it in the cup until morning.

As they told the story, I put my jar of birthday cucumbers on the galley bench and lifted a plate from the top of the prison cup. Inside was the famous bug that had caused such a rift among my crew.

'Don't let it escape!' Josh yelled.

It was just a bug. Did it have to cause such a problem to our harmonious existence?

'There's heaps more of them anyway,' Beau said, as if that was some sort of argument.

It wasn't moving, so I tapped the cup. 'I think it's dead,' I said.

I touched it with my finger. No doubt about it. I looked at Beau and felt slightly sorry. I then looked at Josh as he scratched his bites and felt less sorry for Beau.

'Let's hope they die naturally from all the salt,' I said, in the hope that would put the issue to bed. As long as they weren't in my bed, I thought as I flicked the bug overboard.

During breakfast Josh and I discussed how to film the surfing. Should he get the underwater shots or should I, or was it too dangerous for any of us to go near the surf with scuba gear? We agreed the logistics of filming in the surf were complicated and it was better to get a feel for what it was like before dragging the camera along.

As we chatted, a small dinghy pulled up to say hello. The people on board were from one of the other yachts anchored nearby. They'd come to tell us about a 'dong night' on the outskirts of the village that evening. All we had to do was meet at the home-stay at 7 p.m., earlier if we wanted a meal. Without hesitation we agreed, although we didn't have the slightest idea of what a dong night was.

By the time Steve motored over, the waves had dropped and were looking good for learners. He dropped us at the southern break with his daughter, her nanny and the two men who'd offered to teach us.

We found ourselves with boards in hand entering the water without a clue as to what to do. Stand up and surf was as technical as our instructions got. The paddling was hard work but the waves looked safe – from a distance. It wasn't until I got out there and faced a two-metre wave head-on that I realised what I had got myself into.

On my first wave I paddled and felt the surfboard increase in speed as white water crashed on my left. The water was sucking up towards the curling wave and below, less than a metre from my face, the coral reef raced by. I jumped to my feet and surprisingly found myself standing up. I veered left and raced down the wave. I was riding the wave! Then I wasn't. My dumping was as violent as my ride was exhilarating, tossed about in nature's washing machine until I finally came up for air.

What a feeling! I reckon I was only on my feet for three and a half seconds, but gee it was worth it. I could see how people became hooked on surfing.

I paddled back out to see Beau and Josh taking off. Throughout the afternoon we each had about five dumps for every good ride. A highlight was paddling back to where the others sat on their boards and explaining in detail what had happened on our last wave. Then another swell would arrive and one by one, we'd disappear behind a wall of water leaving the others to wonder if they were going to be OK.

Before we knew it, Steve returned in his launch. One coral cut on Josh's heel, two litres of salt water swallowed and a handful of half-decent rides were sufficient to make us feel satisfied.

As we headed back to *Kijana* I asked Steve about the dong night.

'It's a waste of time,' he said matter-of-factly. 'I've been to them before. The locals dance around and get you pissed, then ask for money.' It seemed a pretty brutal assessment. He was leaving for Kupang the following morning to collect more passengers, so we thanked him again for the surfing and said farewell.

Despite Steve's opinion, we were committed to going to the dong night. It was not just a night out for us, but a chance to get some footage for our documentaries.

We planned to arrive at the home-stay in time for something to eat but somehow managed to get the dinghy tangled in the seaweed farm, so we arrived as everyone was finishing their meal. There were about 20 people gathered at half a dozen tables. The woman who ran the home-stay welcomed us and ordered her daughter to quickly fetch some food.

Half the crowd were yachties, the other half surfers. We scoffed our food in time to board an ancient minibus that pulled up outside. Everyone crammed in until it was set to explode with passengers, forcing six people to climb onto the roof. We were driven north out of town along the main track, coming to a halt at a dry riverbed. The driver announced he wasn't sure if the bus would stay upright as he headed through the riverbed, so would we mind getting out. He didn't have to ask twice. We ambled along, watching in horror and amazement as the bus jolted at precarious angles until it was safely on the other side. We all jumped in and on, and set off again.

We continued on a little further, then took a track to the right, away from the beach. We arrived at a house lit with floodlights. In the distance I could hear the hum of a generator.

Near the house was a bare area that looked like a dusty dance floor, around which dozens of locals sat on homemade benches. As we joined them, an old plastic jug with a matching cup was passed around, with everyone expected to take a stiff shot of a clear alcoholic drink, called sopi. It didn't leave a taste but gave a hot flush, the sort I'd experienced with tequila. It was handed out by a guy with an Australian accent. He was a tall, weather-beaten man aged in his fifties with a broad friendly smile. He reminded me a bit of Paul Hogan, the actor.

Kijana at anchor in Thailand. I never got sick of looking at her sweeping lines.

Me, Mika and Josh.

Beau

Me and Maya (at Maya Bay).

Nicolette

Maria

Swimming with the Yolngu kids in Arnhem Land.

A cheeky face on the beach. We had a lot of fun with Gayili and her family.

Gayili teaching Mika and Nicolette to weave.

Our final night in Arnhem Land. We
could hardly wait for our feast to cook
in the underground oven.

Josh, me and Maria. A typical cockpit dinner aboard *Kijana*.

Arriving in Kupang, Indonesia, felt like we were stepping back in time.

Trying goat brain during preparations for my twenty-first birthday party on Roti.

Some of the Roti kids guarding the dongs before the evening celebrations.

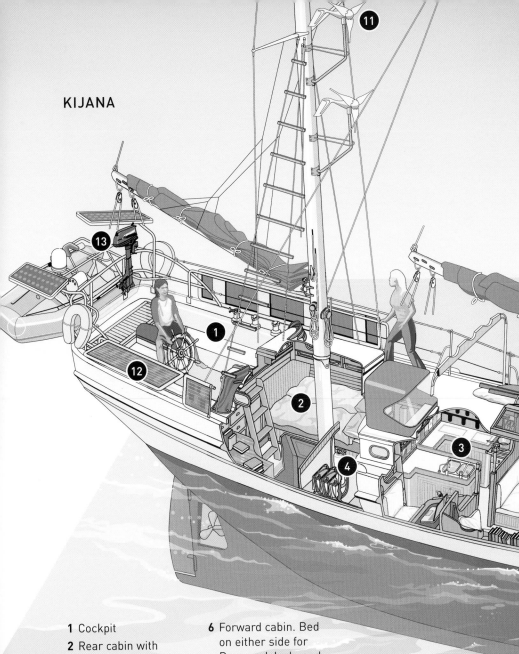

KIJANA

1 Cockpit
2 Rear cabin with double bunk. The girls slept here.
3 Galley (kitchen). Beau's domain.
4 Engine room
5 Main couch and dining room. This was my bed until Darwin.
6 Forward cabin. Bed on either side for Beau and Josh, and the bedbugs!
7 Toilet and basin
8 Anchor well
9 Bow sprit and anchor roller. Dolphins would often play in the water below.
10 Ratlines, used to spot reefs.
11 Wind generators
12 Solar panels
13 Davits, which hold the dinghy out of the water.

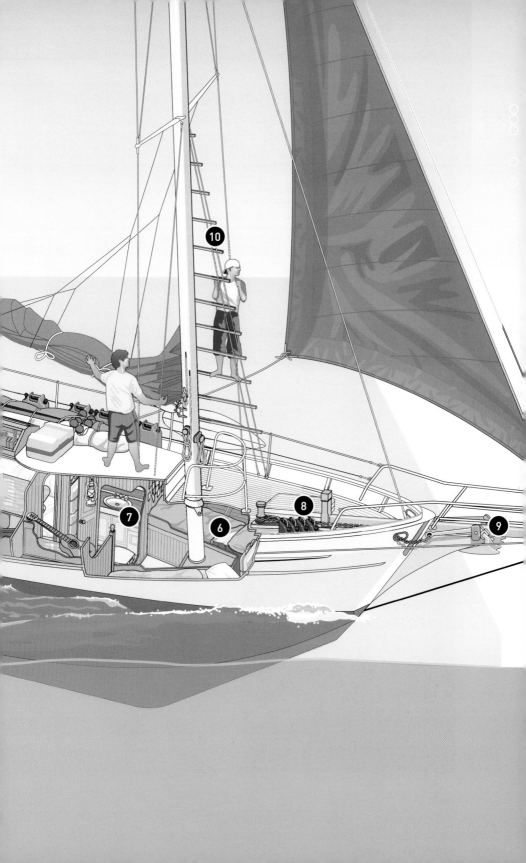

Me peering at skulls in one of the Torajan burial caves.

Josh shaving in the outdoor shower area in Toraja. We got used to doing without creature comforts.

The whole funeral arena was packed with buffalos for the village chief's funeral.

In Toraja, buffalos are sacrificed to honour the dead.

The family of Punans that the Blair brothers had met in the 1970s, and my inspiration for our trip into Borneo.

Grandfather Kila helped us realise what we were really searching for on Kijana.

The canoe trip down the river in Borneo was perhaps one of the greatest days of the voyage but, for me, it also held the biggest disappointment.

Our quest to meet the traditional Punan people took us into the deepest jungles in Borneo, where river travel is the primary form of transport.

Beau and I decided to get a
permanent reminder of our
time in Borneo.

The island of our dreams and the location of Maya Bay in Thailand.

Arriving at Maya Bay.

My best friend and me.

A fleeting moment of paradise – they did exist!

Unfortunately there was no Ben Harper or Pearl Jam on the stereo, just some metal gongs hanging from the branch of a sweeping tree on which the local men tapped a beat. These gongs made a dong noise each time they were hit, creating strange, atmospheric music, and giving the event its strange name.

On the dance floor the local women and men took it in turns to do a traditional dance. Nearly all the dances involved a scarf held behind the head between outstretched arms. The dancers' heads slowly rotated from side to side, like those clowns in a sideshow attraction, while their feet pounded the dusty ground in time to the gongs. The scarf would then be handed to someone in the audience, who would take the floor and attempt to mimic the dance that had just been performed.

Some of the surfers looked like they'd seen it all before, doing the dance very well. One of the younger surfers even had his arm around an old lady as if she was his grandma.

Someone then yelled an order, summoning all the women from the audience onto the floor. Maria joined the group as they formed a circle and proceeded to move in a clockwise direction while they kicked out their legs in a cancan-style dance.

While this was going on, the Australian guy plonked himself down in Maria's seat and surrendered the jug of sopi. He'd had his fill. Despite his drunken state, he introduced himself as Dave and explained that he'd helped organise the night with the family that was hosting the evening. He already knew we were the 'young people' from the ketch, complimenting us on our boat.

As he told us what the dances meant, we realised he actually lived with the family in the house. He explained he was trying to earn the community some extra income by organising these dong nights.

That immediately aroused our interest, so we asked if we could question him on camera. He wasn't keen on that idea, instead changing the subject. He was curious as to how such young people got to be cruising through Indonesia without any parents or adults. We told him about the Kijana adventure and what we were doing. He asked what Kijana meant.

'It's Swahili for young people,' we replied in unison, we'd got so used to answering the question.

'How old *are* you guys?' he asked.

I pointed to Maria: 'She's 22, Beau's 19.'

'I'm 22,' Josh continued, then, pointing at me, said: 'He's 20 ... actually 21 today.' It made me stop and think. He was right, it was so easy to forget. I was 21.

Dave nearly jumped out of his seat in excitement. He called out in Indonesian to an old man standing nearby who came over and listened to Dave explain something.

'This is Samuel,' Dave announced. 'He's the boss of this family.'

The man was small with a pointy face. He smiled at me and put out his hand to shake mine. The man then pointed to a boy walking towards us and called him over.

Dave introduced us. 'This is Rianto, Samuel's son. He's 21 today as well!'

He explained the circumstances to Rianto, who seemed delighted. He made some elaborate hand gestures, then shook my hand affectionately. I introduced Beau, and Josh and pointed out Maria who was still dancing. Dave was still very excited by my news. He continued speaking in Indonesian before turning back to us.

'Are you having a party? You can't turn 21 and not have a party.'

'Well, this has been a pretty good day so far,' I replied.

He continued speaking to Samuel, who was nodding his head.

'We'll organise a party for you,' Dave declared. He was speaking so quickly we could almost see his mind ticking over. 'We can have a few goats and make it a feast for everyone, I know a perfect spot down by the beach. It'll look great for the camera. You can film that instead.'

I wasn't sure what he was more excited about – my birthday or the fact that he'd been able to divert attention from himself. No matter. I was flattered by his enthusiasm. Rianto smiled at me like a brother. It was set.

The following morning I went to meet Dave at the house, as arranged. Daylight revealed the dry and scrubby landscape that had been shrouded in darkness the night before. I passed several small shacks on the way as I retraced the bus route. It was much further than I remembered.

As I arrived at the house, Rianto was sitting on the porch strumming a guitar. His eyes lit up when he saw me. The whole family came out and I was handed a cup of locally grown coffee.

'Is Dave here?' I asked. None of them spoke English but they understood Dave's name. I was shown into the house, which was almost completely bare. The floors were well-worn, smooth concrete, while a few cloth mats and a plastic chair in the corner were the only furniture in the main living room.

I was directed through a door to the right, where I found Dave asleep on a bed under a mosquito net. There were a few books on the windowsill and a single bag, which appeared to amount to his total possessions.

'David,' Rianto softly called. I left the room to let him get up in peace. A short while later he emerged, ducking under a doorway obviously not built for westerners. He was nursing a hangover but still seemed genuinely pleased to see me.

He finished the introductions he'd started the previous evening. Samuel's wife, Shysi, I recognised as one of the women who had been dancing the previous night. Another old man with a friendly smile was called Ahmad. He was Samuel's brother. Then there was Rianto, the boy who shared my birth date; his older sister Empy, who was about 25; her husband Ronny and daughter Aalyyah.

With the formalities over, Samuel and Ahmad led Rianto, Dave and me towards the beach, where they revealed the location they had in mind for my party.

It was a special site, Dave told me. Out towards the water lay hundreds of giant clam shells, each half a metre wide and facing upwards, towards the sky. For more than a century they'd been used to evaporate sea water so the precious salt that remained could be harvested for cooking. The men set to work clearing the hardy shrubs around the area, gathering them into a pile for burning.

While they did this, Dave showed me a half-built traditional hut of about 3 metres by 3 metres. As we inspected the hut, he told me the extraordinary tale of how he had come to be there.

Dave discovered Nembrala as a much younger man. He was like any of the surfers staying in the village, working in Australia merely to get enough money to travel through Indonesia surfing. He met Samuel and his family on one of his visits to Indonesia. Empy was only 11 years old at the time and bedridden with malaria, fighting for her life. With no local health system and very few doctors, there was nothing Samuel could do to help his daughter. The few doctors who could help lived in the major cities and Samuel could never afford their services, let alone the cost of getting her to them. She was destined to die within months.

Her plight so touched Dave that he returned to Australia to resume his job as a bricklayer, returning a few months later with money and a stash of medicine. With Dave's help, Empy slowly escaped the clutches of death and returned to normal health. She was now an adult with her own family. Samuel had thanked him the only way he could – he offered him the site we now stood on. With an ocean view and scrubby surroundings, Dave was in paradise. He now planned to retire and live permanently in Nembrala and the hut was to be his home.

Samuel and his family insisted they build him a big house but Dave refused. All he wanted was a little grass hut, his surfboard and a horse on which to ride to the surf. Their attempt to convince him to get a motorbike was met with a staunch refusal. They used petrol, he argued, and why buy that stuff when a horse could eat from the surrounding bush. He not only looked like Paul Hogan, he lived like Crocodile Dundee.

I asked Dave what had led him to his decision to live a 'primitive' life, as he described it.

He explained how he'd become fed up with aspects of modern life in Australia. For instance, he was sick of busting his gut laying bricks for houses, only to see them demolished within a few years because property values had risen, and a better house could be built in its place. Such waste angered him.

'You spend your whole life building stuff only to see it get knocked down,' he said.

He figured he'd be alive for another 20 years, so he wanted to go out leading a life he believed in. It was an extraordinary story. I wished Josh had been there with the camera.

We both stared out to the water until I finally broke the silence.

'So, how should we pay for this party?'

He looked at me sheepishly. I sensed the topic of money was a difficult one considering what he'd just told me.

'Well, I've had a word to the guys and they can't afford to give away any goats. A month ago half their stock was stolen by a neighbour, so I can't ask them for another two goats. What I was thinking is that you could cover the payment for the goats, and the rest they will cover – vegetables, rice and sopi.'

He paused to think, then continued, his enthusiasm returning: 'Agung will bring the dongs, and that reminds me, I've gotta find Trent. He's married to an Indonesian lady and can play guitar pretty good. So if that's all right with you, I'll give 'em the go-ahead for tomorrow night, then all we have to do is spread the word, yeah?'

'Sounds good to me. How much is a goat?'

'Twenty bucks or so, not much, but it's heaps for them. We'll have them in the morning, so come along and watch them prepare them if you like.'

On my way back I called into the home-stay to invite all the surfers.

While I was away, Beau and Maria had been cleaning the boat while Josh had set insect traps throughout the forward cabin. I told them of the plan and we scooted in the dinghy to the three other nearby yachts, inviting them to come along. Sam and Gabby on the small catamaran already knew. The word was spreading!

We spent the afternoon filming our attempts at surfing, with Josh donning the scuba gear to film the underwater shots. Dinner on board in the cool air capped off another day in paradise. I took a moment to think how far removed this was from the early stages of the trip.

By the morning it was obvious the bug traps would need some refinement. Josh and Beau had battled it out with the bed bugs all night, with Josh embarking on a bug-swiping spree using a library card to collect and squash them. Beau again opted to use a cup to capture them alive. Josh claimed 12 lives, Beau's tally was two. They sat in the cup on the galley bench, awaiting further argument on their fate.

By midmorning we were ready to go. We packed the camera gear and headed along the island in the dinghy to where the clam shells sat in the sun. When we arrived I discovered Beau had with him an empty Mars Bar wrapper which contained the two bugs. He solemnly walked up the beach and let them go in the tall grass. I hoped they didn't settle in Dave's hut.

We made the short walk to where the party preparations had already begun. The women from the nearby houses were already dressed in their best clothes. What immediately struck me was that they all wore the same coloured lipstick. It was an odd sight to see them in the cooking shed, leaning over a searing fire and grinding chilli paste in such delicate attire.

We all had a shot of sopi to kick-start the day, then followed the men to gather the goats.

The goats we were about to butcher had arrived the previous evening by motorbike. Ronny had picked them up from a relative who lived 20 kilometres away. The legs of each goat were tied together and wrapped around his stomach, one at the front and one at the back as he rode home.

The goats were herded from a pen to beneath a tree near the house. Within half an hour the two bleating goats had their throats cut and their blood drained into a bowl. They were then skinned and cut into pieces we could carry. Josh sat transfixed behind the camera as Ronny carried out the work. The best cuts went straight to the women in the shed while the heads and blood were kept by the men.

A fire was lit and a metal bowl placed over the flames. A drop of oil and some crushed chilli and salt began to sizzle before the blood was poured in. The colour was spectacular – bright red with green specs of chilli. It then started congealing and turned black. At this point it was taken into the cooking shed for the women to use in their preparations. Meanwhile, a goat's head sat in the coals, sizzling away until Ronny decided it was cooked. The skull was smashed between two large rocks until the brain was exposed. Seeing as I was the birthday boy I was offered first taste.

'Interesting,' I said as I popped a morsel into my mouth.

It was the only word I could muster that I thought would not offend. Its texture resembled warm baby food, yet it was sort of taste-less. I eagerly passed the skull to Beau, hoping his newfound bug-saving beliefs didn't mean he was going to shirk tasting the goat's brain. He took the skull, possibly out of politeness, and tasted the brain. Always there for me when it matters, I thought.

Maria declined, saying she'd better go and see if the women needed any help. Josh was busying himself with the camera functions – what a professional – but he was not about to get out of it that easily. I reminded him of what he'd said at the start of the trip: 'If it's part of a cultural experience then I'll try it'.

He knew he couldn't get out of it, and reluctantly agreed to a taste. I grabbed the camera to record such a momentous event. He'd eaten crab and fish with Gayili and her children in northern Australia, so it was a logical step to move on to red meat in Indonesia.

'White meat,' Josh corrected me. 'It's a brain!'

The smile and bravado disappeared as he examined the piece in his fingers. It slowly began its journey towards his mouth. He hesi-tated backwards and forwards, wanting to do it but not being able to seal the deal. He dropped his hand by his side, laughed one of his nervous giggles, then closed his eyes and popped it into his mouth.

'I've eaten brain,' he yelled, both arms raised in victory. Ronny and Samuel found this pretty funny, if not a bit odd.

While most of the goat was destined for the evening meal, the back legs were eaten for lunch. Samuel's wife cut a chunk off for each of us and we washed it down with another shot of sopi. It was delicious.

I watched Dave sitting among the old men, listening to them and chatting. He really did fit in. He may have been taller, bigger and whiter but they resembled a gang of wise old men.

'They've really turned it on for you guys,' he told us later, 'I've never seen this much food at the one time, except at a wedding.'

He told us the locals usually only had two small meals a day. For breakfast they would collect palm sugar and mix it with water to make a drink that tasted like honey. It was the same stuff the locals distilled the sopi from. Lunch would usually be rice and a small amount of meat. Dinner was a rare event, so they too were looking forward to that evening's feast.

By early afternoon the number of women in the cooking shed had increased. They were stripping beans, tossing stir-fries and pounding more chilli into paste. It was getting so crowded in the small shelter that more fires were lit outside to accommodate large woks of rice which were stirred by women using big poles.

While this was going on, we helped the younger kids shuttle tables and benches to the party site. A large table was placed in the party area to hold the food and we set up our filming lights for when the sun went down. The metal dongs were already hanging from a tree and two drums rested on a grass woven mat in the middle of the setting. Dave was running around like a mother-in-law, confirming and reconfirming that we would have enough sopi and acting as translator for our questions.

Soon it was late afternoon. There was not much more to do except wait and hope for a good turnout. The kids asked Dave if we could take them for a ride in our dinghy, so I took them for a quick spin before the crew returned to *Kijana* to wash and get dressed for the evening ahead.

We returned to the beach, where the air was heavy with anticipation. The first guests to arrive were Dave's mate Trent and his wife. In Trent's hand was a guitar.

'This is good,' Dave assured me, 'Trent's a good guitar player.' Trent took a seat on the woven mats in the centre of the party area. Ronny sat beside him and started to beat a rhythm on a goatskin drum. Trent began strumming a song and they both began singing what was obviously a well-known Indonesian tune.

All right! I thought. We had a party.

Kids crowded around and joined in the music as more guests began to arrive. It was a party in the truest sense. Everyone felt like an outsider, but that only increased the sense of excitement and after the bottles of sopi were passed around, the conversation flowed.

Dinner was served before dark. I looked around as everyone ate, taking a moment to consider the bizarreness of the occasion. It was my twenty-first birthday, yet I hardly knew anyone. If I was at home I'd have invited nearly everyone I'd ever known in my life, waiting until my old school teachers and relatives went home, before getting plastered with my mates. I never dreamt that I would be in Nembrala, and everywhere around me I would be looking at friendly, yet unfamiliar faces.

I was heartened by the festive tone of every conversation I could hear. Local Indonesians, barefooted and wearing torn clothes were laughing with yachties wearing leather deck shoes and aftershave. Who cared whose birthday it was, it was just a good reason to get together.

As it grew darker Josh repositioned the filming lights to keep us illuminated, while Samuel appeared with a clump of hand-threaded leaves which, when lit, burnt like a torch out of *Indiana Jones*. He dug a hole and propped up the torch with two rocks. While the stark filming lights gave plenty of light, it was the burning leaves that provided the atmosphere.

The night continued, with more drinking, singing and dancing to the rhythm of the dongs. Later in the evening the festivities moved 20 metres or so onto the beach where a fire was lit and Trent belted out some of his best songs. He was a very soulful singer, even if his voice was dirtier than Bob Dylan with a hangover. There must have been 50 people scattered around the flickering light, sitting on top of the rock ledge or playing with their feet in the sand.

I could make out Dave's face by the glow of the fire. He appeared to be lost in a world of sopi, staring blankly into the fire. His eyes broke from their stare as a burning stick snapped and a stream of cinders floated into the air above. As I too stared into the hottest coals of the fire, I remembered something Dave had mentioned to me the day before.

He'd told me of a group of men and women living as God had

intended – unashamedly naked and freely roaming among thousands of square kilometres of virgin forest. They were not figures of folklore, for they really did exist, Dave assured me. They were known as the Punan tribe and lived in the forests of Kalimantan on the island of Borneo. Little was known of them, for sightings were few, but they were mountain dwellers, living in small groups and constantly moving through impenetrable rainforest. They were both feared and revered as the ultimate jungle dwellers. What interested me was that they were able to live the life they wanted, without any of the crap of modern life. They represented everything I yearned to be.

As soon as Dave told me about the Punans, I decided the Kijana mission would be to film these people and let others know that it was possible to live life the way they chose to live. Also, if we could capture them on film then surely our documetaries would be sold. And that ultimately would mean Maya could join us on board *Kijana*. Dave had influenced us more than he probably ever imagined.

The following day, Ronny gave me a lift on his motorbike to the nearest major town to get some money to pay for the goats. Unfortunately, all the banks were shut, forcing me to return to Nembrala with only enough money to pay for one goat. Dave kindly lent me the A$20 to pay for the remaining goat, which I promised to repay by posting the amount to him. I thanked Dave, Samuel and his family for everything they'd done, then said goodbye and returned to *Kijana*.

It was sad to leave our new friends but we had to keep moving.

CHAPTER SEVEN
DRAGONS

WE SAILED THROUGH THE NIGHT AND MOST OF the next day. The wind came steadily from behind and we made good progress. Maria was handling the watches well and she was over her seasickness. Only when the wind got above 25 knots, which was rare, did she start to feel queasy.

The wind, while generally lighter as we got closer to the equator, always seemed to be enough to keep the sails raised and the engine off. This was a blessing for those in the rear cabin. Being so close to the engine room, it was extremely noisy and stinking hot when we had the motor running.

Crew morale was great. We'd had a lot of fun since we left Darwin. But beneath the surface I continued to feel the pressure of expectation on me, the feeling that I could never have too much fun because there was always more work to do, more to film, another update to write and, of course, boat maintenance. There was constant pressure from the office to make quality films to pay for the adventure.

I hoped to solve that problem at our next stop, Pulau Rinca, the island home of the infamous komodo dragon. We sailed for three days, past the low-lying tropical islands around Roti, which made way for the more volcanic and visually stunning island of Sumba. Our challenge when we arrived at Rinca was to capture the komodo dragons on film close-up. In fact, just getting close to such reclusive beasts would be a major achievement.

I was excited about the assignment, but also a bit frightened. We'd heard varying reports about the komodos. They ranged in size from a large lizard to crocodile sized. And they could run – fast! If bitten by a komodo, it was said, the victim would eventually die. Even if one could wrestle with the lizard and get away, the bacteria from the komodo's teeth would eventually poison its prey.

It was hard to tell how much of these stories to believe. I could hardly believe anything could contain enough bacteria to kill a human. Nonetheless, to help us get the required close-up shots of the dragons we decided to use live chickens as bait to attract the hungry lizards. We weren't sure how this would work, but it had to be better than nothing. We had to capture them on film or our visit would be a waste of time.

We anchored *Kijana* in the small harbour of Waingapu on Sumba and made our way to the market where we purchased two chickens and a flimsy cage to keep them in.

Rather than stay in port, we weighed anchor before it got dark and sailed through the night. The chickens made a hell of a noise as they sat on deck, but once the sun went down they thankfully stopped clucking. We made such good progress over the 60-odd miles to Rinca that we were forced to slow down so we didn't arrive before the sun rose.

I replaced Josh for the last watch and, as the sky in the east began to lighten up, I could make out a channel between two mountainous islands. These were Rinca and Komodo Islands. Irrespective of the island names, we'd been told there were more dragons on Rinca.

As morning dawned, the wind died and I turned on the engine to motor the last few miles. The engine noise slowly woke the others and by the time Beau and Josh were on deck we had entered the channel. We found a small, protected bay and dropped anchor. No sooner had the engine been cut than Josh had the binoculars aimed at the shore in search of dragons.

'Can they swim?' Maria asked. It was a good question. I knew the iguanas of the Galapagos Islands could swim.

'Possibly,' I replied. I'm not sure if it was the answer she was after.

'Well, even if they could,' Beau reasoned, 'I doubt they could leap a metre from the water up on deck.' However, he sounded less than convincing.

Josh saw some monkeys playing in seaweed and something that looked like a deer sitting in the shade of a tree – but no dragons.

We spent the morning exploring the island and searching for dragons. It was very dry and hard to believe that anything could survive on it. Only the hardiest of trees prospered while the rest of the vegetation appeared to be dead. The grass was brown and the soil crumbled easily beneath our feet. And it was bloody hot.

As the midday sun reached its pinnacle we decided to pull the pin and return to the boat for a drink and to formulate a plan.

'Maybe we're making too much noise,' I suggested.

Everyone agreed, so we decided to head out in the cool of the following morning when we could travel more efficiently. We also decided to take along the chickens to try our luck.

That night I prepared the backpacks for an expedition deep into the island, packing everything necessary for an overnight stay. If we walked as far as we could, then lay in wait, perhaps the komodos would make their way to us.

We set off early, leaving the dinghy on the beach safely above the high-tide mark. It was a beautiful sight to witness the rays of light creeping over the mountains on Komodo Island and lighting up the peaks on Rinca.

We picked a point that led into the mountains and began our climb. It was rough terrain and the packs threw us off balance. Also, we were carrying two live chickens. We made it to the top of the first rise only to realise the downward trek into the next valley was heavily bushy. The dry bushes scratched our skin and the packs felt heavier and heavier. At one point the only effective way to get through the twigs was to fall into a bush to clear a path ahead.

When we hit the bottom of the valley I recognised the bay as the one next along from where *Kijana* was anchored. Maria looked around, slightly puzzled.

'Weren't we here yesterday in the dinghy?'

I was horrified to realise we'd spent one and a half hours bashing through the bush in searing heat, making enough noise to scare any animal within three kilometres, when we could have got to the same place by dinghy in ten minutes.

We had a short break while I tried to muster up some enthusiasm for the next uphill climb. The sun was now beating down and I had already drunk half my water. Once we got underway we realised this climb was even worse. At times we were on all fours, so steep was the incline.

I was getting increasingly frustrated at what was turning out to be a foolhardy attempt to find the dragons. The soles of my shoes were slippery and gave no traction on the thick layer of dry grass. I looked around to see everyone else seemingly handling the climb better then me. I started to wonder if my pack was heavier than theirs. I came to a large rock in my path. It was about a metre high and there was no practical way around it. I sort of leapt at it in an effort to clear it, pushing off the ground with all my energy only to feel my feet slip out from under me. Like a cartoon character, peddling my feet midair to find a grip, I was thrown off balance and the weight of my pack ensured my chest hit the ground with a thud.

I wanted to cry with frustration as I lay prone on the ground examining the base of the stupid boulder that was just centimetres from my face. Maybe I should've gone around the bastard. My mood was made no better by the fact that Josh had managed to get way ahead of me. He had enough energy to bound back with the camera and film my struggle.

We eventually got to a clearing and let the chickens roam nearby while we munched on some dry biscuits and cheese for lunch.

'We're not going to see anything with the amount of noise we're making,' Josh commented.

At that point I couldn't have cared less about the dragons. I'd banged my knee several times and all I wanted to do was sit still and drink the last of my water. Maria suggested we wait there, and hopefully the dragons would smell the chickens and come to us. Everyone was happy to go along with her suggestion. I was particularly enthusiastic about it.

After we ate, we rigged up a sunshade. The afternoon wore on and the temperature continued to rise, but still there was no sign of any dragons. I stayed under the shade while Josh headed further uphill with the camera, and Beau and Maria went down to the bay for a swim.

I felt like such an idiot, making the crew walk so far carrying so much stuff. It now seemed such a totally inefficient way to find the dragons. I wondered what the others thought. For me to lead the journey, they had to believe in what I asked them to do. Follies like that wouldn't help instil much faith in their leader.

The next thing I knew Josh was waking me. I'd been asleep for a couple of hours. He'd climbed along a ridge as far as he could before it fell away at a cliff face. He'd returned to find me asleep, Beau and Maria still swimming, and the chickens missing.

It was a disaster. I'd lost the chickens, it was now late afternoon and we were out of water – so much for my expedition planning. I felt like a complete fool, but the crew seemed to be able to get a laugh out of it.

We decided to head back to the boat before it got dark. The chickens were long gone, probably in the belly of an elusive dragon, so we bade them farewell.

Josh and I gathered all the packs we could carry and headed for the beach. Beau and Maria would just have to come back for the rest. Once again I was astounded by Josh's energy. He arrived at the beach and had already told Beau and Maria of the plan well before I arrived. I only had the energy to nod as they passed me on their way up the hill.

I found Josh sitting under a tree looking out at the water. I dropped the pack from my shoulder and slumped down beside him. He had a strange smile on his face.

'I know, I'm buggered. I don't know what's wrong with me today,' I tried to explain.

'Nah, it's not that,' he said. 'I just came down, before you got here and … don't say anything …'

'Nah, I won't,' I assured him, intrigued by what he was hiding.

'… and those two were kissing!'

I looked up the hill to where he nodded, as if I expected to see someone other than Beau and Maria.

'Really!' I said, trying to understand what he actually meant. It took a while to sink in.

'Did they see you?'

'I dunno, but don't say anything to them.'

My brain took the next logical step.

'Where they … you know …?'

He laughed, then began to tell me exactly what he saw. I tried not to smile when they returned and we began the hike back to the boat.

I woke the next morning from an exhausted sleep to the sound of loud bangs on *Kijana*'s hull and a woman's voice I didn't recognise. I was startled to see that the sun was already up and *Kijana* was not in the same position as when I went to sleep.

I went up on deck to find a man and woman in a dinghy holding *Kijana*'s safety lines.

'Ya anchor's dragging,' the woman said matter-of-factly.

It certainly was. We were in the middle of the channel. The depth sounder revealed we were in 70 metres of water, not the 14 metres we'd been anchored in. I didn't know what to say back to her. I estimated we'd drifted several hundred metres.

'Ahh, thanks,' I said, sounding like a twit.

Beau and Maria emerged to see what was going on just as I reached for the engine key and ordered the anchor to be pulled in.

Still coming to terms with the situation, I thanked the man and woman again properly.

'We didn't know if you were leaving or what, then we saw you heading for the rocks over there and knew something must be wrong,' she said.

They kindly stayed with us until they were confident we were under control, before wishing us luck and heading back to their yacht.

'Where's Josh?' I asked.

'He went ashore to look for dragons.' Beau replied. Josh was determined to film the dragons, so Beau had dropped him off on the island as the sun was rising.

We decided to drop anchor in the next bay, closer to another yacht, where we presumed the seabed would do a better job of holding us. As we dropped anchor, I realised Josh was going to return to the beach and find the boat gone.

We'd been at our new mooring for less than 30 minutes when a steel-hulled launch with two big outboard motors sped into the bay heading directly for us. I could see half a dozen Indonesian men sitting on its deck. I was immediately concerned. It wasn't a typical Indonesian fishing boat and they appeared to have *Kijana* firmly in their sights. Then, sitting among the men, I could see Josh's long hair blowing in the wind. My immediate reaction was relief. He'd made some friends, I thought.

The launch pulled up alongside and Josh stepped onto *Kijana*, pushing the boat off with his foot at the same time. I searched the men's faces for an answer as to how they had come to have Josh on board.

'OK, thanks a lot,' Josh said in an unusually high tone, as if he was stressed. It then struck me that the men were in uniform and, upon further inspection, I realised two of them were carrying automatic rifles.

'I'll tell you later,' Josh said quietly to me. I put on a friendly face and waved to the men, hoping they'd go away. They eventually pulled away and left. The moment they were out of earshot I demanded to know what the hell was going on.

He explained that not long after Beau had dropped him on the island he had entered the undergrowth and spotted something he thought was a dragon. It quickly disappeared, so he set off in pursuit. After startling an army of monkeys, he finally spotted his quarry, a dragon a couple of metres long. He gave chase but only caught glimpses of it through the viewfinder. Nevertheless, it was a victory. The komodo dragon did exist.

He'd decided to head back to the boat to tell us the good news, but when he got to the beach he was confronted by a band of young men, two of whom carried rifles. They said they were representatives from the police, National Parks and a few other organisations who wanted to see his permit. When he couldn't produce one, they accused him of trespassing. The leader began to get aggressive. The other men roamed the beach working out where he had been and accused him of hiding a dinghy.

Struggling with the language barrier, he tried to explain he'd been dropped off by a friend, but when he went to point out *Kijana*, which should have been 40 metres offshore, she was gone. It only made the men more suspicious. Josh said he would show them the boat he was from if they would give him a lift.

One man remained on the shore, apparently trying to find evidence that Josh was a smuggler, while the others escorted him aboard their launch to search for his alleged 'yacht'. Once they left the bay, *Kijana* quickly came into view. Josh gladly pointed her out, which was the point at which we saw them heading for us.

As Josh began to retell his story to Beau and Maria, I spotted the launch heading towards us again.

'Hide the guns,' I ordered, 'and remember, we're just tourists. Don't mention anything about filming.' I suspected these characters would be willing to pin us on any number of legalities, although I wasn't aware we needed permission to go onto the island or to film.

Josh grabbed the camera to film the confrontation. 'Try to be subtle,' I warned him. 'Remember, we're tourists!'

The launch arrived and we nodded in recognition. Beau and Maria came back on deck after hiding the guns. A short man stood at the bow wearing a bright orange construction worker's vest. I took the line from him and tied them off. I couldn't remember seeing him before, so I presumed he was the one who had remained on the beach searching for evidence. He also appeared to be the leader of the troop.

His English was very bad, made worse by my conscious effort not to understand him. My strategy was to make it so hard for them to do their job that they would leave. I shot curious looks back at my crew, shrugged shoulders and threw in the few Indonesian words I knew. As the man became more frustrated, his voice rose.

'Tourist, tourist,' I repeated. He understood we were tourists but wanted to see our permit. After much haggling, the angry man turned and spoke to one of his men. A beefy chap jumped to his feet and handed his rifle to a colleague, then prepared to step aboard *Kijana*.

I knew that under maritime law a person must request permission from the captain to board his vessel. It was also good manners. But when it came to men in uniforms bearing weapons, none of these points seemed to carry much weight. The man was soon on the deck of *Kijana*.

The leader was becoming angry and began to yell at me. I eventually worked out that he wanted us to buy a permit. I knew a man with a gun could ask any price he liked. Maybe it was better just to pay, no matter how exorbitant the price, rather than have them search the boat and find our guns and computer gear.

Then something happened which triggered a chain of events. One of the men reached out to pass the rifle to the man on deck. As he did so, the ammunition magazine dropped from the gun and fell between the small gap between *Kijana* and the launch. The 'plop' of a metal object dropping into water grabbed everyone's attention, even the angry man. He posed a question in Indonesian and half a dozen bodies moved to peer over the side of the launch to see where the magazine had disappeared.

The tone of the encounter changed dramatically. It went from starforce troopers to Keystone Cops in an instant. The fool on *Kijana* sheepishly inspected the rifle where the magazine should have been, while his mates peered vainly into 12 metres of water.

Their threatening image suddenly dissipated. They were no longer straight-faced soldiers intent on getting the job done, but little boys desperately wanting to get their toy back.

One of the younger men lifted his head and gestured towards his face. He wanted to know if we had a diving mask. Beau went to the anchor well and pulled out a mask, handing it to the intruder on deck. The young man took off his clothes and replaced his balaclava with the mask. With the strap pushing out one of his ears he looked like a dog with a floppy ear, not the frightening invader of a few minutes ago.

He climbed over the side and put his head in the water, but the mask was leaking and he quickly pulled it out again. I motioned to the now not-so-angry man that his colleague had to remove all the hair from his face so the mask could properly seal. He barked some orders and the job was done. We watched for several minutes while the man duck-dived under water, each time returning to the surface empty-handed. I started to feel sorry for them.

'Maybe we should get the dive gear,' I suggested. Beau agreed, even volunteering to do the dive himself. Josh helped him put on the diving gear and the launch was moved away so that he could step in. He released the air in his jacket and dropped below the surface, leaving a stream of bubbles erupting on the surface. I nodded to the angry man and he gave a slow nod back. We waited and said nothing.

Thirty seconds later Beau emerged with the clip in his hands. The men helped him out of the water and Beau passed the magazine over. They immediately began wiping it dry with their T-shirts.

The angry man gave a smile but kept up his stern voice and said we could stay one more night. We weren't allowed to go ashore and we must leave early in the morning and head straight for a town I'd never heard of. He would meet us there and we were to buy a permit for the equivalent of A$15. I figured the price had dropped considerably in the previous few minutes, so I agreed to his offer.

I thanked the man and untied their line, watching as they left with their tails firmly between their legs.

And so ended our quest for the komodo dragon. I can't say I was displeased to leave Rinca and the dragons behind, even if I felt we had failed.

We were unable to find the town we had been ordered to on the chart, so we continued onto the town of Labuhanbajo on the island of Flores. We sailed the entire day, right around Rinca, before arriving at the small bustling settlement on the western tip of Flores. A tiny island off the coast provided sufficient protection for the fishing fleet that called the town home. It was almost dark by time we manoeuvred *Kijana* through the maze of small fishing boats, dropping anchor within rowing distance of the shore.

The following morning I was woken by the sound of Muslim prayers playing over a loudspeaker from a nearby mosque. The fishing boats were leaving port and we noticed that another yacht had arrived during the night.

We had breakfast, then went ashore. Beau and Maria headed to the market to restock our fresh food stores for the four-day sail to Makasar, while Josh and I walked around looking at several fishing boats that had obviously been built by local craftsmen, nestled in the mud at low tide.

On the way back to *Kijana*, Josh and I called by the new yacht to say hello. The entire length of the boat, where the safety lines ran along the edge of the deck, was lined with solar panels.

We gave a yell and were immediately welcomed aboard by a man wearing a sarong. Dave, a fellow Aussie aged in his thirties, was in the middle of cooking breakfast – a big coral trout simmering away in a frying pan. Dave lit the stove and put on the kettle after offering us a cup of tea.

'Quite a set-up,' I said, tapping one of the solar panels. 'How come so many?'

'I need them to move,' he replied. He took us down below and uncovered his engine. 'She doesn't use one ounce of diesel. When there's no wind, it's usually sunny, so I run the electric motor. She's the greenest boat you'll find.'

I asked how often he had to motor. 'Since I got out of Australia, it's been 80 per cent of the time. The thing is, I only get around five hours of motoring for every full day of sun on the panels, so it's been kinda slow.'

I was intrigued as to why he would go to such lengths, so after our cup of tea I asked if we could interview him on camera.

'Sure,' he said. He planned to go to the market but would be back in the afternoon. We thanked him for the tea and headed back to *Kijana* to wait for Beau and Maria with the food.

While we waited I wrote down some questions to ask Dave. Surely it would have been cheaper for him to have a diesel engine, especially with the price of fuel in Indonesia. It was only about 30 cents a litre, compared to one dollar back home. We had solar panels on *Kijana*, but they were only used for lights and charging the computers and camera gear. I was intrigued by this strange man and his unusual set-up.

Later that afternoon Josh and I headed over to interview Dave. He had another fish on the frying pan, this time a species I didn't know.

'Do you mind if I eat during this?' he asked.

'Sure, go ahead,' we said. Josh set up the camera and we were rolling.

It turned out that, yes, it would have been cheaper for him to put in a diesel engine, but Dave considered himself a greenie. The boat was central to that philosophy, so the money he spent on solar panels was worth it, as far as he was concerned.

Ironically, his background was in the oil industry, where he had worked as an engineer on rigs drilling for oil. He pointed out that this gave him a good understanding of both sides of the story. He felt compelled to take up the environmental cause because of his disgust at the way some world leaders disregarded the environment. His anger, in particular, was directed at the United States. As he put it, the Kyoto greenhouse gas protocol had been set up by the United States then, at the eleventh hour, the same nation, which spews out the most greenhouse gases, decided not to agree to cut back on emissions. Australia was another country not willing to 'do its share,' he said.

'You don't have to be all that clever to see that the problem is going to snowball,' he said to the camera. 'Anyone who argues that human impact cannot be proven for the ecological changes taking place has got their head in the sand. A panel of the world leading scientists have released papers confirming they have proof.' He was getting pretty fired up, but quickly calmed down to explain how he was doing his bit.

'Current alternative power sources like solar and wind generation still need more research and development until they're sufficient enough to sustain the world's energy needs. Research only happens when there is consumer demand, so I figure it's worth spending my cash on something that's not yet as good as diesel but encourages the alternative energy industry to get better.'

'Or we could stop using as much energy,' I suggested, deviating slightly from my role as interviewer.

'Yeah, but who's gonna do that?' he asked. 'Not your average person who considers themselves struggling as it is.'

I found myself joining his outrage. If I knew which politicians had such blatant disregard for the earth, I would never vote for them. I made a mental note to register to vote, something I'd never worried about before. We finished the interview and thanked Dave for his time. More importantly, I thanked him for his passionate views. They were more valuable to me than anything we caught on film.

We decided to leave the following morning. We were restocked and keen to get away from Labuhanbajo before our police friends spotted us and nabbed us for not buying a permit. I was pleased to find a healthy breeze when we woke the next morning. Dave had already departed and half the fishing fleet had also left port.

We weighed anchor and sailed out of the bay, heading for the island of Sulawesi, about 250 miles due north. We were heading there because the office had organised for us to spend time with the aid organisation Plan International in the major city of Makasar. The aim was to see Plan's projects in Indonesia and demonstrate how the aid money was being put to good use.

By the time we left Labuhanbajo Beau and Maria had become openly affectionate. In port they'd used the excuse that their cabins were too hot, forcing them to take their mattresses up on deck. A likely story.

The trip to Makasar was expected to take four days, but that was assuming we were able to sail. Alas, the wind died a few hours into the trip, until the sails were doing more damage by shuddering the rigging as we crawled along at $2^1/2$ knots.

I had no choice but to fire up the engine while the others tied up the sails. For the next two days the wind continued to lift then drop. The engine was constantly going on and off, and every time I turned the key I thought of the greenhouse gases I was adding to the atmosphere. However, I knew there had to be a balance. Where did I draw the line between acting responsibly for the good of the world and acting for the success of Kijana? When there was no wind, we were wasting time that could be used for filming. Without film, there would be no Kijana. So we had to go faster than the wind sometimes allowed us, and that meant burning fuel. It was a vicious cycle, for we needed to sell the documentaries to get the money to buy more diesel to film more documentaries. My encounter with Dave had really messed with my mind.

CHAPTER EIGHT
TALKING TO THE DEAD

THE PLAN TEAM HAD BEEN AWAITING OUR arrival and had kindly organised a space in the local docks where we could moor *Kijana*. After inspecting the site, we politely declined. The concrete wharves would grind *Kijana*'s timber hulls away and I didn't trust the driving skills of the huge metal tankers that would be coming and going beside us. Instead we anchored *Kijana* off the main beach, close to the local transport jetty where we could leave our dinghy when ashore.

It had taken us three days to get to Makasar, with about 60 per cent of the trip completed under motor. However, I had more than atmospheric pollution on my mind. We had only four hours of tape remaining, which was dangerously low, so the office had arranged for a box of 20 tapes to be sent to the Plan building for us to collect when we arrived. Also, our three-month Indonesian visas were close to expiring, so we immediately set to work getting a visa extension. Several days later, after accusations that we were carrying false papers, Josh had our passports freshly stamped. This extended our stay in the country for an extra two months.

Like any arrival at a major centre, the first few days were spent restocking the boat's supplies. Makasar had everything a big city of one million people usually offers – two cinemas, a Pizza Hut and a shopping mall. We'd almost forgotten what air conditioning felt like, until we discovered the mall. Maria again helped Beau with the food shopping, while Josh and I caught a rickshaw with our jerry cans to refill the boat with diesel. Each jerry can held 20 litres and we had five of them. Two trips later and she was refuelled.

The next job was water. As in most of Indonesia, we couldn't be sure whether the water was safe to drink or not. We took our chances and filled our water cans, carrying them back to the boat and emptying them into the main water tanks. With each can we poured in we also added a few millilitres of chlorine, hoping it would kill any bacteria.

The next day was spent cleaning the inside of the boat.

It wasn't until the third day at Makasar that we felt *Kijana* was up to scratch and the four of us could catch a rickshaw to the Plan office to begin our tour and use their showers for a decent freshwater cleanse.

Once we felt clean enough to be around other humans, we sat down and met the team at Plan, who explained to us their projects and asked which ones we'd like to see. Our enthusiasm for filming as much as we could was tempered by the fact that our tapes had so far failed to arrive.

Over the next week we travelled through the sprawling metropolis of Makasar, and beyond, to see Plan's work. With money donated by sponsors in wealthier countries, Plan is able to help local communities survive and live a higher standard of life. One of the first places we visited was the local rubbish dump where unemployed people followed around the dump trucks, sifting through the fresh rubbish in search of anything made from plastic. With a basket slung over one shoulder, they would stab at crushed bottles and the like with a sharpened metal rod, swinging their bounty into their basket. Plan organised for the collected plastic to be sent off for recycling, with the money earned going straight back to the collectors, who ranged from old women to young boys and girls. Without this program, these people would have struggled to survive.

Another Plan project was to build water wells in drought-stricken areas to ensure the drinking water was clean from disease-spreading bacteria, while yet another project involved buying ducks for families, who were then taught how to breed and incubate the fertilised eggs. This would not only provide food for struggling families, but also provide some income so they could afford to send their children to school.

Everything Plan did was aimed at serving the community and the money seemed well spent. Their office, for instance, was simple and showed no sign of unwarranted spending. Most of all, we got the sense the workers had a passion for helping the community.

After a week in Makasar our tapes had still not arrived and there was a growing concern that they'd been stolen or lost in the Indonesian mail system. We'd seen everything Plan was doing and I was keen to start the next leg of the trip to Borneo in an attempt to find and film the Punans. But we couldn't leave until the new tapes arrived and none of the local electronics stores stocked the type we required.

The Plan team were invaluable in making phone calls to track down the missing parcel. They were eventually able to find it. Unfortunately it was sitting in Indonesian Customs, with an import tax bill of A$1500 slapped on it. Considering that the value of the tapes was A$1800 it was daylight robbery, especially in our parlous financial situation. We simply couldn't afford to blow that amount of money. In a double blow, we discovered that something was wrong with one of our cameras. A pixelating line had appeared through every shot of our most recent filming. After a few tests, Josh and I realised we had a problem that needed serious attention.

My email to the office broke both pieces of bad news. They agreed with my view that we simply had to get the camera fixed, no matter what the cost. There was a Sony repair centre on the island of Java, which meant one of us would have to fly the camera over to get the repairs done. However, the import tax on the tapes was another issue. The office was as outraged as I was at the charge, vowing to do everything to make the authorities see reason. We agreed that we'd need a week to sort out the mess. If we hadn't untangled the tapes from officialdom by then, we'd probably have no choice but to pay what was clearly a corrupt charge.

Josh left that afternoon with the camera. We hoped it could be fixed in a day, which meant he'd be back in a few days. Now that we knew we would be in Makasar for at least another week, Beau, Maria and I began planning an expedition into the mountains of Sulawesi, which we would embark on as soon as Josh returned. The highland area, known as Tana Toraja, was well known for its funeral ceremonies and strange burial customs. Relatives would reputedly preserve a deceased family member in their home for a few months before they were buried. If we could get that on film, we knew we would have some knockout footage.

It felt good to finally have something to do, for we were growing tired of drifting around Makasar waiting for the tapes.

It was particularly frustrating for Maria. She'd been with us for more than the two months we had initially agreed upon, but she'd fitted in superbly. She was great company, especially for Beau, who I felt, at times, was the loner on board. Not that he wasn't one of the boys, but it was just that Josh and I got on so well and because we both had the challenge of filming, we found ourselves drawn together as a two-man team. Since Maria had come aboard, she and Beau had found much in common and their affection for each other was now obvious to all.

However, all good things must come to an end. It came in the form of an email to Maria from her brother. He was flying out from Denmark to meet her in Australia. She had just three weeks left with us. Of course, she wanted to make the most of the remaining time, but we were stuck until Josh returned.

Makasar was a pretty dirty place and much rougher than Kupang. It was definitely not a regular stopover for tourist yachts. In fact, we hadn't seen any other westerners in the two weeks we'd been there.

The lack of exposure to outsiders meant that the locals knew very little of Australia, or any other developed country, for that matter. Their only knowledge came from what they saw at the movies – for those who could afford to go to the movies, that is.

The sight of a white person was definitely a rarity, especially a pretty, young Danish girl dressed in clean clothes. On nearly every street corner someone would say 'hello mister' to Maria. The rest of us were not immune. 'Hello mister,' they'd yell – beggars, passing cars, stallkeepers, anyone. Male and female, it made no difference. We were all 'mister'. After a while it started to play on our nerves, so we chose to spend most of our time in the privacy of *Kijana*'s decks.

To relieve the boredom while we waited for Josh, Beau devised a way of making a type of homebrew. He took a 20-litre jerry can of water, added 5 kilos of sugar, 1 kilo of diced fruit and a few packets of yeast. After two weeks the jerry can's contents would ferment in the heat of the tropical sun and transform into 'jungle juice', a fizzy, slightly off-tasting fruit wine. At least, that was the plan. Like so many home brews temptation proved too great and Beau and Maria tapped it after only a few days. By late afternoon the pair of them could be found sitting on the bow, jungle juice in hand. Beau would have his guitar in hand, playing out-of-tune Red Hot Chilli Peppers songs while Maria laughed and sang along with him.

I left the others aboard and went in to see Plan to find out the best way of getting to Toraja. They offered to make some phone calls and said I should call them the following day. On the way back to the boat I walked through a lane of stores that sold homemade birdcages and pet birds. I inspected each bird to see if any were an endangered species. Parts of Indonesia were home to the rare bird of paradise, but luckily there didn't appear to be any among that lot.

I figured that we could do with some new faces on the boat, so I paid A$15 for a small cage and two finch-type birds that seemed full of energy. Feeling happy with my purchase, I continued on until I got to the local international telephone shop where I sat the birds down in my booth and dialled Maya's number.

Unfortunately I had no further news on her joining us, despite the fact that Maria was leaving in a few weeks. I told her how frustrating it was waiting for the tapes, then how the camera had broken. She was quiet and didn't appear to be very interested.

I asked her the latest news from home. There wasn't much. She'd visited a pet shop that day and had seen a small Quaker parrot that she liked, but it cost $500. I told her about the cute finches I'd bought for $15. Again, there was little reaction. It was hard to feel close to her when she was like that.

'Maria is leaving soon,' I said. 'She has to meet her brother in Darwin.' We both knew the significance of this piece of news. We were both hanging onto the hope that she could join *Kijana*. I didn't know how best to say what I wanted to say next.

'So hopefully that means we'll be together soon.' I was trying to be diplomatic. I didn't dare say, 'you'll be allowed on soon'. She didn't respond, becoming even more withdrawn in our conversation.

'Isn't that good?' I asked, a little too pleadingly. All I wanted was to hear her happy voice.

'Yeah, well I can't see that will ever happen.'

'Well, we've gotta be positive about this,' I fired back. She needed to give me more support.

'It's easy for you to say, you're the one away from home. I don't think you understand what it's like, living my life for the past six months hoping for something that is never going to happen.'

'Well it's not that easy out here either. I'm doing everything I can, for you ... and me! I've got a lot happening, all right.' I was getting angry, which I knew I shouldn't be.

'Do you actually even want to come?' I asked.

'Yes, of course, but I'm being realistic here. I don't want to keep getting my hopes up!'

She paused to think about what she'd just said, then continued in a calmer tone. 'I'm just being realistic. It's all I can do. I've been thinking maybe it's better if I stop it ... Like, at least that's a definite.' She wanted to end our relationship, there and then. I was millions of miles away from her holding onto two birds and she wanted to call it quits. As if that would make things easier!

The words hung in the air. I didn't know what to say. I wanted her to hang on and trust me a little bit longer. But it was her right to do what she needed to do. I only hoped she was saying this out of confusion and didn't really mean it.

'Maybe it would save *both* of us a lot of pain,' she said. I knew her tone. I knew she was trying to hide the fact she was crying. It hurt me that she was trying to hide it and there was nothing I could say. I wanted the conversation to end. I had nowhere to go with it. I tried to wrap it up as gently as I could, saying a few meaningless things before telling her I'd speak to her soon.

'OK,' she said and hung up.

I returned to *Kijana* with our newest crew members in hand and hooked their cage to the ceiling above the table in the main cabin. Beau asked how it had gone. For a moment I thought he was asking about my conversation with Maya, but I then realised he was talking about our Toraja plans.

'All right,' I told him. 'I've gotta call them back in the morning.'

He and Maria stayed on deck while I got an early night, trying to bury my burden in deep sleep.

In the morning I spent the best part of two hours writing an email to the office detailing the reasons why Maya should join Kijana. I tried to be assertive without disrespecting their predicament. I sent it off, then went ashore to call Plan. They told me a bus travelled daily to Toraja. When we got there we'd have to find our own way though. I noted down the times and the name of the terminal, then thanked them once again.

I arrived back at *Kijana* to find Beau hunched over the computer.

'There's an email,' he said. 'It's about Maya.'

I asked what it said, knowing he would have already read it.

'Not much, the same old stuff.'

He knew what her coming along meant to me.

'It's your trip isn't it?' he said casually, but oh so cutting.

'Yeah, well, I'm working on it, OK!'

It took three more days before Josh returned. I found myself constantly scanning the jetty, waiting for him to arrive. Finally I saw his skinny figure looking out to the boat. I headed over in the dinghy and shook his hand, unable to disguise my relief that he was back.

'Good to see ya,' I said with a huge grin.

'You too,' he laughed back, not at all embarrassed by my enthusiasm. Maria gave him a big hug when we got back, which made me feel better. It had cost A$800 to fix the camera and had been a nightmare to organise. But now we had it and Josh back, and we could hardly wait to leave for Toraja.

The bus departed at 8 a.m. the next day. I emailed Maya, telling her where we were going and that I'd call when we got back. Beau fed the birds while Josh and Maria tied the dinghy on deck. We then hailed a passing longboat to take us ashore.

To our surprise the bus was only a minibus. Even more surprising was that we were the only ones on it. For most of the morning we travelled through flat terrain. After midday we began climbing into the foothills where we stopped at an eating place that looked out over the flats we'd just travelled. After lunch we hit the real hills, and the road became windier. The vegetation became thicker, the higher we climbed and the hairpin bends each revealed some new breathtaking view.

It was late afternoon when we arrived at Toraja. We paid for a night's accommodation at a lodge and locked the camera gear in the room. Maria was feeling ill after the winding journey and opted to remain in the room with the gear while Beau, Josh and I grabbed something to eat.

The town was set in a beautiful location. A deep gorge with a shallow river flowed along the outskirts and there were few cars. We ordered a coffee made from locally grown beans, witnessing the beans being hand-ground in front of our eyes. Despite the thick residue that refused to break down in the boiling water, the coffee was delicious.

We arrived back at the lodge after dinner to be greeted by a man, aged in his mid-thirties, who appeared to be waiting for us. Our enquiries about the funerals through Plan had somehow got back to this man, who offered his services as a tour guide. We could hardly refuse. His name was Gibson and he spoke understandable English, which was a huge bonus for us.

He told us of some burial caves he could show us. We tried to stress that we were actually more interested in filming a deceased person and the process that led to a funeral. He told us we'd like the caves. We assured him we would, then pressed him on the funerals. He knew about the funerals, he said, but wasn't sure if there was one on at the moment. He told us he would ask around. It would cost, of course. The risk was that he'd take our money and only show us the caves. Maybe someone else knew more than he did, but, as he was our only lead, we had to trust him. After agreeing on a figure of roughly A$40, we arranged to meet Gibson the following morning.

The next day Maria was feeling terrible and we feared there was something seriously wrong with her. With Gibson's help we located the town's doctor, who diagnosed a stomach virus, much like the dreaded Bali belly. She was given an injection and ordered to stay in bed. The pain would subside as the virus slowly worked its way through her system, he told her.

We had no choice but to leave without her. I told her to order any food she wanted and I'd pay for it when we returned, which would most likely be in a few days.

Gibson was the most laid-back tour guide I'd ever met, arriving without fanfare and speaking quietly as if he was telling us a secret. Nevertheless, he seemed to know where he was going. As we sat in his van, bumping along a gravel road, we asked if it would be possible to see a dead person. He nodded his head but didn't say anything.

After travelling for 20 minutes we pulled into a parking area where Gibson pointed to a set of steps leading down to what appeared to be a cave, framed by an imposing cliff face. It was obviously the first stop for any tourists visiting Toraja. We walked past stalls selling knick-knacks and hand-carved motifs and headed down the steps. As we approached the cave entrance, we came across some deep recesses carved into the cliff face. In each recess stood life-sized dolls that, Gibson told us, represented the men and women whose bodies lay in the cave, the largest burial cave in Toraja.

At the base of the cliff was an opening large enough to walk through. This was as far as Gibson was going to go, returning promptly to the car. A few locals loitering at the cave entrance offered us torches and their services as tour guides. We declined, preferring to use our filming lights and explore on our own.

Once inside, we came across a very elaborate cave system. The first thing that struck us was the number of coffins. They were everywhere.

They sat on hand-carved ledges that lined the cave walls. Some of the wooden coffins had rotted away to reveal only the thickest of bones – legs, arms and skulls. Offerings were precariously balanced near the remains. Coins, cigarettes, even lolly wrappers, anything of personal value was offered.

Some coffins were bigger than others, and sported elaborate carvings. Others were plain planks of timber nailed together. There were even a couple of small coffins, only large enough to hold a child.

The cave was initially several metres wide and we were able to stand without stooping, but as we got further in the cave began to shrink. We followed what seemed to be the main passage until it narrowed to a small tunnel that looked unnaturally round, as if fashioned by hand. Gibson had mentioned this while we were in the car and, after glancing back at our sizes, reckoned we should be able to fit through. Beau went first, getting down on his hands and knees, periodically setting off the flash on his camera to light the way ahead. Josh went next with the video and I followed with the light.

The further we crawled, the smaller the tunnel became, until we had to do a commando shuffle on our elbows just to move forward.

'Urgh, smell that!' Josh's voice echoed along the tunnel. I sniffed, trying to catch a whiff of the offending odour.

'It must be the smell of death,' he said.

'It sure is!' Beau confessed, 'I just farted.'

We erupted into laughter before realising it was not a good idea to breathe too heavily.

After crawling for about 15 metres, Beau emerged into a large opening where we could again stand. It appeared to be a passageway that led both left and right. Beau turned right, where the passage continued to open up even more. There were no coffins in this area, probably because they couldn't fit through the tunnel. But what it lacked in coffins, it sure made up for in spiders. They were everywhere. On the walls, floor, ceiling, ledges – anywhere they could get a grip – and they were big suckers, some with legs spanning 20 centimetres.

By that stage we'd been in the cave for more than half an hour and had travelled a fair way underground. It was difficult to estimate how far. The way out was not going to be easy, as the paths we'd followed were not marked. There was a maze of tunnels behind us that all looked the same. Who knew which one would lead us out.

I took some solace from the fact that we had a guide waiting for us, who'd presumably miss us after a while and come looking for us. Thankfully we hadn't paid him yet, so at least we knew he would still be there. I asked Beau, as the leader of this expedition, how we would get out.

'Simple,' he said, 'we go back the way we came.'

It wasn't the answer I wanted to hear. 'When do you think we should turn back?' I probed nervously.

'You can go back if you want, I want to see if this passage comes out anywhere.'

Great. My little brother thought I was a scaredy cat. I caught Josh's face in the light. He was thinking the same thing as me.

Despite the lack of coffins in that part of the caves, there were skulls in odd places. The sight of the skulls perversely gave me some comfort, as they refocused me on why we were down in that godforsaken place.

We crawled through another small tunnel, which opened into a large cavern, then into another tunnel through to an identical open area. I suggested there was nothing left to see. Beau didn't answer. Josh thought it was funny. Beau looked at him as if to say the two of us were free to leave, then continued moving forward. The cave led to yet another tunnel, which Beau peered into by using his flash. Josh and I stayed in the opening waiting for him to advise us if it continued. He set off another flash, which disturbed something. It squealed and sent Beau leaping backwards. A dark object exploded from the hole Beau had been peering into. Josh hit the deck and let out an almighty scream, quickly followed by his trademark nervous laugh.

'It's just a bat,' Beau said.

Josh was still laughing. 'Then why'd you jump so far?'

'Yeah, it's just a bat,' I said mockingly. I was only fooling around but Beau took me seriously.

'Yeah, well if *you* want to lead, go ahead and do it!'

Josh's laughing subsided, leaving an awkward silence. Beau didn't say a word as he turned and headed back in the direction we'd come. I knew I'd made a botch of the situation. Maybe I'd dug a little too deep. I was only doing it to get a rise out of him for the camera. Josh knew that, but either Beau didn't catch on or he was fighting something else.

I'd sensed he felt increasingly on the outer when it came to us three guys, especially without Maria around. Leading us through the tunnels may have taken on greater significance for him than I had realised. Until that point of the trip I'd never really let him take control of anything, despite my complete trust and reliance on him.

He made a mockery of my earlier concerns by leading us quickly and easily to the cave entrance. The sunlight brought everything back into perspective and our confrontation deep within the cave was left there, dead and buried. Instead, our stomachs reminded us it was lunchtime. Gibson, like a true guide, knew the best local eating place.

Less than half an hour later we were sitting on a wooden bench choosing from various bowls containing chicken, buffalo and green vegetables. All were presented in different sauces and all looked like they'd been cooked two days previously. Nonetheless, they were delicious, if not a tad spicy.

As we ate, I again asked Gibson about the funerals. He again became coy, replying reluctantly that he may know where a corpse lay, where we may be welcome to visit and film. It would cost us, he said. Of course, we were willing to pay. Where was the dead person and how much would it cost, I asked.

'Cigarettes,' he said, would be sufficient payment. Maybe money was a little disrespectful for such macabre information.

Our destination was 25 minutes out of town, but he knew the way well. On the way we stopped by a stall to purchase the cigarettes. I asked him which brand he smoked. He pointed to one of the clove brands and spoke to the stallkeeper. I beckoned for a packet, but the stallkeeper pulled down a whole carton, completely ignoring me. Gibson, on the other hand, nodded sheepishly but wouldn't meet my gaze. I watched dumbfounded as he scuttled back to the car with his spoils. This bloke was good, no doubt about it.

The car climbed further into the hills along another dirt track until it stopped, seemingly in the middle of nowhere. We would walk from there, Gibson announced. He then hit us with a bombshell. He was taking us to his family who would show us his deceased grandmother.

I immediately felt bad for the way we'd pressured him. No wonder he'd been reluctant. Suddenly it didn't feel right to be paying to film a dead person. I looked at Gibson and his carton of cigarettes and immediately felt like a gravedigger. Hardly a word was spoken as we followed him down a path through a small forest of bamboo. It felt like a funeral procession already.

The bamboo cleared and a wooden house came into view. It was built on stilts and below it an old man was hammering away at something. Next to the house were two traditional rice huts. Their distinctive rooves were typical of many we'd seen around Toraja.

While the local houses were basic, the rice huts were intricately built, with shards of bamboo sticking out the end of the roofline, like pan pipes, and motifs of buffalo figures painted in red, white and black. No two designs were ever the same, but they all had the very distinguishable arching roof.

We learnt that the roof was designed to resemble the spiritual ships on which the Torajan people believed their ancestors had arrived from the stars. It was this belief that made death not a tragedy but a celebration, for it signalled the deceased's return to the heavens above, to the place they called paradise.

Gibson greeted a man, who he introduced as his father. As Gibson explained why we were there, we politely stood and smiled, hoping his father would not be put off by our request. We also hoped he would not admonish his son for bringing us home. The next half an hour went by awkwardly as the old man appeared to ignore us. It wasn't until Gibson asked me to hand over the cigarettes that we got to shake hands with his father.

The old man took things very slowly and had a friendly smile that made me feel OK. Gibson's mother emerged and we were introduced. She then handed each of us a strong black coffee made of Torajan beans. Gibson then told us we should wait while they 'got ready'.

We finished our coffees, then Gibson invited us to enter the house. He lingered behind as we climbed the steps towards the entrance. I moved as gently and as precisely as I could, taking off my shoes at the top of the steps.

'Follow her,' Gibson said, pointing to his mother. He seemed awfully uncomfortable, as if we were about to walk in on a ghost. We followed the old lady along a passage, until we got to a doorway. She held open a curtain covering the doorway and ushered us into a small room. Beau went first, followed by me, then Josh with the camera filming.

Lying on the floor on the far side of the small room was the corpse, wrapped in sheets and covered by a blanket, with only her mouth and eyes exposed. I nearly bumped into Beau who had stopped not too far into the room, with Josh still trying to get in with the camera.

Gibson's father shuffled past us. He beckoned to us, indicating it was OK for us to come closer to the body. Josh was filming, while Beau didn't quite know if he should start taking photos or not.

'How long has she been here?' I asked the old man, breaking the silence. He didn't understand me, instead shouting to Gibson who was elsewhere in the house.

'What?' came Gibson's muffled voice through the thin walls, as if his father had asked him if he'd done his homework.

'How long has she been here?' I began, starting in a loud whisper and ending in a shout.

Gibson relayed the question back through the wall to the old man still standing beside us. He shouted back in Indonesian and smiled at us.

'Two months,' came invisible Gibson's translation.

What was up with Gibson, I wondered. Was he scared of ghosts or did he feel embarrassed at bringing tourists into his family home? Perhaps he wasn't allowed in the room. It was such a crazy scene I didn't know if I should feel relaxed or on edge.

The old man certainly didn't appear worried. In fact, he seemed overly casual about the whole affair. He smiled at us as he began pulling back the blanket to reveal the skinny body of his deceased mother-in-law wrapped like a mummy in cloth. The body had been preserved by injecting formaldehyde to retard the decaying process, which gave the family up to a year to save funds for her funeral.

We gradually moved closer, inspecting her face and trying to decipher which were her mouth, eyes and nose. Her face was a dark blue and looked as if it would sound hollow if tapped. The only other exposed part was her fingers, which stretched out from long sleeves. Everything about the body had shrunk. She looked like she could have been dead for 20 years. Only the bright coloured material she was wrapped in gave any indication of how recently she had died.

It was fascinating to actually examine a dead person and contemplate what it meant to be dead. I was surprised to find I didn't feel spooked by what was before me. The old man manoeuvred the blankets around as if she were merely asleep. Josh held the camera while I crouched over the body and explained the preserving process while Beau stood quietly against the wall, his hands clutching his camera at his crotch. I don't think he was enjoying himself.

'She doesn't look very happy,' I flippantly said to the camera. It seemed this was no place for jokes, for Gibson's voice startled me.

'She can hear what you say,' he warned through the wall. 'Speak to her, tell her how well she's looking.'

I looked apprehensively at Josh and his camera.

'She looks pretty good doesn't she?' I said, nodding at the lens in an attempt to be as convincing as possible. Josh was smirking behind the camera.

'Seriously though!' I said loudly, so everyone could hear, including grandma.

We got the shots we needed as quickly as we could, then Gibson's voice came meandering through the wall.

'It's time for her lunch.'

It struck me as an odd thing to say.

We took that as our cue to leave, and thanked the old man. We helped drape the blanket back over the corpse before leaving the room. It was one thing to read about the Torajan way of dealing with death, but another to actually see it for yourself. I left the room feeling honoured to have experienced it.

There was no sign of Gibson in the house. We eventually found him sitting on the porch staring out at the nearby hills. It was our chance to ask all the questions that had been running through our minds.

Gibson explained that in Torajan culture, the grandparents were the primary carers of the grandchildren. The old lady was more like Gibson's mother than his grandmother, we learned. He would have become too upset if he'd come into the room with us.

He explained that during the time the body was in the house it was treated as if it were still alive, hence Gibson's insistence she could hear us and that it was time for her to eat. Family members visited and spoke to the deceased, keeping them company until the funeral, when it was believed the spirit left the body. Only then would their deaths be mourned.

Gibson then told us his father knew of a funeral to be held in the next few days much further out of town. His family knew some people who lived close to where the funeral was going to take place. We would be welcome to stay with these people and attend the funeral, if we wished. It didn't take long for us to agree. We thanked Gibson's parents and headed back to the car.

It took us an hour to get there, along a very winding and bumpy road, climbing even further into the mountains. We passed rice fields on either side of the road where women sat, hunched over, planting new rice seeds, their ankles deep in a mixture of water and mud. Buffalos were often tethered near the houses, chewing their cud and swooshing flies with their tails. Due to the spiritual importance of the buffalo, they were a family's most prized possession, Gibson explained. They were always well fed, washed by hand daily, and allowed to roam free during the day. Of course, their happy lives came to a spectacular end when they were sacrificed, as we were to discover.

We arrived at the village late in the afternoon, stepping from the car into another round of introductions. Gibson appeared to know the people very well. The man and woman looked like they too could have been Gibson's parents, so I wasn't surprised when Gibson revealed this was actually his home. Confused, but not surprised.

We spent the afternoon walking through the surrounding hills. It was a hive of industry. Children and women carried sacks of rice from the field to a communal grinding machine that prepared the rice for storage.

We returned to the house to find Gibson sitting on the porch, chatting with his 'family'. A freshly killed chicken was stewing on an open fire. As the sun went down we sat on the floor of the family house and ate dinner by candlelight.

As we ate I asked Gibson about the funeral preparations. He told me they were taking place about a kilometre away.

'When will we be able to go there?' I asked.

'Now,' he said. I was surprised, for I presumed it would be a day-light event. After dinner Gibson led us through the dark, down the side of the hill and past yet another rice hut until ahead of us we could see a few lights. Then came the sound of chanting. This was it – the preparations for a full-blown Torajan funeral.

We came across a clearing 30 metres wide by about 150 metres long. Along each side of this area were more than a dozen rice huts, arranged so that people could view the events that would unfold in the clearing. It seemed that some huts had been built especially for the occasion. The front of these buildings looked like any normal rice hut, while the rest of the building remained unfinished.

Gibson came across a family he knew sitting under one of the rice huts. The father, Paulus, invited us into his family's hut so we could watch a circle of men and women swaying from side to side and chanting like Tibetan monks.

The eldest son of the family, Ronny, was our age but only Paulus spoke understandable English. He introduced us to his wife and youngest son, Budi.

Paulus was a well-to-do man by local standards, wearing gold-rimmed glasses and shoes with socks. He seemed out of place considering the subsistence living of the locals. Paulus took a shine to our small camera, asking to have a look at it as Josh explained about the filming we were doing. Paulus then proudly pulled out his camera from a top pocket to show us.

'Where are you parents?' he asked.

'We are travelling alone, just us three, and one other who is sick in Toraja. We're staying up the hill,' I told him.

'Will you be staying for the funeral?' Paulus asked.

'We'd like to,' came our reply. 'Who should we ask for permission?'

He smiled and translated our question to his eagerly awaiting family.

'This is my funeral,' he finally answered.

I knew he didn't mean it was *his* funeral, but he was clearly overseeing the event.

The deceased person we were honouring was actually an important local chief. Anyone who knew of him would attend the funeral, with thousands of people expected to pass through the funeral grounds over the next four days. Paulus and his family had flown over from Borneo, where he worked as an engineer for a timber company. His relationship with the deceased was not clear. He never explained it and we thought it too rude to ask.

'You can stay with us if you like,' Paulus said.

Gibson wasn't fussed by this, so we accepted Paulus's offer. I paid Gibson for his help, then we said our farewells and he headed back down the mountain. It was the last we saw of him.

Paulus's house was located near one end of the clearing. There seemed to be several families staying in the house. Paulus said they were his family but I wasn't so sure. I wouldn't have been surprised if he now considered us part of his family. Needless to say, we were welcomed by all the occupants. We found a patch of floor in the corner of the house and put our bags down not far from where a man and woman were already sleeping. We decided to do the same, for it had been a long day.

The next morning we found Ronny, who asked us to breakfast. Paulus appeared and joined us on the floor for rice, coffee and buffalo pieces dipped in a tomato and red chilli sauce.

The four-day funeral, we discovered, was to begin that day. We couldn't believe our luck. Like any major event, there was a scurry of activity on the funeral site. Dozens of men hauled long bamboo poles as they raced to finish building the rice huts, while live animals were being carted left, right and centre.

The noise outside the house reminded me of a livestock show. The pigs were the loudest, protesting at being strung upside down on thick bamboo. When each animal was lifted from the ground, the vines that were lashed around its body tightened, sending the pig berserk. Its high-pitched squeals conjured up frightening images of someone being slowly tortured with a hot iron.

After breakfast, Paulus took us beneath the house to proudly show us his family's buffalo, which was to be sacrificed during the funeral.

The Torajans believe that the deceaseds' spirits are carried by a ship pulled by the spirits of animals slaughtered at the funeral. The buffalo, as the ultimate working beast, is best equipped to drag the ship through rivers and over mountains, finally arriving in paradise. The more buffalos sacrificed at the funeral ceremony, the more pulling power for the ship, which means a greater chance of arriving safely at the heavenly destination.

However, not everyone can afford to offer a buffalo. One buffalo is equivalent to a year's wages for many locals. Those who can't afford a buffalo often bring a pig. We even saw a deer and a pony roaming the funeral grounds. The poorest families can sometimes only afford to offer a couple of chickens. It'd be a fair effort getting to paradise on the back of a chicken's spirit, I thought.

Paulus explained how his family's buffalo would be one of many sacrificed.

'Every buffalo here?' I asked in disbelief, for everywhere you looked there were buffalos. I estimated I saw at least 40 buffalos during my time there.

'Yes, every buffalo.'

But before they were killed, they had another use, Paulus added. 'Bullfights!' he announced with a smile.

These were held each afternoon of the funeral on an old rice field further down the hill. After lunch we followed hordes of people down a road to where the field opened up. People scrambled for any vantage point they could find. The owners of half a dozen buffalos proudly walked their beasts to the edge of the field, waiting their turn to fight. Bets were placed and two animals were brought together. Initially they didn't seem interested in fighting, possibly due to the sheer number of people standing around shrieking with excitement. The owners then led the buffalos directly into each other. Once their heads collided, it was on. They charged at each other, their horns locked together as they battled it out. This went on for about a minute, each buffalo giving no quarter until eventually one could take no more.

Pandemonium broke out when the bloodied loser of the bout suddenly turned tail and charged towards the crowd, hotly pursued by the victor. Men, women and children leapt for their lives as the frantic loser tried to find an exit from the field. It eventually leapt down an embankment on the far side of the field and charged through some fairly substantial growth to get away.

After the scores of bets were settled, two more combatants were led onto the field for another violent contest.

Josh, despite his vegetarian views, was in his element, for suddenly he had so many interesting things to film. Luck had finally turned our way and we couldn't afford to waste it.

That first day of the funeral was mostly spent deciding which parts to revisit to film. It was exhausting and when night fell, immediately after we ate our evening meal with Paulus and Ronny, we rolled out our beds, in the same spot we'd been eating, and fell asleep.

I woke some time later to the sound of chanting. I must have been asleep for only a couple of hours, for the room was still lit by its solitary electric light bulb. I'd heard music in my dreams, only to wake and realise it was actually happening. I listened for a while, then noticed Josh, too, was awake.

'I thought I was dreaming,' I said, loud enough for only him to hear.

'Yeah it sounds amazing doesn't it! Should we get up and film it?'

My body had adjusted to sleep mode and all I felt like doing was letting the chanting carry me back to dream land.

'I just want to enjoy it,' I said. 'Hopefully they'll do it every night.'

'I'm a bit concerned about the tapes,' Josh said, well awake by now. 'I could easily use the last 80 minutes tomorrow.'

It was something that had also been on my mind. We agreed that now that we knew the quality of the footage we could get, there were some tapes on the boat of footage from earlier in the trip that we could afford to tape over.

'Maybe we should wait and see how much we use,' I urged. 'If necessary, I can catch the bus back, get the old tapes and check on the boat at the same time.'

'Good idea,' he said, satisfied. On that note I closed my eyes and tried to imagine what the next few days would bring.

The following day it was obvious we were going to run out of tape. Josh was becoming very selective with what he shot, but there was still so much to cover. We needed tapes urgently and the only option was for me to make a quick dash back to the boat. If I missed the sacrifice that was just bad luck. Beau and Josh would be there to film as much as possible.

I hitched a lift back to Toraja at lunchtime on a truck that had just dropped off a load of people at the funeral. Maria was surprised to see me suddenly appear on my own.

'Where's Beau and Josh?' she asked. I explained everything, finishing with the need for my dash to the boat. I asked if she wanted to meet the guys at the funeral or come back to the boat with me. She was feeling slightly better but was still rushing to the toilet and had a constant headache. All she felt like doing was lying on a bed, so she opted to return with me to Makasar and check into a hotel that had air conditioning.

I felt sorry for Maria. There is nothing worse than feeling sick in a Third World country. Except seasickness, perhaps. Maria had experienced both and I admired how little she complained.

We found a bus heading to Makasar that afternoon and piled our bags in. It was another long road trip. Maria sat next to the window, her head glued to the glass, trying to sleep through the ten-hour ordeal.

It was well into the night by the time the bus finally arrived at a hotel for her to check into. I told her I would see her in a few days' time. Hopefully, by then, the tapes would have arrived from Customs and we could get her out of that place.

I headed straight for the boat, happy that the long drive was over and looking forward to a good night's rest. I was relieved Toraja had uncovered some interesting footage and I looked forward to calling Maya with this small amount of good news. Every piece of good footage was one step closer to her joining Kijana.

I got to the jetty in the dead of night and found a boat-owner willing to drop me on *Kijana*. After a solid sleep I was up early and packed two 40-minute tapes into my bag. In the mad dash to make the bus, I forgot to check the seed and water levels in the birdcage. I think my mind was also a bit muddled by the thought of another ten hours bumping along a winding road ahead of me.

I arrived in Toraja late in the afternoon and caught a lift back to the funeral site. I found the guys among the growing crowd and Josh lunged at the spare tapes in my hand, ramming one into the camera. I was not a moment too soon.

They'd been working hard while I was away. Beau had taken eight rolls of film and Josh had run out of tape. I was relieved to discover I hadn't missed the buffalo sacrifice, which was to be staged the following day.

The following day we witnessed the biggest bloodbath imaginable. It had been one thing to see a pig sliced open on a bush track, but an animal the size of a buffalo was a different matter. The crowd cheering gave the experience a chilling dimension. As distressing as the scene was before us, it was exactly the sort of thing we'd set out to experience on the journey of Kijana.

The sacrifice began at about noon. Thousands of people gathered around the clearing that was lined by rice huts. In the middle of the clearing was a large and intricately decorated rice hut. It was here that the chief's coffin lay. Near this hut was a pole. A buffalo was led into the centre of the funeral area and tied to the pole while a man commentated over a loudspeaker, rambling on and on. His enthusiasm appeared to rub off onto the crowd, for the atmosphere was electric.

The crowd then hushed as the slaughterman approached a beast with a sharp machete in hand. With a whip of the blade he slashed the neck of the unsuspecting animal, sending the crowd into raptures. The buffalo reared up on its hind legs, gushing blood from its neck like a burst water pipe. It sprayed everywhere, some of it onto the crowd, who watched in awe. A few seconds later and the beast lost balance, toppling sideways with a thud. The next buffalo was then led to the pole, cruelly forced to stand lashed beside the body of its dying friend.

More than a dozen times over, this was repeated, with the beasts often landing on the other dead buffalos. Pretty soon the dusty ground was converted into a dark brown mud from the many litres of blood that had been spilt.

Then, as another buffalo entered the arena, something triggered a commotion. The man leading the beast appeared to have a sudden change of heart and gestured that he wanted to take the buffalo away. Other men attempted to take the reins of the buffalo from the man, who I presumed was the owner, but he pushed them away. Another man dressed in a uniform stepped in. They discussed the problem for a moment between themselves. The owner was shaking his head and was visibly upset. While this was going on the fellow on the loudspeaker decided to put in his two bob's worth.

A man, who appeared to be a friend, walked over and took the distressed owner's arm, leading him away. The crowd seemed to approve of this and his buffalo was tied to the pole.

Moments before the deed was to be done, the owner reappeared from the crowd and approached the slaughterman. With what looked like tears in his eyes, he took the knife from the slaughterman's hand and proceeded to cut the buffalo's throat himself. It reared up in anger, for the cut wasn't deep enough, with only a small dribble of blood spurting out. The buffalo thrashed around, and the crowd roared while the man tried to make a deeper cut. He made a real mess of it. It took three other men to lasso the buffalo around the horns to hold it still so a decent cut could be made. As it fell to the ground, the owner returned the knife and walked off. This was enough for me. Beau and Josh were also happy to get away from that repugnant scene.

Back at Paulus's house, Josh logged onto the computer to update the web with our most recent photos. Two emails greeted us. Both contained good news. The first, from the office, had the news we'd been waiting for – the tapes were waiting for us in Plan's Makasar office. We were free to leave.

'Borneo here we come!' I declared.

The second email was from Mum. It said that Maya had left a message asking me to call. She had some 'good news to tell me about'. My mind went into overdrive. Suddenly, the buffalo massacre was pushed to the background as I wondered what the 'good news' could be. Maybe the office had called her and agreed that she could join *Kijana*.

We hurriedly packed, then thanked Paulus and his family for their wonderful hospitality. His final act of kindness was to direct us to a van heading back to Toraja.

It took an hour to get into town where, luckily, we were able to find the bus returning to Makasar. It was leaving in an hour's time, giving us just long enough to find something to eat and buy a couple of celebratory Bintang long-necks for the overnight trip.

It may have been my fourth trip on that winding road, but that made it no easier. For ten hours we jolted and swerved our way down from the hills until, in the early hours of the morning, a loud screeching sound woke us from our awkward half-sleep. The noise came from the rear axle dragging along the road. We piled off the bus to discover a wheel had fallen off. We were thankful it hadn't happened on a hair-pin bend near Toraja.

We were even happier when we realised we were within sight of *Kijana*. We grabbed our gear, carrying it the remaining 200 metres, then waited until the sun rose and the early morning longboats started work. After five days away, we were back home aboard *Kijana*.

At 9 a.m. we took our dinghy ashore to surprise Maria, who was over the moon to see us. We paid the hotel, then dropped into Plan for the tapes and to say farewell. Finally, I stopped at a phone while the others went to prepare the boat.

'Hi, it's me,' I said, when Maya answered the phone.

'Hello,' she replied. Her voice was fresh with excitement, unlike our last conversation.

She asked how it had been at the funerals.

'Great,' I replied, then realised that it probably sounded odd to describe such an experience as 'great'. 'I mean, really good filming.' I went on to tell her about the dead grandmother and the caves, and the thick Torajan coffee. She laughed when I told her about the wheel falling off the bus.

'How are the birdies doing?'

'They're fine,' I told her. She was such an animal lover I didn't dare tell her that our newest crew members hadn't handled our absence from the boat as well as we'd hoped. One was dead when we got back and the other was so close to death that I had to put it out of its misery.

'Mum said you've got something exciting to tell me.' I was jumping out of my skin.

'I do,' she said. Her voice bubbled in a way I hadn't heard for a long time. 'The other day Mum and I were shopping, and we passed that same pet shop, so I went in and the same Quaker parrot was sitting on the front desk chewing a pen. It was so cute, it didn't fly away or anything. Anyway, Mum bought it for me.'

'Wow,' I managed to say. I had to force myself to respond, to try to hide my disappointment.

'So now we've both got birds,' she cheerfully added.

I was totally blown off-course. This was the 'good news'? I covered my tracks by asking some questions.

'Is it a girl or boy?' I asked. She wasn't sure, but she was going to get one of its feathers DNA-tested.

'I've called him Luis anyway.'

It was a challenge to sound enthusiastic, but the more I asked about the silly bird, the more I enjoyed hearing her tell me about it. He was green and about the size of a budgie, she told me.

I felt stupid for thinking that maybe she'd been given permission from the office to join me. Surely the office would have told me first. But as I listened to her talk, slowly my disappointment turned to relief. I knew I loved her, but being so far apart it was easy to forget why. Without knowing it, she'd just reminded me why. It was, as she'd said, good news.

CHAPTER NINE
GOODBYES

IT FELT GOOD TO BE MOVING AGAIN. AT FIRST we hesitated raising *Kijana*'s sails. It had been more than a month since we had been on the water, causing us once more to forget the routine of life at sea. But by the second day everything was back to normal and we were making good progress towards the city of Balikpapan on the east coast of Borneo. It was there Maria would leave us, flying first to Bali, then back to Darwin to meet her brother. Knowing their time was limited, Beau and Maria stayed close. During dinner she sat between his legs, and Josh and I even coerced them into a kiss in front of the camera.

It was tropical sailing at its best. On studying the chart, I determined that if the wind remained constant we'd arrive in the next four days. After Maria left, we'd then continue another two days' sailing north, and enter the delta that spreads out along the coast from the Mahakam River. Thirty miles inland, nestled on a bend in the river, is the town of Samarinda. The Mahakam, which stretches inland into the centre of the island, would be the launching pad into the wilds of Borneo in our search for the Punans.

I spent most of the days leading up to our arrival reading books about Borneo. I became familiar with the names of the main rivers, the cities where we could deck ourselves out with supplies, and studied every map I could find, comparing locations of reported villages and the rivers that led to them.

Of everything I read, I was particularly taken by one account of an encounter with the Punans. It was written by two brothers, Lawrence and Lorne Blair, who explored the region in the 1970s. They trekked for almost a month into the remotest parts of Borneo accompanied by guides carrying their film gear. They eventually came across a group of Punan families camped at the junction of two rivers. The following excerpt, from their book *Ring of Fire*, describes their discovery:

> *The older men and women came cautiously down to the bank to greet us. They wore vivid loincloths, were latticed with tattoos, and great clusters of earrings dangled unashamedly from their long earlobes.*
>
> *At first they were aloof as we squatted together in the strangely empty longhouse, but as the evening wore on the population silently expanded. Sinewy, exquisite, bare-breasted women crept in like does to peer at us from the edge of the circle, their wide-eyed babies cradled on their backs peering over their shoulders.*
>
> *There were about thirty-five families here, each with their individual compartments opening on to the long communal veranda. To avoid being eaten alive we had to be individually introduced to all the hunting dogs. About ten of the families had been living here for five years, yet still relied more on hunting and gathering than on their rudimentary experiments with growing dry rice. The rest spent most of the year still wondering freely through the forest, sheltering during the heaviest rains at any number of abandoned longhouses, such as these, scattered through the jungle.*

I read the account over and over until I drove myself crazy. I scanned every map in fine detail looking for the town or location of Suleh, the name of the village where they had found the Punans. It was on the Long Eut River. I found neither. In a way I was happy with this. The journey of Kijana was teaching me that nothing worth achieving came easily. We'd just have to find our own path into the interior.

On the evening of 12 October, our fourth day at sea, Josh received an email from his sister. It contained news that was a world away from my visions of living peacefully with the Punans. It was news that would change Kijana dramatically.

The tourist town of Kuta, on the Indonesian island of Bali, a place we'd all visited, had suffered a series of horrific bomb blasts in the heart of its tourist strip. The targets included the well-known Sari night club. Her email told us that possibly hundreds of lives had been lost, with many of those Australian tourists. The death toll eventually rose to 202, with 88 Australians killed. More than 300 people were injured.

We were stunned. It was impossible to comprehend the scale of the disaster unfolding a little way over the ocean from where we were sailing in peace. Another email from the office told us that the Australian Government had issued a warning to all Australian citizens to leave Indonesia, as it was classified as an unstable country for westerners such as us.

We arrived at Balikpapan, a city of about 500,000 people, the day after the explosions and unceremoniously dropped anchor in muddy water. We were unsure what to do next. Going ashore had taken on a whole new meaning.

For some reason we felt compelled to head to Bali. I didn't know why I felt drawn to the scene of such tragedy. Perhaps it was a way of reconciling within our own heads why someone would do such a thing to young people like us. We made the decision to go. As Maria was due to fly back to Darwin anyway, Josh and I decided to fly with her to Bali the following day. From there she would continue on to Australia. Beau would remain on board the boat to keep guard. We hoped to be away for only a couple of days.

The next day, Beau dropped us at the beach and wished us well. I felt bad for leaving him alone, but someone had to look after *Kijana*.

In hindsight, because of the volatility in Indonesia during the days after the bombings, perhaps I should have stayed. Beau and Maria said a final goodbye, then we were off to catch our flight. We didn't actually fly directly to Bali, instead, flying to Surabaya, on the island of Java. From there it was a ten-hour bus ride through the eastern tail of Java, crossing over to the island of Bali. We decided to make this strange detour because of the strong warnings against tourists entering Bali. We didn't dare fly directly into Denpasar, the Bali airport, for we could have run the risk of either having our camera gear confiscated, or even being refused entry into Bali. At least this way we knew we would get where we wanted.

We arrived in Poppies Lane, two blocks from the blast site, late at night, three days after the terrorist attack.

After an eagerly anticipated sleep in an air-conditioned room the three of us rose soon after sunrise and made our way to the bombsite. The bright sunshine did little to lift the mood of Kuta. As we walked we encountered shop-owners beginning the laborious task of cleaning up, sweeping piles of rubble against shopfronts that had been badly damaged, even though they were several hundred metres from the centre of the blast.

We arrived at the bombsite to find onlookers standing behind a flimsy barricade. Disbelief hung heavily in the air as tourists and locals meandered about, whispering to each other and pointing to objects that caught their attention among the rubble.

We found an alley next to where Paddy's Bar once stood. Peering through the gaps where windows once were, we could see into the burnt-out remains. Metal stools lay on their sides, the plastic tops melted onto the floor. What struck me was the array of high heeled shoes that had been piled together awaiting collection by the Australian police sent to investigate the explosion. It was hard to believe that only a couple of days earlier hundreds of young people, just like us, had been partying there.

We continued along the alley, then turned left and followed another road that brought us out onto the main strip directly across from the Sari Club.

A burnt-out car was parked beside the road where yet another barricade prevented us from walking out onto the street. There we stood, staring at the mess in front of us.

It was a scene of utter devastation, which I still find difficult to put into words. A peculiar, indescribable smell wafted through the air. We remained silent, afraid to consider what that smell could be. We were not the only ones there, with groups milling at every vantage point.

'I wonder how many people are still missing?' I finally asked.

No one felt the need to answer me, for no one really knew.

I glanced at Josh. He hadn't said a word since we'd been there. He stood, arms folded, with tears welling in his eyes.

For some time we stood there, each in our own world, trying to come to terms with the scene in front of us. I couldn't contemplate why a human being would scheme to do such a thing to others, to people our age.

On the way back to the hotel we popped into an internet café to find an email waiting for us. It was from the office urging us to get back to the boat as soon as we could. Beau had been threatened by some intruders in our absence, forcing him to sleep on deck with a machete by his side. He desperately wanted to know how much longer we would be. That was all the information we had. My mind was in a spin. What the hell was going on? The world seemed to be spiralling out of control.

As we left the café Josh saw Gabby and Sam sitting on a motor-bike, our friends from the small catamaran who'd come to my birthday in Nembrala. We ran up the street to where they sat, engrossed in a map.

'Hey!' Josh yelled. Gabby swung around and instantly recognised us.

'Hey, you guys, what you doing here?' she said in her infectiously friendly Chilean accent. It was an emotional reunion for two groups who'd known each other so fleetingly. Gabby explained that every friendly face they saw was 'like the best time we've seen them, because we are just happy that they are alive'.

They recounted their experiences on the night of the bombing. They had planned to meet friends at the Sari Club but Gabby was feeling sick 'so we waited until it was late, then we felt the explosion. It shook me so hard that I wanted to be sick!' Gabby explained.

She then continued with a startling revelation.

'Dave, you know, from Nembrala, he is somewhere, but we have not seen him since the explosion.' Stupidly, my first thought was that I still owed him $20. The ramifications of what she'd said then sunk in. Could Dave have been killed or injured? For months I pored over the lists of injured and dead, but never came across his name. I sent off the $20 I owed him and it has never returned to me. I have had no way of contacting him since, so I can only presume he survived and is still happily working on his retirement hut.

Josh and I had our final meal with Maria before we farewelled her at the airport. I was sad to see her go, for we'd shared the best of Kijana with her. We would miss having her on board. I certainly knew Beau was going to miss her desperately. Their long chats on deck and giggles had held him together. Now it was just us three guys again.

Something about her departure, coupled with Beau's alarming email and the awful mood following the bombing made me feel like Kijana was slowly beginning to erode.

In the morning Josh and I made the ten-hour bus ride back to Surabaya for our return flight to Balikpapan. We stepped back on the deck of *Kijana* four days after leaving her. It felt like an eternity. As always, it felt nice to be back. But there was no time for relaxing after Beau told us of his experience.

The day after we left, he'd been sitting on deck when a number of fishing boats began circling *Kijana*, yelling out in a threatening manner. That night he felt compelled to sleep in the back cabin, facing the steps with the rifle by his side.

The following morning he was visited by a boatload of men. They demanded to know what he was doing in their port. They refused to believe him when he said he was on his own.

'We could come and cut your throat and no one would ever know,' they said mockingly. With the bombing fresh in his mind, he had no choice but to believe them. When no further crew came out of hiding after such a provocative threat, they began to believe Beau's story that the skipper had gone to Bali for a few days. The men then introduced themselves as police.

'When the skipper returns, tell him to come to our office,' one of them warned a very scared Beau before departing. It was early evening as Beau told his story, much too late to go to the police station. I also didn't relish the idea of being interrogated, so we decided to leave at first light the next day.

Later that night, as we prepared for an early morning departure, Beau approached me and said he wanted to 'have a talk'. We weren't the types to have serious chats together so I became alarmed. We went below deck where he abruptly announced he wanted to leave Kijana. It all came out, everything that had been brewing since he first did his block in Darwin over his smoking – the 'fakeness' of the filming, the control of the office, the way Maya had been blocked from coming on board. He was also struggling with his own identity. All those Buddhism books had given him the urge to seek enlightenment, to the point where he felt he couldn't find it aboard *Kijana*. He was confused, angry and scared. He was crying and I was in shock. Never did I imagine Beau would leave me.

I suspected he was feeling the pressure of being alone and afraid while Josh and I were away in Bali. But I told him it was OK. He could do whatever he wanted.

I knew there was some original opposition from the office to Beau coming on the trip, that he was hitching a ride on my coat-tails. To have him pull the pin now would surely bring some degree of resentment towards both him and me. But all I cared about was that he would be OK and, for the first time in the trip, I didn't care what the office thought. I admired Beau for sticking to something he believed in and I told him I was glad he'd made a decision.

However, his departure presented a major problem. Slowly *Kijana*'s crew was whittling away. We were already down to three from the original five. We needed Beau to sail *Kijana* and I really needed him to help us find the Punans. So I played my ace.

'Do you think you could stay on until India? I've been reading about the Buddhist temples up north. You could leave us there and it would make sense filming-wise.'

He shrugged his shoulders. 'Yeah I s'pose.'

During all this I'd been looking at him through the lens of the camera. I felt heartless. It was an extremely intense conversation, but the camera had come between us. I forced myself to switch it off, to stop being a filmmaker and become a brother. I wrapped my arms around him for the first hug I could remember ever giving him. He was so much bigger than me. I squeezed and held tight. He put his arm on my shoulder. I held on, each second feeling like forever. I felt terrible for leaving him alone to look after the boat.

I was the first to let go, sensing his awkwardness at what we'd done. I looked at him and said thanks, then headed off and locked myself in the toilet where I burst into tears.

The next morning we weighed anchor and raised the sails, heading north, bound for Samarinda. We never looked back to see if the police gave chase.

A slight breeze blew from the coast where some menacing clouds sat, trapped by the mountains of Borneo, like a chained dog threatening to bite.

The water was calm and a dry smoky fog drifted by, making it hard to distinguish where the ocean finished and the sky began. Every now and then we'd spot a tugboat towing a barge piled high with dirty coal or felled logs from the forests of Borneo. Empty barges would overtake us on their way to Samarinda to collect a new load of produce.

In a way, these barges became our guides, for our chart was proving next to useless. The detailed chart we'd used on our approach to Balikpapan ended a few miles north of the town. All we had was a chart that contained little detail. It was also a photocopied version, which increased the risk of not accurately showing the location of any reefs.

With a crumbling crew and little guidance, I'd be forgiven for thinking everything was against us. Yet, the menacing strip of land to our left gave me all the hope I needed. In there, somewhere, lived the Punans, hiding from the loggers and miners in the deepest, darkest corners of the island. It was that simple thought that powered *Kijana* forward.

The wind died as the sun disappeared for the day, forcing us to start the motor in the hope we would arrive at the entrance to the Mahakam Delta some time in the morning.

I rose at 3 a.m. for my shift, giving me three more hours to think.

'There's a light over there. It's been there for about ten minutes. The depth is still unreadable,' Beau said as he headed off to his bunk. I made a coffee and was sitting on deck when the bright beam of a spot-light suddenly appeared, seemingly pointed in our direction.

It couldn't be a lighthouse as there was nothing marked on the chart. Even our poor chart would show a lighthouse. It had to be a vessel of some sort. The search beam stopped but the light Beau had referred to earlier continued to grow brighter. The blinding flash of the spotlight appeared again, passing over *Kijana*.

'Holy shit, it's getting closer,' I said to myself. It was impossible to tell how far away it was or whether we'd been spotted. I suspected we had, for the light grew as it got closer.

I was becoming worried. The International Maritime Bureau, which keeps track of these sorts of things, consistently pinpoints Indonesia as having more pirate attacks than anywhere else in the world. My heart began thumping as I realised we had several lights on and whatever was out there was heading our way. I was unsure whether I should wake Beau and Josh. Hopefully, I was being overcautious.

I leapt downstairs and switched off all our lights. Pirates or police – or anyone for that matter – I didn't want to meet them. However, I knew that extinguishing our lights was a sure sign to any would-be pursuers that the battle was on. I grabbed a packet of matches and headed back to the cockpit, revving the motor to full speed and changing our course 90 degrees so that we were heading towards land. In the darkness I hoped they wouldn't be able to find us.

The spotlight appeared again, pointing in our direction. I could see the light but could they see us? Was it a small boat 200 metres away or a big boat one mile away? I still couldn't tell. If they could see us with their light and had a bigger engine, there would be no escape if they did, indeed, intend to meet us.

The engine screamed under the strain of pushing the boat along at eight knots. Without lights I couldn't even make out the cockpit seat I was sitting on, let alone anything ahead of us. Or, even worse, the depth gauge indicating what was below us.

I ducked down, lighting a match out of sight of the other boat. The cockpit lit up for an instant before the match blew out. I lit another, this time closer to the depth gauge. Whereas before it had been too deep for the sonar to pick up the depth, the digital display now read 20 … 19 … 18 metres. It was decreasing with every knot of speed *Kijana* gained in escaping the mysterious pursuers. I knew land was at least 15 miles away, so the only logical conclusion was something I hoped I'd never have to confront again – a reef!

I dashed downstairs. 'Wake up, wake up! Leave the lights off!' I screamed, then raced upstairs and slammed the engine throttle from full ahead into reverse. The engine didn't like it at all, the gearbox letting out a clunk of disapproval.

Images of nearly losing the boat off the Queensland coast five months previously came flooding back to me.

'Leave the lights off,' I yelled again, before realising Josh and Beau were already at attention on deck.

'Check the depth.' I ordered, shoving the matches into Beau's hand. The water around us bubbled from the turbulence of *Kijana*'s big hull slowly moving forward at about three knots.

'I think they're following us,' I said to Josh. 'Get the gun, the big one.'

I never thought I'd ever have to issue such an order. Beau's match lit the way for Josh to make his way down the stairs towards the gun locker. He then lit another to look at the depth display. I leant down to see it reading 1.1 metres. The depth of *Kijana*'s hull below the water line was 1.8 metres. We should have been sitting on something! Yet, I could still hear water passing the hull over the scream of the reversing engine.

'How come we're still moving?' Beau asked, taking the thought directly out of my head.

As Josh stepped into the cockpit with the gun, *Kijana* came to a gentle standstill. I pulled the throttle back and looked over the side for the telltale sign of breaking waves on a reef. Instead, the ocean was relatively flat as *Kijana* sat comfortably in the middle of a black abyss of water. It was quieter now the engine was in neutral. In fact, it was quiet enough to hear the metallic clicks as I loaded bullets into the barrel of the gun. The thought of actually feeling safer with a gun in my hands made me sick.

'I didn't feel us hit anything, did you?' I asked.

'I don't think there's anything here,' Josh replied.

As we watched the light of the boat, I told the guys what had happened as they slept.

'Maybe it's a tug spotlighting its barge.' Beau suggested hopefully. I somehow couldn't agree.

'What about the depth? You saw it say 1.1 metres before the match went out – or was it 11?' I asked Beau.

'It was 1.1,' he said. Things weren't making sense. Beau lit another match. This time the reading was 50 metres.

'That's impossible,' I said, looking at the readout in disbelief. I turned off the engine so the other boat couldn't hear us, then we sat in the cockpit watching the light. It continued to shine its searchlight intermittently, until the main light grew smaller and further away.

Eventually we felt comfortable that they'd lost us and had given up. We decided to make a run for it. We started the engine again and ever-so-slowly began motoring, resuming our original northern course. The depth remained constant at about 50 metres, which gave us enough confidence to rev the motor and increase our speed. As we did, the sonar went haywire, jumping from 13 metres to 60, back to 50 and so on. There were still no obvious reefs marked on the chart, so we could only conclude the sonar was receiving an electrical surge when the motor was revved, sending the reading crazy.

I felt stupid, but at least it explained what had happened. The light, however, remained a threatening mystery. We remained on deck with the gun, and the lights off, until the sky began to lighten and a new day dawned.

It was afternoon by the time we arrived at the entrance to the massive delta where the Mahakam River spread out as it entered the sea. We motored as we followed the deepest lead to the river proper. It was extremely unpredictable, as we knew our depth sonar was unreliable. A few bumps into the shallows of the river only added to the anticipation of getting to Samarinda.

After many kilometres of nondescript low-lying bushes lining the riverbank, we suddenly encountered some houses. They grew more frequent until we eventually came across Samarinda nestled in a long curve of the river as the last light of the day escaped us. With a population of more than 500,000 people, Samarinda's prosperity is based upon timber, oil and mineral exports. It had the feel of a wild place, just as the guidebook described it. It may not have looked like the most inviting place we'd ever come to, but a part of me was glad of that. No pain, no gain, I reminded myself.

Nearly every house along the river was built over the water, most with jetties leading out a few metres from the bank. We tried to find an empty space at one of these jetties but the river traffic had already arrived home for the night, taking up every space. Some jetties had two or three boats tied to each other.

There was no other option than to anchor in the middle of the river next to two large tankers. It wasn't an ideal anchorage, for one tanker had a man aboard welding who was sending a stream of sparks into the water, while the other looked like it had been abandoned.

We dropped anchor and cut the engine. When our noise ceased, the local noise kicked in. From each riverbank a loudspeaker blasted Muslim prayers out of time with each other. Our location midstream made it seem like we were sitting between two speakers of a stereo that was playing the same song but out of synch.

We stayed up late that night, making sure neither tankers were dragging anchor and threatening to crush us. As I sat sipping Beau's jungle juice and watching the steel monsters either side of us, I thought of what lay ahead of us. Since meeting Dave two months previously at Nembrala, my focus had been on locating the mysterious Punans, and finally we were at Samarinda, the launching pad for our search.

The expedition was vital for the Kijana adventure. The office seemed to think we could just turn these adventures on and off, scheduling one neat adventure each week to fit in with our filming schedule. But it didn't work that way. At least our expedition into the forests of Borneo should have provided enough footage to impress the office.

However, I knew what we planned was not going to be easy. The accounts I'd studied were enough to tell me that. The Blair brothers, who I quoted earlier, trekked for months into the jungle, accompanied by 20 local guides, before they found the Punans. They searched thousands of square kilometres of dense jungles for small tribes who did not call anywhere home and rarely left any calling cards when they moved on. When they did finally discover a tribe, they were only the second outsiders to ever set eyes upon them. The account was 30 years old and much could have changed in that time. And the location names were not on any map I could find.

The interior of the island was so dense with jungle that the only means of getting in were by light aircraft or riverboat. However, both had their limits. Planes need an airstrip to land, yet these are often washed out by heavy rains. The riverboats are at the mercy of rapids, which grow more frequent the further inland the rivers wind. Also, they can only pass after heavy rain, when there is enough water to cover the boulders that dot the riverbeds. An option was to carry the boat around any rapids but this would require a light boat that could be lifted by the three of us. However, storage space was limited on a small boat, and we wanted to avoid buying fuel inland, as it was extremely expensive and scarce in the areas we needed to get to.

Our best option appeared to be to buy an old derelict riverboat, patch it up and head up the Mahakam River as far as time would allow. Our Indonesian visa had already been extended to the hilt and was due to expire in a little over three weeks.

We began scouting possible boats, looking for something we

could carry around rapids. However, every boat we saw was in good nick. They were freshly painted and sported newish-looking long-tail outboards on the back.

Eventually we came across a boat that showed promise. It lay half-submerged and was still tied to a jetty. The engine had been removed a long time ago, which suited us, because our plan was to bolt our outboard onto the back. We pulled up in our dinghy and held onto the jetty while we inspected it. As we did, more and more people came to inspect us. Few foreigners visited that part of the world, so we received special attention.

We asked who the owner of the boat was. They either didn't know, or didn't understand us. Eventually, someone appeared to understand what we were asking. Josh stayed to look after the dinghy while I was led along the jetty, through the back door of someone's house, right past a family eating a meal on the floor and out the front door to a road at the front of the house. The man I was following jumped aboard a motorbike and motioned for me to sit behind him. Having been in Indonesia for more than three months, I was accustomed to hitching rides on motorbikes. What I couldn't get used to was putting my arms around a bloke's waist. I'd leave them there for a few seconds so as not to offend, then, on the first bump, I'd opt to try my luck and hold onto the back of my seat. Of more concern, in this case, was the fact that I had no idea where I was heading with this stranger, who couldn't speak English.

After riding for about ten minutes we stopped outside a shop. We entered to find a large man dressed in a robe, lounging on his side and snacking on peanuts. It was like a scene from the Roman days. The two men spoke, then the big man looked at me and, in broken English, asked if I would like to sit. He told me he was the owner of the boat and asked why I was interested in it. I gave him a sketchy outline of our plan, being careful not to give away too many details. I said I'd like to know how much it would cost to buy or even rent. He declared five million rupiah would secure it. His men would help raise it from its watery grave and patch the holes. That was about A$750, which was way too much, so I suggested one million rupiah on the proviso that

I return the boat in three weeks. He agreed, so I arranged to meet his men the following afternoon.

It felt good to finally have a plan. Beau began gathering supplies, while Josh organised the camera gear and worked out what to take and what to leave. I resorted to the guidebooks again to work out where the hell we were going.

I knew we had to head towards the centre of Borneo, because that was the general area where other explorers had found the Punans. But the maps of the interior were clearly marked 'survey incomplete'. It all came down to a bit of a wild guess. I flicked through a well-leafed guidebook one more time. Suddenly I saw something that was to change the course of our adventure.

At the bottom of a page outlining air routes around Borneo was a name that rang a bell. 'Long Suleh', it said. Long meant village, while Suleh meant – I had no idea. But I knew I'd seen the word somewhere before. Samarinda to Long Suleh it said. An airline by the name of MAF flew the route, but it had no times or dates. I racked my brains as to where I'd come across the name.

I put down the guidebook and reached for another. It was the account by the Blair brothers. I found the section about discovering the Punans. I was getting excited. I read down until I found what I was looking for. That was it! Suleh. It was the village near where they'd found the Punans. I checked the guidebook again for the flight details. Yes, it certainly said Samarinda to Long Suleh. This was despite it not appearing on any of my maps. All of a sudden we had a change of plan. I showed Josh my discovery, then we piled into the dinghy and went to find the airline.

The Samarinda airstrip was as I expected – very basic. Several buildings lined the bitumen runway and a refuelling truck was parked on the grass. The MAF hanger was the last building along. It was only when we got there that we learnt what the initials meant – Mission Aviation Fellowship. If that wasn't the name of an airline for adventure, I was yet to hear of one.

On the wall of the office hung an old laminated map that had been pieced together using aviation charts to make up the entire island of Borneo. At the end of one flight path from Samarinda, marked in pencil, were the words 'Long Suleh'.

Bingo. We'd accidentally struck gold!

The MAF was funded mostly by churches and generous benefactors to allow remote areas of the globe access to the outside world. The cost of a flight for a villager was heavily subsidised, while we westerners paid full fare to keep the fellowship alive. However, they could offer what we were looking for, so we happily coughed up the money for three tickets to leave in a few days. It may have been more expensive than our riverboat plan but it meant we could get there in hours rather than weeks, which was vital with our visas due to expire.

Now that we had changed our plans, I dropped off an envelope containing 100,000 rupiah to the family who lived by the riverboat we'd earlier organised to rent. I asked them to pass it on to the owner, with the message that there'd been a change of plan and here was a little compensation for his troubles. The last thing we wanted was an angry businessman taking out revenge on *Kijana* while we were away.

To prevent anything untoward happening to *Kijana*, the airline helped arrange for a local to live on board in our absence. He happened to be the brother of one of the MAF employees and a member of their church, so I was confident we could trust him.

A few days later we arrived at the MAF hanger at 8 a.m., our packs holding everything we expected to need for at least three weeks.

As we were the only passengers, our packs were weighed and placed on the last two seats of the plane, a single-engine Cessna that could seat five passengers and the pilot. The pilot was an American, named Peter, who'd flown mission planes all around the world. He, his wife and two children, had lived in Samarinda for three years. He was surprised to see three young men wanting to be taken into the wilds of Borneo.

'Not many people go in,' he told us after our introductions. 'We take mostly only supplies and villagers coming out if they get injured. I did take one anthropologist in once, but that was a few years back.'

We weren't sure if we should feel honoured or worried.

All we had to hope for, Peter warned us, was a clear runway at the other end. If we ran into heavy cloud cover, landing would be impossible, and we'd have to fly home and try again another day.

Peter outlined our flight plan, which took us over the low-lying forests along the coast, then up into the foothills and eventually to the highlands, where the rivers began their long journey to eventually become major rivers like the Mahakam.

We took off and circled *Kijana*, which looked like a mere speck on a trickle of muddy water. The 'Mighty Mahakam' didn't look so mighty from that height. We flew north-west, over a carpet of dense forest. The noise of the engine made talking impossible. A tap on a shoulder and a pointing finger was enough to let each other know about a view worth sharing.

As the mountains began to form, great scraggly peaks passed not far below us. Deep gorges were evident only from directly above. It seemed a miracle that beneath the sea of trees below were small tribes of men, women and children untouched by 'civilisation'.

As we flew over a ridge, Peter pulled down his microphone and proudly announced: 'waterfall'. What would have been a towering cascade of solid water if we'd been on the ground, appeared as a tiny white tear in the green canvas of treetops that spread as far as the eye could see. It was a scene that made me feel we were truly heading to the end of the earth. Who knew what we would find there.

CHAPTER TEN
LOST TRIBE

FACES. TINY LITTLE FACES. FIRST ONE, THEN another, followed by a few more. Soon they were everywhere. After an hour in the air, Peter had put us safely down on a dirt runway, scratched into the forest on the top of a small hill. As the dust from the propeller began to settle, the faces began to appear – mostly children, but then women wearing wide-brimmed sun hats they'd made themselves. They'd been waiting not for us, but for the fresh supplies of fuel, salt and washing powder. It had been three weeks since the plane last landed here.

Peter swung open the aircraft door, jumped out and landed on both feet like a cat. He wasted no time in unloading his cargo, for he could see his customers were pretty keen to get their hands on the goods. Beau, Josh and I struggled with our seatbelts, then hesitantly emerged from the craft to be immediately surrounded by the wide-eyed locals. Peter explained to the crowd who we were as he continued passing cardboard boxes to the many helpers, and asked in Indonesian if they would lead us into town and find us someone to stay with.

No sooner had the dust settled and the boxes been unloaded, than the aircraft propeller was again spinning and Peter and his noisy aircraft were off, set to return in two weeks to collect us. As he rose into the air and disappeared, the noise of the plane was replaced by crickets and chattering children.

We found ourselves led along a dry dirt track to the centre of the village. As we arrived, a dozen men halted work to watch the arrival of the new visitors. These people were not exactly the naked race I'd imagined. They were mostly clad in worn-out denim shorts and stained T-shirts. The men were attempting to tip a pole, freshly cut from the local forest, into a hole in the ground, directly behind a smaller pole that already supported a suspension bridge that crossed a river.

This was the Long Eut River and a little further down it joined another estuary. The village was right where the Blair brothers had described it, at the intersection of two rivers, yet the people looked nothing like they'd described. I imagined them to be more ghostlike. These people looked and dressed like many people we had met during our travels through Indonesia.

Along the riverbank several women looked up from their washing while their children, covered in soap suds, danced about, oblivious to our arrival. We were directed by our young leaders to the porch of a house built on the river's edge. The smell of smouldering wood wafted from inside. Some of the men ceased work on the bridge and began to mill around us. It became evident that no one spoke English, but they did speak Indonesian, which we could, by that stage, understand enough of to communicate the basics.

We asked if there was somewhere for us to sleep, drawing blank expressions. Only when we made the universally understood sign of tilting the head and closing our eyes did we get a response. Chattering erupted as many of the men pointed at a middle-aged woman who stood with her hands on her hips. I immediately got the feeling it was her porch we were standing under.

While this commotion went on about us, my eyes darted from face to face. I caught glimpses of what looked like typical Punan features, but predominantly these people resembled the Dyaks, the coastal dwellers found around Samarinda.

As I scoured the faces I saw, standing away from the adults among a small circle of girls, a face that was definitely not Dyak. She looked markedly different from everyone else we'd seen so far. She had to be a Punan, I figured. My spirits lifted considerably as I stared at her.

My concentration was broken by the arrival of a young man who squeezed through the growing crowd. He had a different build to the sweaty workers around us who all sported well-trimmed bodies. He was stocky, with slightly flabby arms and wore a clean white T-shirt.

'Good afternoon,' he said in an unnatural fashion, as if he had learnt his pronunciation from a Buckingham Palace butler. 'My name is Charlie.' At last, an interpreter! We immediately explained that we had arrived on the MAF plane and were wondering if there was anywhere we could set up our tipi.

He spoke to the woman, her arms now folded, who appeared to be the centre of the village's universe. She glanced up and down the river, then gave a snigger as if she'd just had a disgusting thought. She replied to Charlie, who stared at the ground, nodding his head until she finished. As she spoke I turned my head to sneak another look at the Punan girl, but she was gone.

'Are you a scientist?' Charlie asked.

'No, we are students,' I replied. It was the easiest answer to give people, considering none of us had a profession and 'student' was widely understood.

'What do you study?'

Josh held up the camera. Charlie gave a nod of recognition.

'We are looking for Punans,' I volunteered. 'Do you know where we can find them?'

Charlie translated our question to the woman, but we didn't have to wait for her answer. She began shaking her head halfway though the question.

'Are there any in the forest?' I asked.

The woman's reply this time was more elaborate, relayed to Charlie for about a minute.

Finally, Charlie translated for us. 'Yes,' he said.

'How many days to get there?'

Again, Charlie relayed the question and the answer.

'They walk back to the village in the afternoon.'

I was stunned. We looked at each other with excited grins. Surely we couldn't have stumbled across a lost race with such ease. The woman addressed Charlie, who translated for us.

'You can stay here, with Shian. She will look after you. The next MAF plane won't be for a few weeks.'

I smiled at the lady. Her face lit up and she smiled back, changing my impression of her immediately. She showed us upstairs to a room where we could sleep. Charlie sat with us for a while as we talked and looked out over the second-storey balcony at the river below.

The men had gone back to work, for we could hear them heaving on long ropes to get the pole into place. From our vantage point we could see the children watching their fathers and grandfathers working hard. A few of the cheeky boys were imitating them, pretending the rope went slack then toppling backwards to great laughter.

Shian's daughter, Ahyena, entered the room and gave us fried plantains, a type of sour-tasting starchy banana that turns to the texture of potato when cooked.

Charlie revealed he was the only person in the village who spoke English. He was from the coastal town of Tarakan, north of Samarinda, and was employed by the Indonesian Government to oversee the building of suspension bridges in remote areas of Borneo. He'd been in Suleh for five months building the bridge the men were working on.

With accommodation arranged, it was time to explore the village. Charlie bade us farewell and told us he'd catch us later on. We crossed the suspension bridge to the other side of the village where the dwellings were much more simplistic compared to our 'guesthouse'. Most of these huts were fashioned from rough-sawn forest timber, with tin metal roofs and a small verandah, where the occupants would sit weaving baskets or preparing food. I calculated the average dwelling to be a meagre four square metres, about half the size of the average bedroom at home. I also figured, by the number of huts, that the village had a population of about 200 people.

It didn't take long before we had a growing line of children following us. Josh found it most amusing. One particularly cheeky boy walked next to us, his head rubbing our arms. He then dashed off and did a flying karate kick, making sure to land facing us so that he could see if his performance had been noticed.

'Nama?' Josh asked.

'Tommy,' he answered.

'Nama Josh, nama Beau, and nama Jesse,' Josh said, pointing to each of us. This set off a chain of introductions among the 30-odd children around us. We heard all their names, except for one girl. She looked very serious, too serious for a girl her age, and froze whenever we looked at her. Josh asked her name again but got no reply. All the children stared at her, which only made her more determined to defy the game.

'Gimme five,' Josh said, putting out the palm of his hand in an attempt to break her defences. All the boys began yelling at her, willing her to play with us.

'Gimme five,' Josh repeated.

A smile slowly crept across her face, then she slapped his hand. The rest of the children went wild, hooting in excitement. To the kids at least, we were the hottest property to visit Suleh in a long time.

The entire village could hear us coming simply because of the noise of the children. We walked past a group of women sitting by a smouldering fire, weaving rattan baskets. An older man chipped away at a solid log, shaping it into a canoe. On the riverbank nearby lay half a dozen finished canoes. Upstream, an old woman with saggy boobs knelt in the shallows of the river, washing herself. She quickly reached for a sarong when she noticed three foreigners among the children. Aware of our intrusion, we turned and headed back along the river.

We came to a landing built just above the water level. Suddenly a barrage of small naked bodies swept past us as singlets and shorts were thrown into the bushes.

Within seconds, our entire following was in the water. The boys scrambled from the water back onto the platform and formed a neat little line. One by one they jumped into the water, doing their best to impress us. Tommy led the procession, jumping off with one of his karate kicks. The second boy jumped out and spun 360 degrees before hitting the water, the next a somersault, and so on. As each performed his trick, the next in line moved forward, paused for a second as they thought of something original, then leapt in.

The girls, meanwhile, had waded further out, away from the splashes, and were watching us cautiously. When we caught their eyes, they giggled and ducked under the water.

When it came time to leave, little effort was put into getting dressed. Most merely clutched their clothes to their bodies as they followed us up the river embankment, battling each other to get in front of us. At the top of the embankment we found Charlie. The Punans had arrived from the forest, he announced.

We followed him until we came to a hut where an old woman hobbled out with a woven basket strapped to her back. Inside the basket appeared to be two cucumbers.

This lady was a Punan, Charlie told us. She stood still, staring at us as we stared at her. It reminded me of looking at an animal in a zoo. The situation wasn't exactly how I'd imagined it would be. She looked like every other old woman we'd seen so far. Her face was extremely wrinkly and she stood with a hunch. If she was a Punan, I doubted she was full-blooded. The only outward sign that she was part of the lost people were her ear lobes. They stretched down to her shoulders, where copper rings had once been worn. To the Punans, stretched ear lobes were a sign of beauty. Other than this she seemed no different.

As I looked at her I couldn't help feeling disappointed.

As we walked back to Shian's house it became clear that when Charlie had told us the Punans returned from the 'forest' each afternoon, he actually meant the farmers who returned from a day's toil in the local fields. They may have been Punans, but they no longer lived the Punan lifestyle that had so captured our imagination.

I was devastated. It appeared that the only Punans left had been persuaded to give up their nomadic lifestyle and integrate with the Dyak villagers. Of course, I had nothing against the Dyaks. It was just that their lives were similar to ours. With two weeks until our flight out, we had no choice but to bide our time in Suleh. Shian said we were welcome to remain at her house. Gradually our disappointment at our Punan experience changed as we got to know the village and its people better.

Shian was the perfect hostess. We may not have been able to speak to each other, but she knew how to keep us happy, serving up a steady stream of breakfasts, lunches and dinners. They were sensational, and made all the better by the fact that all ingredients came from the surrounding land and water. We had fried fish from the river, rice, cucumbers and corn from the fields and wild deer and pork hunted in the jungle by Shian's eldest son. And all were prepared locally – very locally. It was no surprise to walk to the toilet at the rear of the house and find half a deer gutted but complete with skin and hoofs, lying on the bare timber floor. It would remain there for several days until it was consumed.

Shian cooked the most delicious meals I've ever eaten. The smell of chilli, nuts, salt and oil would waft throughout the house from the open fire she cooked over. Smoke filtered out through specially designed outlets at the pinnacle of the ceiling. She'd slowly cook the pork in her wok for a couple of hours before serving it up. It tasted and smelt so good that even the once-vegetarian Josh began to crave it. He quickly gave the rice the flick and would hoe into the pork and deer along with the rest of us. To see the once-so-strict vegetarian munching away on a gristly bit of wild boar, complete with hair sprouting from it, was a sight to behold.

How he'd changed. He was a long way from the clean-shaven boy I'd first met in Melbourne in that dark editing suite more than two years ago. In fact, none of us looked the same. Constant strenuous activity had defined our muscles; all of us wore stacks of facial hair and our skin was a healthy brown.

Suleh, Charlie explained, was actually two villages, one on each side of the river. The Indonesian Government, in its wisdom, had looked upon the local highlanders as a national embarrassment. How could they expect to become a developed country when they still had natives living in the Stone Age? Their answer was to pull together different villages and make it easy for them to become 'civilised'. They paid for bridges, subsidised washing powder and helped build the churches and schools (one for each village).

While a few locals have found jobs with a logging company, which means spending a lot of time away from the village, most make a meagre living by selling handicrafts to stores in Samarinda. The most popular items are parangs (bush knives in a wooden sheath) and rattan baskets. Peter the pilot had told us Suleh has a reputation for making the best baskets in all of Borneo. A basket costs nothing to make, only time. The rattan vines are collected from the forest, then left to dry for a few weeks. Once dry, flat strips are shaved off the vines to produce a very strong, almost flat, material that can be bent, wound, tied and woven to become extremely durable baskets. Attach two straps and they become a Borneo backpack. Everyone has one. Farmers carry their vegetables in them, hunters take a parang in them when hunting, and firewood is brought into the village using them.

From Samarinda, these handicrafts are sent to places such as Bali, where tourists pay a high price for them. It's ironic that in this most remote of places, a small basket-making industry will most likely suffer the economic impact of the Bali bombing. Our attempt to get to the ends of the earth clearly wasn't far enough away to escape the troubles of the world.

The locals are paid very little for their effort, so it takes a long time to afford the things that make life easier. At the top of the list for most is a canoe, which allows locals to travel up and down the river to hunt and collect rattan vines. For those with a canoe, a long-tail outboard motor is definitely worth saving for. It's called a long-tail because of the long shaft from the engine to the propeller. This allows the propeller to be lifted quickly over rocks and rapids. However, once you have a motor you also have to be able to afford the fuel, which doesn't come cheap in those parts, costing A$1.50 per litre compared to 30 cents on the coast. Chainsaws are also highly sought after, as they can be used to clear fields for rice paddies and cut timber for huts.

As our faces became familiar around the village, the locals became more relaxed around us. One day, as we wandered the streets, we were invited to a villager's house for lunch. We knew we had to accept, as it was an honour for them to feed us, almost a statement to their peers declaring their popularity. This became evident when we realised the woman who'd invited us didn't even want to eat with us. Instead, she ushered us into a back room were we waited on a bench seat. In a corner a baby monkey was tethered. It was still young enough to be looking for a mother – anybody would do. In this case, it was Beau. It reached up to him in a way that no one could resist. When he leant over, its long arms hugged him.

Out came three plates from which we could choose fried river fish, vegetables in a thin white sauce and, of course, steamed rice. Our hostess laid the plates on the table, smiled at us, then left us alone in her dark and dingy abode.

We looked at each other, wondering if she would return to eat with us. We eventually assumed we should start. Lucky we didn't wait because she didn't reappear.

After eating our fill, there was still no sign of her. So we climbed under the table and awaited her return. Not long after, she entered the room only to find it empty. From under the table we could see her hesitate while she tried to figure out where her guests had vanished to. On the count of three we burst out from under the table with the loudest 'Boo!' we could muster.

In utter panic she bolted out of the house and onto the porch where her family and friends were chatting. Immediately we felt guilty that perhaps we'd gone too far with our shenanigans. But once we heard her laughter from the porch, we knew we were safe to step outside. News quickly spread of what had happened, and we watched as the incident was re-enacted by the woman to a growing crowd.

After a few days we were amazed how much we were able to understand what was going on around us without speaking the language. But sometimes we had to ask Charlie about something we didn't understand. We noticed that occasionally a couple of dogs would start howling, then more would join in until every dog on both sides of the river had joined the chorus. Josh asked Charlie why they howled together. He responded, very seriously, that they were spooked by ghosts.

Despite the disappointment of being told all the Punans now lived in villages, I was not convinced. I continued to see the distinctive girl from the day we arrived. Her parents must share her Punan features, I figured, but we never saw any adults carrying those characteristics.

One afternoon Beau was having a sleep and Josh was out walking about through the village. I was downstairs at Shian's at the pool table, which served as the local hangout. Shian had just topped up my coffee, while I watched her husband, Abraham, the local policeman and Charlie playing a game, when Josh rushed in and sat down. I could tell he was excited.

'Guess what?' he asked breathlessly.

I was in a playful mood, so I strung him along.

'Um ...' I said, while I thought. 'You were just walking back from the gardens and you saw a naked Punan with a blow dart gun scamper off into the forest?' I teased.

'No' he said, 'but close.' I stared at him, thinking that he was now taking me for a ride.

He then blurted out his story. He'd wandered over the bridge, to some huts near where Charlie had taken us on the first day. He'd been invited to sit on the porch of a family's house while they tried to engage in a conversation. It wasn't what you'd call a fast-moving conversation until one of the teenage daughters produced an ancient Indonesian to English dictionary. Josh took the dictionary and found the Indonesian word 'asli', which meant 'original or traditional'. Going backwards and forwards he wrote the question on paper to ask if there were any original Punans in the forest. They read his Indonesian and the daughter took down the mother's response.

He handed me the piece of paper that carried her message. The words that stood out were Original Punans, Grandfather Kila, Rattan and Metun.

'So does this mean a guy called Grandfather Kila is an original Punan?' I asked Josh.

'As far as I could understand, two days ago Grandfather Kila left for a place called Metun to deliver raw rattan to some original Punans.'

'How far away is Metun?'

'I don't know,' Josh replied.

'Then how do we get there?'

'I didn't get that far. It was hard enough getting this.'

When the game of pool was over, we told Charlie, who translated Josh's discovery to Shian. She appeared totally uninterested in our search for Punans, to the point of being reluctant to help us. Maybe she didn't want her house guests to leave. Or was our information about Metun misleading and she knew it?

We pressed Charlie for information, but he was not the local expert. All he knew was that Metun was too far to walk and, besides, there was no track leading there. Grandfather Kila would have travelled by canoe.

Shian interrupted, wanting to know how we would eat if we went there. We explained that we had a camp stove and we would be all right.

That appeared to convince her that we were fair dinkum, for she suddenly became a bit more forthcoming with information. She told Charlie the name of a man who might take us in his canoe, but we'd have to pay him. Fuel for the long-tail engine was expensive and you could always expect to lose at least one propeller on long river trips.

We woke Beau to tell him the exciting news before following Charlie through the village until he found the canoe man, Elijah, down by the river. Charlie made the request on our behalf.

After negotiating a price, Elijah agreed to take us. However, the river was too low for a canoe to get to Metun. If there was sufficient rain that afternoon to raise the water level, we may be able to leave early the next day. If we encountered no problems, we might arrive before nightfall.

It was our biggest breakthrough since discovering the MAF, and re-ignited our hopes of discovering real Punans.

The daily downpour arrived that afternoon, as it had each afternoon we'd been in Suleh. But we knew that only a morning inspection would confirm whether we could leave for Metun.

That night we packed our bags, filling them with hope more than anything. After dinner Beau and Josh went to sleep, while I sat outside on my own for several hours, listening to the insects and watching the village lights turn off one by one. I was too excited to sleep.

As I sat, lost in thought about what lay ahead of us, a few dogs on the other side of the bridge began to howl for no apparent reason. Suddenly, every dog in the village joined in. After a few minutes of howling, the dogs went silent. Just as they did, I heard the door to our room open and I turned to see Beau come around the corner.

'Can't sleep, hey?' I asked. 'Did you hear the dogs?'

He sat with a bewildered look on his face and gave half a laugh.

'Something really weird just happened.' I knew by the tone of his voice that something was troubling him. He continued. 'I've been awake for about 15 minutes. I *was* asleep, kind of half-dreaming when I heard, or *thought* I heard a voice say to me "wake up".'

As he spoke I remembered Charlie's story about ghosts spooking the local dogs, and felt the hairs on my back standing upright. Beau continued:

'I opened my eyes to see stuff moving around the room – like shadows. You know, it's dark in there so it didn't look like anything I recognised; it looked like something was moving. Then I looked over at Josh. He looked like he was moving his arms around in the air in front of his body. I said, "Josh are you awake?" but he said nothing. I didn't know if my eyes were playing tricks or not so I waited probably five minutes, while the shapes kept moving. I called his name again louder, but he was asleep. Then the moving stopped and shortly after those dogs started howling.'

'Shit,' I said, goose bumps now extending along my arms. 'Were you scared?'

'Not really. It was weird. But I swear someone told me to wake up, that's why I noticed it in the first place.'

He seemed at ease, which put me at ease. After he had a cigarette I followed him back to our room and set up my bedding. Before blowing out the candle, I went to my bag and pulled out the book by the Blair brothers. I scanned through the paragraphs I'd highlighted, which described the Punans:

The shyest, most jungle-wise of all the tribes, they wandered with the migratory seasons of their game, hunting monkeys and flying squirrels with poison blow darts, spearing pig and bear, making instant shelters at night, and moving on at dawn; men, women and children, scrambling fast and silently through primary forest so dense that no other tribe could follow them ...

I skipped ahead until I found what I was looking for.

They were thought of as a fey and ghostly people, barely human ...

I couldn't explain it and Beau certainly couldn't. I blew out the candle, yet I was certainly not about to fall asleep. Maybe I was reading more into what had happened than it deserved. Nevertheless, I kept my eyes open and ears straining to hear the voice Beau heard. None came before I lost the battle and fell asleep.

I woke to the sound of Josh opening the camera cases and found myself scattered over three sleeping mats. Beau asked Josh if he'd been moving his arms in the air during the night. He had no idea what Beau was talking about. He hadn't even heard the dogs!

We repeated Beau's story of the night before.

'Ah great!' Josh said in mock indignation, 'I'm possessed.'

We wandered downstairs still laughing at Josh's reaction and said good morning to everyone. Shian handed us coffees and began to speak to us in a jumble of English and Indonesian words. Until then our communication had extended to 'makan' meaning food. But this morning she seemed determined to ask us something. It required our three brains to work out what she was asking.

We slowly pieced together her words and were suddenly stunned when we realised what she was asking – 'Did you hear the dogs last night?'

We looked at each other, and my goose bumps returned. Of all the things she chose to communicate with us, why would it be this? What did she know? Unfortunately, we never found out.

After breakfast, we dashed down to the river where we found Elijah preparing his canoe.

Through Charlie, Elijah advised that the river level was high enough for us to travel.

We rushed back to get our bags and say goodbye to Shian, confirming with her that Elijah would return to Metun in a week to pick us up. She gave us a hug and some of the locals gathered to wave us off.

We plonked our packs in the middle of the canoe and piled in around them. Elijah got in the front, armed with a paddle, while a boy named Ramblas, who could have been his son, started the long-tail engine. We were off in search of the Punans. Children waved from the bridge and adults raised their heads from their jobs to watch us leave.

My imagination was racing with images of what we would find in Metun. I was also conscious of the importance of what we were doing. The cost of flying to this remote area of Borneo needed to pay off. We were setting out on an incredible adventure, something that would breathe new life into the journey of Kijana and get the office off my back. I was the happiest I'd been for a long while, for I felt we were on the verge of discovering something very important.

The canoe was a metre wide at its widest point, and about six metres long. Apart from our three packs the boat was fairly empty. A shotgun, parang, an aluminium pot and a small bag were all that our river guides had brought along.

Elijah kneeled at the bow, occasionally digging his paddle into the river to help the canoe along, or using it as a rudder to navigate the winding river. I was surprised at how fast the forest on either side of us passed by. We were travelling downstream and the current, combined with the engine, shot us along like an arrow.

Initially, we sat bolt upright, not daring to move in case disaster struck. If someone made a quick shift of position, one side of the narrow canoe would roll towards the water, threatening to capsize us. Even the smallest movement would be detected by Elijah, who'd shoot a glance at us as if to say, 'Watch it. I felt that!'.

The river was alive with activity. Butterflies flashed in and out of sight as their wings caught the sunlight with each flutter. Crickets chirped in orchestras that came and went. Each bend in the river casually slipped by, revealing another scenic masterpiece. No stretch was ever the same. The river would swing violently left, then right, its banks separating into a vast expanse of water, then converging to form a narrow fast-flowing channel. The masterpiece was ever-changing, yet always original. I was spellbound and wanted it to go on forever. I glanced at Beau and Josh. They were lost in the same world.

No longer were we sitting to attention. Rather, we had slumped around the canoe, each a counterweight to the other. Josh's shoulder was wedged against the side of the canoe with his arm dangling above the water. His fingers intermittently broke the water's surface, like creepers dangling from a sweeping branch. Beau sat with his back against the opposite side, his head higher above the water and his weight compensating for Josh's outstretched arm. I sat in the middle, but slightly to Beau's side. I subtly shifted myself to the centre of the canoe, a smidgen closer to Josh's side. Without comment he pulled his arm back into the confines of the canoe to rebalance the vessel, while continuing to stare at the shore. We were like a finely-tuned machine – an orchestra of our own! Wow, I loved my crew.

We passed a tree teeming with monkeys, then shortly after came across a makeshift camp opposite an adjoining estuary. Surely this wasn't Metun already? It took a few minutes to realise Elijah had stopped for a break and to catch up with friends. I looked up the estuary. It was a lot narrower than the river, with bumps on the surface of the water indicating stones below shallow water. The main river continued flowing steadily ahead. I had no idea which way we would go.

From his bag Ramblas produced a cardboard box which contained neatly packed half-size bottles of whisky, which he handed over to the campsite residents. Was this a centre for smuggled goods, where shotgun shells and alcohol were traded out of the eye of the head honchos in town? Or was this some sort of bribe that allowed us to pass. I never asked, as I doubted anyone wanted to talk about it. Besides, I was happy not to know for it only added to the suspense of getting to our destination.

After 15 minutes it was time to climb back into the canoe and continue on our way. Ramblas started the engine and pushed us off.

We turned and headed upstream into the estuary. This new river grew smaller with each kilometre. It was now a test of Elijah's and Ramblas's skills to negotiate their way.

We came to a section where the forest opened up. Across our path lay a huge fallen tree. Elijah made a desperate motion with the paddle for us to duck our heads as Ramblas aimed for a gap under the trunk. Like piano keys, we each ducked in turn, rising to look back and marvel at how we managed to squeeze through. As we did so, we felt an enormous jolt that nearly sent Ramblas overboard. An unbearable screeching sound indicated something was wrong. Ramblas quickly lifted the shaft from the water to reveal the propeller missing. Elijah paddled us to a beach of small rounded river stones to investigate. It was, as Shian had predicted, a busted propeller.

'Broken,' I said.

Ramblas nodded and pulled a spare from his bag. Not only had we lost the propeller but the sheath covering the shaft had split, giving rise to all the noise.

Elijah and Ramblas got to work fixing the shaft. A length of bamboo was cut and some rattan vine was stripped to form a strong twine. The bamboo was placed on the shaft and the twine wrapped around it to keep it in place.

As Elijah and Ramblas worked, Beau stayed in the canoe, sucking on a cigarette, while Josh convinced me to go for a swim. We walked upstream and let the current drag our bums over the rocks. It reminded me of those Japanese torture shows you occasionally see on TV.

We got back to the canoe but the guys were still slowly shaping the bamboo. They didn't appear to be in a hurry to get it done, so I picked up a stick from the edge of the forest and started whacking small river stones towards Josh, who was still swimming. I'd throw a stone in front of me, then swing, making sure if I did hit him it wouldn't do too much damage. He quickly headed for shore, both for his safety and to have a crack as well. The closer he got to the bank, the more I missed and the faster I tried to hit them. Then one connected and went in the opposite direction. Josh laughed.

I kept swinging until gradually I got into a groove and started to hit every stone I threw.

'Hey Josh,' I yelled at him, 'Check this out!'

He covered his face expecting one to fly straight at him.

'Nah, I'm not aiming for you any more.'

I swung with all my might, hoping to impress. It landed by my foot.

'Wow, I didn't even see that one land,' he said sarcastically.

'I was getting every one of them just before. See how many you can hit.'

I tossed him one of my selected stones. He took a stick and swung but missed.

'It's all about timing, hey!' he said.

I focused and missed again. I thought back to what I'd been doing before and remembered I hadn't been thinking about hitting the stone, but rather, I was thinking about the result – the stone flying through the air. So I thought about hitting the branches on the other side and swung. A crack rang out that even turned Beau's head.

'Cool,' I thought. Gayili was right. 'Only think of what you are looking for,' she'd told us four months before in Arnhem Land. 'What you think about will happen.'

As this line bounced around my head I swung again. Bingo! A few seconds later I heard a nice neat plop on the far side of the river.

It hadn't made much sense at the time, but Gayili's words were now ringing true. Every splash proved her point.

I tried to explain my revelation to Josh – don't focus on the process, imagine the result and your body will do the rest.

'I think I get what you mean,' he said. Sure enough, on his second swing he connected. It hurtled above us, at what appeared to be the speed of sound and landed in the forest behind. Our success rate rose to about 80 per cent. The next challenge was placement. We tried to hit a boulder at the water's edge on the other side. It didn't take too long for both of us to succeed. It was an amazing feeling.

I felt this major discovery was a sign for what lay ahead in Metun. As I stood there with Josh, I had never felt closer to him. And I'd never felt so alive and buzzing with anticipation. I'd read about life-defining moments, and at that moment, I believed was experiencing one.

Beau dragged me back to earth when he called us back, as the repairs were finished. Minutes later we were on our way again, weaving in and out of obstacles for a couple more hours. I didn't want this trip to end, for it was as close to paradise as we'd experienced so far on Kijana. I was almost disappointed when, seven hours after we left Suleh, I noticed a change in the dense forest and on our left a clearing the size of a football field opened up – we'd arrived at Metun.

As we walked up the riverbank, a heavy sense of dread came over me. It didn't look anything like I imagined it would. Metun turned out to be a derelict logging settlement, with a dozen or so small corrugated tin huts where the employees were housed. Rusted machinery lay hidden in the regrowth surrounding the edges of the clearing.

We found Grandfather Kila weaving rattan on the verandah of one of the shacks. He looked up at us from under his Adidas baseball cap. His old face looked fragile but friendly, with large freckles on his cheeks and the odd rogue whisker sprouting from his chin. He looked like a Punan, with distinctive Punan features and stretched ears, as did another older man and their two wives, who were also weaving rattan. But they weren't the Punans we'd pictured and, to the camera, they looked like any other clothed Indonesians.

Scattered around the clearing I noticed half a dozen other younger men, who I assumed were linked to the local logging company. They meandered about, as if waiting for something to happen.

After exchanging smiles with Grandfather Kila and his companions, I attempted to ask if there were any other Punans living in the area.

Elijah and Ramblas may have been good canoe drivers but were terrible at English. One of the younger men was summoned to translate for us.

'Yes there are other Punans,' the young man said, relaying Kila's response.

'Where are they?' I asked.

Kila raised his hand in answer to the young man, then motioned towards a road in the corner of the clearing that I hadn't noticed until then.

'How far is it?' I asked. The translator didn't even bother asking Kila.

'It's too far,' he said. 'You will need a ride with a logging truck.'

'When does the next truck arrive?' I asked, looking around at what I assumed was old machinery no longer in use.

'Not for a long time,' he said. 'There was a landslide and the road is blocked.'

I wondered how long this logging camp had been cut off. It looked like years.

This was the end of the road – literally and figuratively. A landslide was a landslide – there was no way of getting past the actions of Mother Nature.

Perhaps I was being unreasonable expecting a tribe of naked men and women holding blow darts to descend from the surrounding mountains. I began to realise this would most likely be as good as we could expect to find, in Suleh anyway. We had stumbled across a different world to that discovered by the Blair brothers all those years ago. Our visa ran out soon and we were getting further away from Samarinda and *Kijana*. Also, we had to meet Peter at the Suleh airstrip in five days' time. Who knows how long we would be gone if we headed up that road.

Through the translator, Grandfather Kila asked a very good question: 'Why are you here?'

'Asli Punans,' I said directly to him. He nodded his head in recognition, sensing my obvious disappointment.

We asked Elijah if we could return with him to Suleh that afternoon. He pointed to the dark clouds approaching, heralding the afternoon downpour and motioned that we would have to stay the night.

A young man showed us an empty shack where we could sleep. A generator was started just before the heavy rain began to fall. It powered a television in the shack next to us from where we could hear the younger men watching Indonesian porn. I sat on our bedding thinking about Shian's cooking and wanting to be back in the village. I then thought about her reaction when we told her we were going to Metun. Perhaps she knew all along that we would be disappointed by what we found.

Through our doorway I could see Grandfather Kila sitting on the verandah weaving rattan, oblivious to the rain. When the rain stopped he stood up and walked over to our hut. In his hand was a blowgun and tied to his polyester shorts was a bamboo case in which were some poisonous darts. He motioned with his hand for us to follow him into the forest. We followed him over a hill to where a sheltered platform looked out over the river and forest canopy. Unable to communicate, we were puzzled as to why we were there.

Grandfather Kila sat looking out at the trees as if meditating. After about 15 minutes we heard a great crash on the opposite side of the river. After straining our eyes we caught a glimpse of a family of monkeys several hundred metres away. They appeared to be much too far away for Grandfather Kila's blowgun to claim a victim. Nevertheless, he loaded a dart into the small opening of the pipe. He waited for a monkey to emerge from the branches, took aim and, with a woompf, shot the dart from the gun. It disappeared out of sight somewhere over the river. Fortunately for the monkey, it fell well short.

Grandfather Kila turned to us and nodded, us as if to say, 'That's how we used to do it.' He appeared to be trying to make up for our disappointment by giving us at least a glimpse of what we had come to see. I wished I knew enough Indonesian to thank him.

The next morning we woke to find one of the old women chopping up a monkey. For a split second I wondered if Grandfather Kila wasn't as frail as he looked. But Josh set me straight – he'd seen Elijah return with the animal on his back and shotgun in hand.

We packed up our bedding and waited for Elijah to begin the return trip to Suleh. Grandfather Kila emerged from his shack wearing a construction worker's hat. His stretched ears looked even stranger hanging under the hard plastic. They wobbled as he shook our hands.

I wondered what he thought of us three, coming so far to meet him. He was a funny man but, to him, we were probably even stranger. We were probably the first white men he had met who wanted him to be something from the past, rather than trying to change him into something of today's world.

The return river trip was like drifting out of a beautiful dream and waking up in the real world with all its problems. I didn't want to leave. I'd fallen for the notion of living the life of a river trader, with no business pressures, threats of terrorism or reefs to crunch into.

During a stop on our return river trip, I wandered into the bush to survey the landscape. We had stopped by a small creek that flowed into the main river. I followed it up to where there was a small water-hole and stood there imagining washing dishes with Maya. I picked out two large trees on either side of the creek that could support a sus-pension bridge, and noted that where the creek joined the river was a small inlet, just the right size to keep a canoe and long-tail motor safe when the rains came and the river flooded. I knew it was a pipedream, but I needed something. I could no longer carry my dream of finding the original Punans.

Back at Suleh, Shian greeted us with a big smile and served a steaming meal of deer and rice. She made no mention of our short-ened trip.

We had four days before we were due to fly out. These were spent tracking down the only person in the village – an old woman – who could do traditional tattoos, so Beau and I could have a permanent reminder of our time in Borneo.

She patiently mixed coal with water to make the dye while a growing number of children peered from every vantage point they could find to witness a dying art. I asked her to draw a traditional design on my forearm, while Beau asked for his to be placed closer to his elbow. We had no idea what the designs represented.

For several hours she hunched over us, tapping away with her homemade stick, repeatedly dipping the needles in the dye. The younger children began to imitate the actions of the old woman, making pretend tattoos on each other's arms. It was a heartening sign.

Just as Suleh had made an indelible mark on Josh, Beau and I, we hoped our visit had taught them something. Maybe, just maybe, one of those kids would begin to take an interest in this lost art. Maybe someone would now realise the Punans were becoming a truly lost race. Maybe some of the teenagers would opt to stay in Suleh to continue the local traditions, rather than be forever lost to the bright lights of the coastal cities. Maybe.

The next day the sound of civilisation flew circles over the village. It was time to go.

CHAPTER ELEVEN
THE BEACH

OUR RETURN TO THE RELATIVE CIVILISATION of Samarinda was marked by relief as I saw *Kijana* anchored in the same spot on the river where we had left her, as Peter circled the aircraft in preparation for landing.

But my relief turned to horror when I discovered that, with just one day left on our already extended visas, Samarinda didn't have a Customs office. It meant we couldn't get our passports stamped to leave the country. That, in itself, didn't pose a major problem. The real drama would come when we tried to enter another country without the appropriate papers. It would surely guarantee that no other country would accept us. The closest Indonesian Customs office was in Balikpapan, where the local police were probably still waiting for us to visit them.

Although we knew our visas would have expired by the time we arrived, we had no choice but to return. So we stocked up on fresh fruit and vegies and arrived at the Customs office in Balikpapan two days later.

We nervously explained our case to the officer, who miraculously understood our situation and gave us official clearance. We wasted no time in getting back to *Kijana* before the police realised there was another foreign yacht anchored off the city. We then left Indonesia after four months cruising its waters.

Our route took us from Balikpapan down the east coast of Borneo until we could turn west into the Java Sea. We would continue around the bottom of the island towards Singapore, then up the Strait of Malacca through the hundreds of islands along the coast of Thailand, finally arriving at the holiday mecca of Phuket, and the beautiful Maya Bay.

The first four days of sailing passed without a hitch. The wind was constantly on the beam, pushing us along at a good rate of six knots. But as we rounded the southern tip of Borneo, just off Banjarmasin, we hit a patch of light wind. We sailed as much as we could until it died completely, forcing us to reluctantly turn on the motor just to keep us moving forward.

During that leg, Beau's imminent departure played heavily on my mind. I still didn't want him to leave, but I knew our failed attempt at finding the Punans hadn't exactly instilled in him any new reason to stay with *Kijana*. I had to admit that since he had made his decision, he seemed more relaxed and at ease with himself. I casually sussed him out and, yes, he still planned to leave once we got to the Buddhist temples of Northern India. To get himself into the groove, he planned to undertake a meditation course off the coast of Thailand, which he could travel to when we arrived at Phuket.

An email arrived from the office raising the issue of finding further crew. The usual suggestions were made – someone outgoing, non-Australian and preferably female. New crew were so distant from our needs at the time. The three of us had shared so much that we'd become a tight unit. I was worried a stranger would struggle to penetrate it and remain an outsider for the duration of their time aboard. Also, having to teach a new crew member how to sail and the possibility of having someone who didn't pull their weight was a thought that made my insides squirm. Maria's good work had failed to heal the scars of my earlier experience and I didn't trust myself to be gentle with anyone who didn't fit into life at sea.

The email also made comment that the footage we'd sent so far was not up to scratch. This annoyed me because the office didn't seem to understand that we couldn't just create adventures that would provide good footage.

I spent a day thinking about how to answer the email. It had made no mention of Maya joining the trip, something that offended me. I was quiet all day to the point where Josh approached me in the evening as I stood at the bow, wanting to know what was wrong, so I told him.

The idea of new crew was also playing on his mind. Our bond had become so strong that the thought of stepping back a notch for us to make way for new crew was really bothering him. But he knew how much it meant to me to have Maya join us, so he threw his full weight behind me.

'We've gotta get her on board, don't we!' he declared. Those few words meant so much coming from him. Knowing I had Josh's support made such a difference, and I knew it would also carry weight with the office.

'Tomorrow we should send them an email from both of us,' he said. I nodded and did my best not to show how much it meant to me.

The next day we emailed the office asking for Maya to join us and telling them we'd look for another crew member in Thailand. We figured there'd be plenty of backpackers who would be suitable, we wrote.

Meanwhile, the north-west monsoon had hit and we were motoring almost 50 per cent of the time. We ploughed into the wind and waves, revving the guts out of the engine to make any headway. Our progress was a meagre 80 miles a day. Checking emails in this weather was a nightmare, requiring one person to point the satellite antenna at the imaginary spot in the sky where the signal strength came from, while another person on the computer dialled up the connection. Each time we went through this process to find the cupboard bare. Finally, an email arrived from the office, merely informing us they were considering our request.

The rain clouds came and went, but all the while the grey sky remained. It was on these types of days that the crew relied on each other more than ever. We would sit for hours huddled in the cockpit, dodging spray behind the bimini, and talk about anything that came to mind. After so long together, we'd covered most topics, so our conversations tended to be pretty weird. Jokes were repeated and themes explored to the nth degree, to the point where only a word needed to be uttered for the others to understand. We were clutching at straws but these were desperate times – any chortle in a storm would do.

However, despite our ready supply of laughs, the same could not be said for our fuel. We were becoming increasingly concerned that we may run out of diesel. *Kijana* had the capacity to hold 400 litres of the stuff spread over two tanks, one on each side, but even though we'd left Samarinda under full capacity, the engine had been guzzling it down to get through the weather. I was constantly using the dipstick to check the diesel level, calculating that it would be touch-and-go as to whether we would make it to Thailand with our current supply.

The next refuelling point was at the start of the Malacca Strait, opposite Singapore on the Indonesian island of Batam, which was a solid week's sailing away. We needed the wind to change direction so we could raise the sails and give the engine a breather. Also, the buffeting of the wind and waves was taking its toll on our equipment. One of the braces holding the wind generators had buckled under the constant rocking, snapping the spinning blades and spraying shards of carbon fibre across the deck. Luckily, no one had been on deck at the time or they could have suffered a serious injury.

Then, amid our worries, an email arrived from the office. They'd thought long and hard about our request, and had even spoken to Maya herself. They believed it was too early for her to join the crew, considering the delicate timing of our pitches to the television networks. But they conceded she could fly to Thailand for a short visit.

It wasn't the answer I wanted, but there was at least a tiny glimmer of light at the end of the tunnel. That same day the wind slowly changed direction to come from the north-east, then continued to die down until there was not even enough breeze to stop the boom from slapping. However, the calmer conditions allowed us to at least drop the engine revs, reducing the fuel consumption considerably.

As we approached the beginning of the Strait of Malacca the wind was up and down, forcing us to use our last few drops of diesel to limp into a marina on Batam Island for refuelling. Three hours later we departed with full tanks and an even more depleted bank account, and joined the heavy flow of traffic entering the narrow channel between Indonesia and Singapore, which is one of the busiest shipping channels in the world. This required even more diligent watches to stay out of the way of the thundering tankers who cared little for small wooden yachts.

The wind continued to shift in all directions as though it was determined to make it difficult for us to travel. We used the sails as often as possible and managed to keep engine use to a minimum after we left Batam Island.

Unlike the shifting wind, my thoughts were focused on just one matter. I emailed Maya that we hoped to arrive at Phuket in five days' time, which was probably a little too optimistic. She replied that she would book her flight to arrive in Phuket the day we did. I'd set us a fierce challenge to travel about 800 miles in only five days, but I was determined to get there as quickly as I could. I didn't care what the wind had planned for us. If it wasn't going to help us, then the engine sure as hell would.

Plotting our position had never been more important. It reminded me of those last few days I'd spent aboard *Lionheart* before arriving home. I tackled the art of navigation with renewed vigour. Josh and Beau seemed to feed off my excitement and together we really got stuck into sailing as quickly as we could. Each centimetre on the map was a small victory, and every hour I would calculate a new ETA and make adjustments to keep *Kijana* on course. It was no mean feat, for the shipping channel along the coast of Malaysia threw up many obstacles, not the least being the long lines of fishing nets and trawlers which had the nasty habit of working at night without lights.

We entered Thai waters on 29 November 2002, and late that afternoon spotted, in the distance, the island of our dreams. We re-checked the chart to confirm excitedly that it was Phi Phi Lae, the location of Maya Bay. On that first brief sighting, it certainly appeared the way we'd imagined it – the first thing on the trip that had. It was a small victory, but a victory nonetheless.

Our visit to that island was to come later. First, I had an important rendezvous. We continued on another 25 miles to Phuket Island and as the sun set and the wind died, we motored into Patong Bay. Without worrying about Customs, we dropped anchor and launched the dinghy for the short trip to shore. Maya expected to see us in the morning but I wanted to surprise her at the hotel that very night. I grabbed my Borneo backpack and threw in a razor, toothpaste and soap. It had been 17 days since we'd left Samarinda and the thought of a shower was sending us crazy.

As Beau and I stepped into the dinghy, Josh suddenly changed his mind and decided to remain on board. Throughout the entire trip us guys had shared every exciting moment together. Landing in a new country was always cause for celebration, if for nothing else than to get clean and have a nice meal. It would be the first time the three amigos hadn't shared the excitement of a landfall.

We tried to convince him, but he was adamant that he wanted to stay and get some sleep, which I found hard to understand. But I had other things on my mind, so Beau and I headed ashore in the dinghy and caught a taxi to the hotel.

Once inside the hotel foyer I used the phone at reception and dialled Maya's room, pretending I was still at sea. After confirming I would meet her in the morning, we climbed the stairs to her room, knocked on the door and hid against the wall. Sensibly, she took a while to open the door, a single girl in a strange country and all that. Eventually she opened it, and as she did I peered around the doorway to see my lovely girl standing in her pyjamas with a twinkle in her eye. I felt embarrassed by the stupid grin on my face, but there was nothing I could do about it. I was that happy! At that moment Kijana felt a world away.

CHAPTER TWELVE
TROUBLE IN PARADISE

THAILAND BROUGHT WITH IT ALL THE trappings of western life we'd long forgotten. We felt guilty, dirty even, indulging in the luxuries of modern life – soft drink, spicy Thai meals and cheap pirated CDs. But after a few days of indulging, we soon tired of consumerism and yearned to get back to the business of Kijana.

We were kick-started into action by Beau's need to find his way to the other side of Thailand, where his meditation course was due to begin in a couple of days. It took us a while to work out the best way there – a bus to the mainland, then a train to the east coast of the mainland where the eight-day course of mind-cleansing was to be held.

We said our goodbyes and arranged to meet at the island of Phi Phi Don, the biggest island next to Phi Phi Lae, the location of *The Beach*. From there we would make the triumphant sail into the lagoon of Maya Bay, all four of us together.

In Beau's absence, Josh, Maya and I sailed to the other side of Phuket Island, docking at a rather fancy marina and setting to work, giving *Kijana* a well-deserved clean. She had done a mighty job powering into the monsoon, so the least she deserved was a bit of TLC.

The marina was strangely located in an estuary that could only be accessed at high tide when there was enough water to cover the mud-flats. Despite this odd impediment, the marina was a major facility, with more than 100 yachts berthed along the marina fingers, a couple of restaurants and dry-dock facilities.

Over the three days we were berthed there we took all the carpet outside to dry, wiped the shelves, restocked the galley, and washed the sheets and pillows.

The three of us worked well together, and there was a sense of achievement as *Kijana* was spruced up. Even if we were struggling to get good film for the documentaries, seeing *Kijana* in tiptop condition made me feel better. She was a major investment for the project and had to be looked after.

After completing our work we decided to sail to Phi Phi Don, where we would hang out and wait for Beau. As I paid the hefty marina fees I asked the shipwright for some advice on how to get out of the marina. Entry and exit had to be timed with the tides and I was heart-ened when he told me we were leaving at precisely the right time.

'Just follow the river the way you came in,' he told me.

I stepped aboard *Kijana*, confident and happy with her condition, and excited about the islands we would visit in the coming days. With a clean boat I was keen to show Maya the best side of sailing.

I took to the helm after warming the engine and yelled out to Josh, who was still on the jetty, to untie the mooring lines. Josh stepped aboard just before the gap between the boat and the jetty got too far as confidently as any experienced seaman I'd seen. Watching him, I was even more confident that when Beau finally left us in India, Josh and I could maintain our vessel and command her safely.

However, my confidence soon evaporated when I felt a strange sensation as we motored into the first bend in the river. It was the dull feeling of *Kijana* wedging herself into a mud bank in the corner of the river. So much for our boating prowess!

'Shit,' was all I could muster. I shifted the engine into reverse, hoping to back out of the mud, but she refused to budge. Even revving the bejickers out of the motor made no difference.

We could see the tide sucking the water out to sea, slowly dropping the level around *Kijana*'s hull and holding her tightly wedged into the bank. It was at that point I noticed the masts leaning ever-so-slightly towards the mangroves trees on our port side. It wasn't much, but it was enough to cause panic. The tide was dropping so quickly that if we didn't get off the bank, our newly cleaned vessel would be left high and dry, pathetically leaning on her side until the tide returned in about six hours. How would that sound to the office? I could just see their take on it – *Kijana* had run aground because I was too busy ogling my girlfriend. Great!

Josh radioed the marina office for assistance. At least they didn't have far to get there, for we'd failed to travel more than 100 metres from the jetty. The shipwright and his crew arrived within five minutes in a powerful diesel tugboat. They attached lines to every point possible and gave the tug everything she had. But nothing would work. All the while, *Kijana* continued to lean further and further over as the rush of water from the river gathered pace. We reached the point where it was no use trying to pull *Kijana* out of the mud, for the tide was too far gone.

I looked at the shipwright with pleading eyes. 'It's OK,' he said trying to reassure me, 'it's happened to other yachts quite often.'

Then why the hell didn't you warn me, I felt like asking him. Instead, I asked what the 'other yachts' had done. He told us to tie ropes from the top of each mast to an old rusting abandoned barge on the other side of the river. This, he said, would stop the yacht toppling over onto her side completely. With an outgoing tide, no vessels could get in or out of the marina, so our ropes weren't going to cause any problems, he said. We just had to make sure we got them down by the time the tide returned or else we'd cause a traffic jam of yachts.

The shipwright left us with the frantic job of stringing lines to the opposite bank before the lean got much worse. For more than an hour we crisscrossed the river in the dinghy, tying ropes to the barge, until we began to feel like spiders spinning a web. When we finished, *Kijana* looked like our poor insect victim.

To complete the experience it began to rain, so we scrambled aboard *Kijana*'s deck, which now lay at a 45-degree angle. Below deck we began moving everything to the port side of the cabin to prevent anything falling off shelves and causing damage. The tide was so low by that stage we were able to walk around the exposed hull, which, from a distance, looked like a beached whale. We were even able to inspect the barnacles growing on the propeller.

There was nothing we could do except wait for the water level to rise when the tide came back in. Actually, there was one thing we were able to do – get some footage. Josh ran around like a madman getting shots from every angle.

While Josh stayed on board getting footage, Maya and I returned to the marina for a few hours. Josh later recounted how difficult it was to cook on a stove tilting 45 degrees. Why he even embarked on such a project was beyond me.

We arrived back as the incoming tide began to return the water level to its former depth. As surely as she went over, *Kijana*'s masts began their journey back to an upright position. By this stage it was late afternoon and the day was escaping us. If we didn't get her off the bank during the small window of high tide, she'd be stuck there all night in a repeat performance.

Soon a queue of incoming yachts was waiting for us to unravel our mass of lines draped across the river, and get the hell out of the way. The shipwright's tug returned to provide some extra oomph and, with *Kijana*'s motor revving, we slowly slid off the bank and into the safety of deeper water. As the yachts passed by, we were faced with the decision of which way to go. Although the tide was at its highest, the poor light prevented us attempting an escape. We'd sure as eggs hit another bank in the darkness, so we reluctantly headed back to the same jetty we'd departed from only that morning, and tied up for the night. Even on that return trip of 100 metres we managed to hit another bank, overheating the engine as we extracted ourselves from another near disaster.

By time I stepped onto the jetty I felt relieved, but also pissed off at our mishaps. Despite the poor information we'd been given, I blamed myself for what had happened.

While Josh and Maya prepared a cold meal for dinner, I set about cleaning the fuel filter, which was the main suspect for the overheated motor. After halting the fuel flow and unbolting the cap, I stood on the jetty as I wiped out the muck from the filter. In keeping with the day's events, I knocked my hand against the wharf and dropped the filter's glass cap into the dark water below. It disappeared within seconds, along with any hope that my nightmare day was over. Hell, I was mad. It meant we'd be wasting more time, when every day that went by was one less that Maya and I would share together. Time was too precious to waste being stuck in mud. In the back of my mind I told myself everything would be OK once we got to Maya Bay.

The following morning, I managed to get hold of a second-hand filter cap and by the time I'd fitted it, the tide was at its peak. We managed to cautiously snake our way down the river without incident until we finally hit the open seas. From there it was a four-hour sail to Phi Phi Don and, hopefully, paradise. I was never so glad to see an open expanse of water.

As we got underway I wondered what Maya thought of life on board, how she saw herself fitting into the crew and whether she still wanted to take the plunge and join the trip permanently. Up to that point we hadn't discussed it, preferring instead to merely bask in each other's company. Of course she wanted to stay on, she told me when I asked her. As long as she was with me she'd be happy! How could I not love this girl.

However, her resolve was soon tested when she began to feel sea-sick after a few hours at sea, her longest stretch yet on *Kijana*. While *Kijana* rode the waves without a hint of repercussions from her episode the previous day, Maya was going green in the face. I couldn't help but be reminded of those first days of the trip and the experiences of Mika and Nicolette.

I could see Josh's reaction and knew what was going through his mind. It was the same thing going through mine. However, this time I was more sympathetic. And so was Josh, who promptly fired up the engine to get us to Phi Phi Don quickly to end Maya's suffering.

After four hours on the water we were close enough to spy the intricate details of the cliffs on Phi Phi Don. We planned our visit as a two-pronged attack – Phi Phi Don was to be the fun of the bars and backpackers, while Phi Phi Lae would be the natural beauty of *The Beach*.

As soon as we stopped and dropped anchor, Maya immediately felt better. And when Josh spied the shops and bars of the main strip, his spirits lifted as well.

'I can smell the ladies from here,' he declared as we got ready to explore the shore.

We were surprised by how much activity we found on the island. We'd heard there were a lot of bars, but nothing like the number we found. There was everything from dive shops and cafés to street stalls cooking crêpes and piling them with exotic fillings before our eyes. We even passed a few restaurants where the diners ate in silence, watching none other than Leonardo Di Caprio on the very beach that lay a few miles from where we stood. We obviously weren't the only ones to be lured here by a Hollywood film. Since the film's release in 1999, tourism to these islands had skyrocketed. It had always been a popular place, but was now even more so.

We found a small place to eat dinner, then settled at a club and hit the dance floor. There were backpackers from all over the place – England, Germany, Australia and the United States to name a few. Everyone was there for a good time, so conversation was easy and soon a small group had formed around us.

Towards the end of the night Maya and I wandered off to find a crêpe stall for dessert, but when we returned to the club Josh had disappeared. We headed back to the dinghy, presuming he'd be waiting for us there, but there was no sign of him when we got there. We sat and waited half an hour until Josh's distinctive figure came striding towards us. We'd all drunk our fair share of Red Bulls and whisky, but Josh walked with an intensity that I instantly recognised meant that something was wrong.

He said nothing when he arrived, instead grabbing the dinghy and attempting to pull it into the water on his own. I thought it a strange move, for he knew it was way too heavy for one person to drag, so Maya and I grabbed the other side and helped heave it into the water. After we started the motor and began the 100-metre trip back to *Kijana*, I asked him what was wrong. His face was deadpan, his eyes watery red.

'Nothing,' he said, then immediately changed his mind. 'Where were you guys?'

'We came back after something to eat but couldn't find you,' I explained.

He said nothing in response. We arrived at *Kijana* and stepped aboard, with still not a word uttered. Josh was obviously pretty pissed off at something. He'd either been in a fight, which was highly unlikely, or he felt abandoned by Maya and me. Either way, I felt the issue needed to be resolved, so I quizzed him again.

'Are you sure you're OK?'

He didn't answer but stepped back over the safety lines and into the dinghy and in a drunken slur announced he was going off to think.

As he started the outboard, I yelled out for him to stop, but he ignored me. He may have needed time to think, but this was plain dangerous. I yelled out even louder but he didn't bat an eyelid. It was the first time he'd ignored an order from me. I was very worried, for I'd already hit one of the shallow reefs in the dinghy earlier that day.

As he began to swerve off uncontrollably into the darkness, I took a flying leap off the deck, managing to grab hold of one of the inflatable hulls while the rest of my body dragged in the water. He had such a head of steam that he ignored my plight and revved the engine as hard as he could, dragging me along as I tried to keep my feet away from the spinning propeller. I was being just as stupid as Josh, and I knew I wouldn't have done it if I was sober, but the stakes were high, for Josh was in no state to control a speeding dinghy. I eventually managed to drag myself into the dinghy and yanked out the safety key which immediately shut the engine down.

'If you want to go, you can row,' I yelled, jumping back into the water with the key in my hand and swimming back to *Kijana*. By the time I clambered back on deck I could just make out the sound of oars dipping into water. I looked at Maya but didn't know what to say to her.

'He went that way,' she offered, pointing into the darkness. There was no moon and I could no longer hear the splosh of the oars, so he could have been anywhere by then.

'At least he's not gonna kill himself,' I said rather dramatically, hoping to justify my reckless heroics.

'Maybe you should go and talk to him,' Maya said. I wholeheartedly agreed with her, for I cared deeply about Josh. But the truth was I didn't know what to say.

We sat in the dark contemplating what had just happened when, from across the still water, came the heart-wrenching noise of uncontrollable sobbing. I knew it was Josh.

I wanted to hug him and apologise for taking the key. I wanted him to know it was OK, that if he felt like he was losing a friend since Maya had arrived, he hadn't. Having Maya on board changed nothing for me. I loved her but Josh was always going to be my first mate. No one could replace what he had brought to *Kijana*. I wished he'd realised that before.

When the bright sunlight woke me the next morning, the last thing I wanted to do was get out of bed. I was hungover and unsure of Josh's fate. I was relieved to find him in the front cabin sound asleep. He didn't rise until after lunch, which was incredibly late for the man we'd dubbed Mr Earlybird.

He immediately apologised for the mess of the previous night. I said I was sorry for taking the dinghy key, but he didn't remember anything about that. In fact, he didn't remember much of anything, other than the fact that he had 'regrets', so nothing further was said about the episode. But I knew it was all about Maya. As much as he tried to hide his feelings for my sake, having Maya aboard was having a bigger effect than I ever imagined.

The three of us spent the rest of the day doing everything in our power to ignore the previous night's events as we pottered around the boat, cleaned, checked emails and went ashore to look at the shops. Two emails arrived that day. The first was from Beau informing us he was returning to the boat early. There was no explanation, just a note to say he'd catch a ride on a ferry and be back aboard *Kijana* the next day.

The second was from the office. They'd seen the pictures we'd sent back of our river mishap, and demanded to know how we'd managed to get *Kijana* grounded.

They also 'advised' us that it would be best if the images weren't put on the website or given to any media. It was outright censorship. I believed we needed to show as much of our mishaps and adventures as possible for people to see the dangers we faced. I knew that would be the sort of adventure I'd follow. But I didn't have the energy to object. It was the same story, the same one since hitting the reef and the reason why Maya was only here for a 'holiday'. I knew what their answer would be, so it simply wasn't worth it. I no longer felt I had a say in how the trip was run.

Beau arrived the following day, and I was never so glad to see him. It was a reminder of how much I was going to miss him when he left permanently. The meditation course had been intense, he told us, too intense for his liking. After four days of not being allowed to look any of his fellow meditators in the face, he'd decided to hightail it and return to the relative calm of *Kijana*. He told us that he'd realised he needed more training before tackling such a full-on course.

I didn't have the heart to tell him that things had been pretty intense on board in his absence. In fact, he never found out, but he arrived back to an extremely subdued crew and must have figured something was going down.

We weighed anchor to sail the short 20-minute trip to *The Beach*. As we approached the beautiful island of Phi Phi Lae, the mood was heavy. Josh was still consumed by his worries about his relationship with me, and Beau was obviously affected by his Buddhism experience. I had my own concerns. I was increasingly worried about Maya. She'd been with us for just over a week and I feared that I would start to view her in the same light as Mika and Nicolette, with her seasickness and gentle ways on board. However, instead of shutting her out, as I had with the Mika and Nicolette, I was forced to face the problem because, ultimately, she meant as much to me as the trip.

The softness of her touch, the very thing I loved about her, was obviously not suited to my style of adventure. I was scared at the thought of her being on board. If I'd caused so much heartache and pain for Mika and Nicolette, then it wasn't beyond me to do the same to Maya. The harshness of what we were doing called for adventurers, not passengers.

The past week had slowly made me realise that I couldn't spend my life searching for lost tribes or beautiful beaches if I wanted to be in love. It would have to be one or the other.

And then there was Josh. I'd envisaged exploring the world with Josh for at least the next two years. Now I seriously questioned how that was going to work. We'd developed not only into best friends, a term I hadn't understood until meeting him, but I relied so much on him. I couldn't physically continue with *Kijana* if he wasn't by my side.

We passed through the cliffs guarding Maya Bay and were suddenly faced with our dream – *The Beach*.

We'd finally arrived in paradise, yet it didn't feel like it. The beauty of the bay seemed to intensify the depression we'd sunken into.

I had done everything in my power to get us to that point of the journey, even things I felt pretty ashamed of, believing everything would be OK once we arrived. For instance, I hadn't stuck up for Maya and demanded she join us earlier. She was forced to find out through the newspapers of a 'mystery blonde' joining us in Darwin, while she sat at home wondering what the hell was going on. I didn't have the guts to be straight with Mika and Nicolette because the office needed time to think. I'd ignored Beau's pleas for the trip to be undertaken for the right reasons.

Maya Bay was a massive disappointment. There must have been a dozen dive boats and twice as many Thai longboats pulled up on the shore, with the beach covered in sunbaking tourists – once more, it was not how I'd hoped and imagined it would be.

I felt disorientated. I knew we were *at* paradise but as I stood on the shore the magic of what I expected to feel was missing.

We spent the day exploring the beach until, as the sun made its journey towards the horizon, the last boat motored back to the bright lights of Phi Phi Don, leaving the beach empty. We lit a fire on the sand, as we'd dreamt of doing for so long, and began our attempt at creating the vision that had burnt so strongly in all of us. But no matter how hard we tried, we were on a hiding to nothing. The warm light flickering from the flames did nothing to lift our spirits.

Beau suddenly demanded to know why everyone was in such a heavy mood. I didn't really want to start unloading all the shit in my head, and I didn't want to dredge up the Josh incident of the previous day. So I offered the lame excuse that we were sad that Maya only had a couple of days left before her time was up.

All that succeeded in doing was sending Beau into orbit. He unleashed a torrent of abuse at me. Everything came out. Being forced to hide his smokes, every decision influenced by the office, the constant gloom because Maya wasn't allowed to join us. He nearly exploded at me.

'It's your trip more than anyone's. It fucking pisses me off. You talk about all this stuff ... you know – about living your dream – you're full of shit! When you first told me about this trip I thought it was brilliant, 'cos we were doing it *our* way. I don't believe you anymore. You're in love but you won't stand up for her. You're a fucking wimp ...'

His words cut deep and I could see the look of horror on Maya's face. But I should have expected it. Just as I could rely on Beau on the boat, I could also rely on him to force me to face anything too awkward and confronting.

He continued his tirade: '... and we're meant to be filming *everything*, why don't we film this, it's been the fucking *real* trip ... but no one will ever know ...'

Josh immediately fired back.

'Beau, the reason you are here is because there's an office back home working their arses off so we can all be here – they don't get paid unless we make the docos to sell. We have to do what they want sometimes because they're the reason we're out here. If you want me to film you being a drunken dickhead I'll do it, but that won't get our docos sold, *OK!*'

It was an argument that had been presented to Beau many months earlier, yet he still found it hard to accept. To him, having to set up shots for the camera made things fake and betrayed the true meaning of the trip, especially when we asked him to repeat an action. It went against everything he was aiming for on a spiritual level.

Beau was livid, this time with Josh.

'See that's what I mean, out of everything we've done, why not film this. It's probably the most important discussion we'll have.'

'We're out of tape,' Josh replied. I knew we weren't, for we had plenty of tape, but Josh wanted to get Beau off his case.

I jumped back into the fray in an attempt to calm things. 'Beau, I know what you're saying but you've said it over and over. I get the point ... You can stop, OK. If you don't want to act out something for the sake of capturing our experiences, then don't. But understand that Josh and I have to! We can't always be as "real" as you!'

I knew as soon as the words came out of my mouth that it was a mean thing to say, but he was bringing up more problems than I was willing to face.

'That's it,' he declared, 'I'm going, I'm leaving as soon as we get back to Phuket. This trip is fucked.'

I knew he meant it and I knew he was right. Kijana had a lot of problems, not just the obvious financial ones, and they were only beginning to surface. I was mostly to blame that it had come to this, for throughout the trip I'd run away from our problems. When something came up, instead of confronting it, I'd let it fester. My problem was that I was always in the middle. I couldn't please everyone. Taking one side meant opposing another, as I'd just shown by ridiculing Beau. The thing I wanted the most – peace and harmony – appeared to be impossible to attain.

We solemnly tossed sand on the fire and headed back in the dinghy to *Kijana*, heading straight to our cabins without so much as a whisper. Maya seemed too shocked to offer me any solace. It was the worst night of my life, far worse than any of the early nights on the trip. Everything that made up my world felt damaged, and I felt paralysed by what had happened.

The tourists returned early the next morning aboard the first longboats, crawling and sprawling over our broken dream. I didn't care – they could have *The Beach*. I wanted to get away from Maya Bay as fast as we could to leave our awful experience behind, so we set sail without setting foot on her shores again. Anyway, Maya had to return to Phuket to catch her flight the following day, with Beau intending to go through with his threat and leave soon after.

Josh untied *Kijana*'s mooring line from the buoy while I started the motor and pointed the bow towards Phuket. It was an awful trip, with no one speaking unless absolutely necessary.

By the time we arrived in Phuket we were back on talking terms, but it was strictly a logistical conversation – where to anchor, the time of Maya's flight and where Beau should call the office to tell them of his decision to suddenly leave.

That night Beau and Josh wandered off separately to get dinner at one of the many food stalls on the island, while Maya and I wanted to make the most of our time together, spending it in the comfort of a hotel on the other side of the island. As we sat down to dinner, she wanted to know what was going to happen. I assured her it would work itself out.

'But how?' she asked.

'I don't know, it just will, OK. Trust me!'

She continued to push but I had no more answers. I became agitated by her questioning until I eventually snapped at her. She burst into tears and stormed off down the street, which made me feel even worse. When faced with tears by Mika and Nicolette I'd never known what to do, except be annoyed. But Maya's tears affected me differently. I followed her out of the restaurant in utter distress. In my head I knew she was being an annoying emotional girl, but, unlike with Mika and Nicolette, this time I cared.

Back in the hotel room I apologised for making our final night together so miserable. I still couldn't answer her questions about how I was going to solve the trip's problems, but once we kissed I at least felt better.

The following morning we returned to *Kijana* to collect Maya's bags, then Josh, Maya and I grabbed a taxi to Phuket airport, leaving Beau to pack his bags for his flight home the following day.

When it came time for her to board the plane, Maya and I shared our last few moments together. She tried to hide her tears, while I wished mine would come. But they remained locked away by some biological survival system, switched on while I maintained my air of being the unaffected leader of Kijana.

As she walked through the security gates, Josh yelled to Maya at the top of his voice: 'Your genital herpes cream is at the bottom of the small backpack. Make sure you apply it during the flight.' She broke into a smile, which broke my heart, then disappeared onto the plane.

Beau had packed by the time Josh and I got back to *Kijana*. I held no grudge against him, for I knew he needed to go. The compromises made to be on *Kijana* were too much for him and I was proud he'd taken a stand for something he believed in.

The office hadn't said much when he'd told them he was leaving, but I knew the departure of yet another crew member was killing any chance of selling our documentaries. Their immediate concern was that Josh and I find new crew as soon as possible – a concept a million miles from my mind.

Our last night as a trio would have been too uncomfortable and confronting for us to spend together, so we accepted an invitation to join a group of yachties at a barbecue on the beach. We ate dinner, then mingled with our dining companions. Most of them were older than us – tanned women with short hair and wrinkles and husbands cradling a beer and chatting about self-steering systems. It was interesting conversation but not what I was seeking. Chatting about our next port of call seemed too surreal, and explaining that Beau was heading home in the morning even more so.

One of the Australian couples was being visited by their son, Jake, and daughter, Mandy, who were both around our age, so we spent most of the time sitting with them. When it got dark and the mosquitoes started to bite, the oldies headed to bed, so the five of us decided to make a night of it. Jake wanted to hit the nightclubs of Patong, while Mandy came along to keep an eye on her younger brother.

We hailed a passing passenger truck heading for Patong Beach, the well-known sleazy area of Phuket, with its night markets, strip shows and restaurants. We climbed onto the luggage racks on the roof without the driver seeming to care. The refreshing evening air blasted through our hair as we climbed the hills and passed the beaches lining the coast. It was a moment of pure freedom as I watched the landscape pass us by.

Looking around at Beau and Josh, I reflected on the times we'd shared the same feeling. Like the relief of making it off the reef, having pulled through together. It had been a spiritual experience and no one else could understand that feeling other than those who had been there. Or the adrenaline of shooting a wild pig, then the sudden guilt at what we'd done; our joint frustration at the girls; whacking the river stones in Borneo and the solitary nights on watch knowing the rest of the crew were safely asleep under one person's command. These were the real moments of paradise – things we'd shared together, not places we'd sailed to.

My thoughts were interrupted when the driver stopped on the main strip of Patong, signalling for us to jump off. We joined the hordes of tourists, families, backpackers and Thai hustlers on the crowded footpaths.

After we'd wandered into an open-air bar, Jake asked about our adventures, so we happily recounted tales of places we'd visited and things we'd seen. Jake and Mandy stared wide-eyed at our recollections, obviously envious of what sounded like the ultimate adventure. Not surprisingly, Mandy asked why Beau was leaving. I shrugged my shoulders, not wanting to go into it, preferring to leave it to Beau to explain. He struggled to put his reasons into words and began to get frustrated. Mandy and Jake looked on as Beau worked himself into an angry state as he told them about 'fakeness' and Maya. I stayed out of it. If Beau wanted to bring it up, then he could deal with it himself. Josh cut in, telling Beau he was starting to rant and rave.

'We just want to have a fun night,' Josh said. I agreed. We'd been through all this before, and all I felt like doing was having one last memorable night together.

'Just give it a rest, OK Beau,' I said in a pissed-off tone.

But he wouldn't, turning his attention to me and continuing where he left off from at *The Beach*.

'I thought this trip was about being honest ...'

I said nothing in response, so he continued.

'Do you love Maya or not? Why don't you stand up for what you want?'

I could feel Josh's rising anger and glanced at our new friends, Mandy and Jake, embarrassed by what they were witnessing.

I turned and began to walk away, but Beau ran and grabbed me in a bear hug.

'Answer the question!' he yelled.

'Get off me,' I said, as I prised his arms apart and attempted to walk off again.

I'd taken three steps when I felt a blow to the right side of my face. I turned around in time to register it was Beau, just before his second punch connected with my cheek.

Never in my life had I been punched, and never in my wildest dreams did I expect the first punch would be thrown by Beau.

'What the fuck do you want?' I screamed like never before. It came from the bottom of my lungs, its primal twang seemingly sobering up every partygoer within 50 metres.

Before he could answer, two security men interrupted, asking us to leave the bar area.

'I just want to talk to him,' Beau tried to explain as they looked to me with a puzzled expression. It hadn't looked like much of a conversation so far.

'OK, we'll go outside,' I said to them, trying to maintain some composure.

We found a wall to sit against and I prepared for a God-almighty argument. I was going to give it to him, cut him down to size, tell him what a little shit he was and how he was as much to blame for Kijana's problems as anyone. But Beau had run out of steam. He couldn't put a sentence together, let alone an argument. Instead, he began to sob, gasping for breath as if he'd been thrust under a cold shower.

The only way to describe it was that something inside him had broken. All that anger, confusion and disappointment – it had exploded inside him and here was the result. Any aggression I felt towards him disappeared in an instant. He was no longer a crazed boxing Buddhist who I should be afraid of, but just a confused boy who needed someone to share his troubles with.

After a minute or so he was able to speak. He explained, through his tears, that he wanted to know if we were still friends. He wanted permission from the captain to leave the trip and he needed confirmation that he was making the right choice. He wanted me to face the problems that had existed on the trip since the day it began and he needed a brother who cared as much about him as he did about me. A punch was the only way he knew how to say all of that.

I realised then that I faced a monumental choice. If I agreed with Beau, and gave my blessing to him leaving, I was conceding that leaving was the right thing to do. It was a case of choosing between forgetting all our woes and forging ahead with Kijana versus Beau and Maya.

I was standing at the biggest crossroads of my life.

Throughout the trip I'd taken inspiration from the Yolngu custom of leaving the sick behind when survival of the tribe was the priority. It was why Mika and Nicolette departed, and why Beau now had to go. They had to be cut out for the good of Kijana. I now realised I was one of the sick people. It was no use blaming everyone else for Kijana's woes. I was the one who had made all the promises and selected the crew. Kijana may have been my dream, but now I was standing in its way.

All of a sudden, the person I thought I was – adventurer, leader and wanna-be visionary – disintegrated. I felt the complete opposite of all of those things as my own sobbing overtook the noises coming from Beau. He was taken aback by my breakdown and stared in amazement. I'd never been so open with another human, not even my brother. My emotional tap had been turned on and I felt like I was washing myself clean.

Children stopped to look at Beau and me, a pair of blubbering, filthy waifs slumped in the gutter, until their parents yanked them away. We sat together for a few minutes not saying a word. I then pulled myself up and told Beau I was off to an internet café to email the office.

I had crumbled under the weight of Kijana and had decided to leave the trip. A part of me felt so relieved. Another part was terrified about what I had to do next. The journey was over, ten months into the expected three years, and now I had to try to explain my reasons to everyone else.

CHAPTER THIRTEEN
NO REGRETS

Hi Jesse,

*Wanting to write you a quick note. I apologise for last night.
I remember saying to you that you were a 'DICKHEAD'. I really
do think the opposite of this. I can't really say how I'd be in your
shoes at the moment.*

*Even though I lose my temper sometimes I want you to know
that if you ever ask me something, like if you need help or whatever, I will always stand with you and support you in ways which
I think best.*

*I feel this trip has brought us closer together and I like hang-
ing out with you bro.*

Do what you think best.

Beau

His plane was in the air by the time I received this note, which
he'd left on the cabin table of *Kijana*. His words only confirmed my
decision to end my role aboard *Kijana*.

Josh had taken it pretty well when, earlier that morning, I told him I was leaving. As with everything on the trip, he accepted my decision, even if he didn't understand my reasons. I had battled side by side with him for what seemed an eternity and time after time he had shown faith in me, willing, if you like, to lay down everything in the name of our shared vision.

When I told him I was leaving, I felt I was abandoning him. I knew deep inside he'd feel confused and in despair. He put up some resistance, making suggestions as to how we could make it work if we continued. But my mind was made up. It was over. I desperately wanted to take him home with me, but he wanted to fight on, like the true adventurer he had become, choosing the open ocean to continue the Kijana dream.

As you can imagine, the office was in a state of shock as they digested my decision. They couldn't understand why I was leaving. We decided that Josh would return to Melbourne with me while we sorted out whether he could continue with a new crew. We found a safe anchorage and left *Kijana* under the watchful eye of a nearby yacht, then flew back to Australia, a few weeks before Christmas 2002, to meet with the office and try to forge a new plan for the Kijana adventure.

As I walked through the sliding doors of Melbourne Airport, the irony struck me. Few people saw me off aboard *Lionheart*, yet 25,000 greeted my return. Thousands farewelled us aboard *Kijana* and two people welcomed us home – Josh's mum and my dad.

We stepped into our respective cars for the ride home and, for the first time, it hit me that Josh and I were heading our separate ways. The next time I saw him was a few days later at our first meeting with the office team. A heavy mood hung in the air, adding to my feeling that I'd let everyone down.

I glanced at the shelves lining the wall, filled with legal binders and promotional material for Kijana. They were simply more reminders of how much work had been put into the project to make it happen. I was glad when we decided to adjourn to a nearby pub for our discussions.

I confirmed to those present that Kijana was over for me. I could not make my part of it work, I told them, so I had no choice but to leave. The office no doubt felt dumbfounded. Everything they had been working towards was in jeopardy. It was suggested that Josh keep going with *Kijana*, something I encouraged. He knew how to sail her and could competently captain her with a new crew. I would have felt proud if he'd continued. But over the next few months we discovered the reality was, without an injection of funds, *Kijana* wouldn't be going anywhere and no one wanted to further support a journey where the skipper had resigned. Talk about pressure.

The office suggested I remain as a figurehead, with another skipper aboard to take the pressure off me. But that wasn't going to solve my issues. I struggled to convey the reasons why I could not return. My heart was no longer there, I said. For me, the journey was over and I needed time to heal. Being the skipper was irrelevant. I would pay everyone back, I promised. I preferred to have nothing than to carry the burden of Kijana.

Everything I thought I had been working towards disappeared with my decision that night in Patong. I wrote to the sponsors and friends of the project thanking them for their help and apologising for my inability to captain *Kijana* to success. After it was publicly revealed the trip had finished, negotiations with the television networks immediately fell through. We were up to our ears in debt. And hanging over our heads was the threat of legal action for not fulfilling our obligations. I wasn't surprised. With all the contracts and deals we had promised, to get the trip going, I'd expected as much. All I could offer was to forgo my share of the sale of the boat, which at the time of writing had yet to be sold.

For nearly a year, I negotiated the split of the Kijana Partnership. Everything I had put into Kijana, along with all my proceeds from *Lionheart* were used to pay others. The only thing I wanted out of it all was the hours and hours of footage, photos and diary entries, so I could explain what happened on the journey. It was the only thing I cared about.

My decision cost me a lot more than money. I lost many good friends I'd worked with to get the trip up and running, and my reputation was damaged. I didn't get time to see much of Beau after we returned and I felt I'd permanently scarred my friendship with

Josh. Without him to make me laugh, my life felt empty. If it weren't for Maya, whose softness nurtured me, I would have been a lost and lonely soul. She may not have been able to hold a sail in a storm, but she could save my life in a much less obvious way.

I wished I could have seen that I was leading Mika and Nicolette on the wrong trip. It was my trip and it suited me. Realistically, it would suit few others. I apologise for what I put them through and for not being the type of skipper who could accommodate them. That inability is something that still haunts me.

The first time I caught up with Mika was weird. A few months after I returned we decided to meet up and clear the air. It's taken nearly two years for me to feel comfortable around her. I hope she reads this and understands why things happened the way they did and we won't have to talk about them ever again, except to look back and have a laugh about it all.

I haven't spoken or had any contact with Nicolette. She flew home to the United States a few days after she left *Kijana*. I've wanted to write to her and apologise for the experiences I put her through. However, like many good intentions, I've never got around to it and probably never will. This book, I hope, will explain why I acted the way I did and said the things I said.

Maria continued travelling after she met her brother in Darwin. I hear she is back in Denmark, where she has bought a flat and is attending fashion school. I'm grateful for the time she spent with me aboard *Kijana* and only have fond memories of our time together.

Beau returned and immediately began working as a labourer for our uncle. He helped me with some money for the first few months I was home, until I got my life together. He hasn't become a monk, although he did cut his hair short. However, I think his haircut had more to do with his job than anything. Still, he maintains an interest in Buddhism, even plonking a small statue of Buddha in the garden of the house he bought after working hard for two years. He also has a girlfriend, who keeps a smile on his face. We don't see much of each other, nor do we feel the need to. But I know he'll always be there for me and me for him.

Through no fault of his own Josh was forced to return home with nothing, struggling to comprehend why his dream had ended. He spent a year working on an Australian feature film and shooting wedding videos to get by. For a long time it seemed the best part of Josh had been left aboard *Kijana*. Our friends noticed a big difference in him compared to the Josh they knew before the trip. For a long time we only really saw each other around our group of friends and even then we didn't have much to say to each other.

About 12 months after we arrived home, I phoned Josh, not sure what to say, but wanting to say something other than an obvious 'sorry'. My voice trembled as he answered and I said 'Hi'. He hurriedly told me he couldn't speak but would call back. I waited, but the phone never rang. I was scared that I'd hurt my best friend beyond repair and it would never be the same again.

Instead, I got an email from him shortly after, saying everything I wished I'd known how to write myself. I could have paraphrased what he wrote and signed my name at the bottom, but it would never have had the same heart.

Hey Jesse,

I don't want to be a pain in the arse, but my head is racing and if I called you to explain I'd probably forget what I wanted to say, or start crying before I could get it to make sense. So I'm writing it.

I don't know how to write it without being 'on the nose' so I'll just chuck it all down here before I over-think it, and you can take from it what you will.

I miss you Jesse.

I could end it there and just write: from Josh, but I'll write a few more paragraphs to explain the weight behind those words. If they're in my head they'll only spill out backwards one night in a drunken stupor, so I'd prefer to get 'em out on paper.

We lived a fucken weird time together Jess, 10 months crammed in a boat and there's stuff I want to say sorry for, and stuff I hope you remember and stuff that I don't ever want to forget. We'll talk about it when the time is right, and some things will probably never be said.

Waking up in the morning I close my eyes again and wish I could sleep all day. Some of that's because I wish I was waking up on the boat, ready to crawl up the stairs and fall over the side. But a lot of that is the fact that you're not just a few feet away, about to wake up too.

When we hang out you make me laugh, and think, and I hope I do the same for you. I haven't felt that flow in a long time now.

That said, I'm looking forward to catching up. But I don't want you to think of me as another Kijana loose end that needs tying up.

Don't get me wrong. I know you think highly of me and I know we're good friends. I think you sum it up in one of your old diary entries, you say: 'Josh wants me to talk and open up more but I don't feel like it 'cos I want to be like that with Maya.' And I understand that. Just that I don't have a Maya to come home to.

I don't want you to call me every day and make me feel better. I don't need that. You and Maya will be off living in LA or huts in Borneo some time soon enough and I don't want to miss you when you're gone as much as I miss you when you're only a suburb away.

I don't regret a single day of preparation for the trip or any moment while it was going. I hate how people look at me now and smile an understanding smile as if I've just been through hell. It wasn't hell. It was the hardest, and best two years of my life, and I don't give a fuck that the boat's just in Thailand. I'm proud it came this far.

I hope what we had together on Kijana didn't end when the trip did. History in a friendship can be a real bitch. But I hope we stay friends forever, not just mates.

Sorry I was sad when you called, I just miss ya.

Your friend,
Josh

PS Don't reply to this email fuckwit. I know you hate doing it. We'll talk soon.

People have asked me whether Kijana was doomed from the beginning, whether it was too big, too ambitious, surrounded by too much hype and too commercial. Well, consider this quote by American author and critic Alexander Eliot:

Life is a fatal adventure. It can only have one end. So why not make it as far-ranging and free as possible?

We know that growing up and living life is doomed from the beginning, but that's no reason not to embark on it. It's the same with Kijana. The warning signs for Kijana may have been there from the start. Hell, you only have to look at our original inspiration, the film *The Beach*. It portrayed the image of paradise we were searching for, yet we all overlooked the fact that it had a tragic ending. But that shouldn't be a reason not to embark on Kijana. How would we ever know it would end the way it did if we never took the risk and embarked on the trip in the first place?

To say Kijana was a failure is like saying the death of a village chief in Toraja is a waste of a life. As with the Torajan funerals, I see the end of the trip as a time to reflect on the moments of happiness and bliss during Kijana's life even though some, surprisingly, came in those worst times. I could never label the journey a failure.

To all those dreamers and would-be adventurers, don't be deterred by my experience. I'll always encourage anyone to follow the call of adventure in the quest to be somewhere or someone better. Do it with all your heart, and don't listen to those who say it can't be done. It's just that *they* can't do it. Commit everything, aim high and follow it to the point where all you care about are the bare essentials. To borrow the words from one of Mika's diary entries: 'I have learnt that paradise is not a pretty beach and freedom is not just five friends sailing around the world.'

Of course I could rattle off a list of things I wished I had done differently, but it kind of ruins the point of what the journey was about. Things were done the way they were and it was all part of what was in store for us. I now know more about who I am, as distinct from who

I wanted to be. I have fond memories of very close friends, with whom I feel proud to have shared the most important journey of my life.

I thought I was leading the journey, but in fact it was leading us, and I am thankful for where it took us.

ACKNOWLEDGEMENTS

I wish to thank the following individuals and organisations, without who Kijana would not have been possible.

John Allin
Maria Anderson
Michael Barrett
Damien Bear
Eliza Bellmaine
Jayne Bendroph
Bruce Bird
Lawrence Blair
Tracy Brady
Gerry Bryant & crew
Siobhan Caffery
Jon Carnegie
Sam Cavanagh
Katie Cavanagh
Tony Chew
Blanche Clark
Paul Currie
Samantha Currie
Dan Davies
John Devers
Peter Devers
Anna Dusek
David Eades
Nicolette Fendon
Lewis Ferrier
Darren Finkelstein
Michelle Field
Neil Flavel
Amelia Ford
Gayili & family
Ed Gannon
Jenny Geddes

Peter Godfrey
Michael Green
Phil Gregory
The Harris family
Yappa Helen
Geoff Henderson
Sue Hines
Rick Jackson
Bev Knight
Maya Knight
Holly Kramer
Jules Lund
Beau Martin
Kon Martin
Louise Martin
Dave McKeogh
Dave Meredith
Lyn Moore
Tracie Olcha
Steve & Julie O'Sullivan
Rebecca Park
Richard Parkin
Jenny Pullan
Paulos Ranti & family
Tim Reid
Chip Richards
Martin Richmond
John Rolland
Lisa Saad
Carly Schmidt
Josh Schmidt
Lesley Schmidt

Michael Schoell
Flip Shelton
Michael Shultz
Susie Stott
Barry Streete
Nick Theofilakos
Mika Tran
Sam & Gabby Valderrama
Myrna Van Pelt
Fabio Versace
Rowena Vilar
Wadu
Pauline Webster
Melissa Whiltshire
Joanna White
Ralph White
Noel Wright
Gary Woodyard
Mandawuy Yunupingu

Sponsors
The Alfred Hospital
Apple Computers
Design Wyse
Environment Australia
Go4 Web Design
Herald Sun
Mars
Mercury Marine
Nike
NRMA
Sandringham Yacht Club
Sony
Tag Heuer
Telstra
TXU
William Angliss

Special thanks
AGFA Film
Australian National Maritime
  Museum
Beyond Capricorn crew
Birds Bees Trees & Things
Cameron's Metaland
Chroma Media
Cummings Flavel
Deakin University
Doquille Perret Meade
Filmplus
GME Electrophone
Igloo Design
Lightstream Films
Lizard Island staff
Lonely Planet
Mission Aviation Fellowship
Morgans Hotel
Newcastle Fire Services
Novotel
Plan International
Reach Youth
RDF
Royal Australian Navy
Snowgum
Victorian Government
Working Dog

The indigenous and local people
of Australia & Indonesia who
took us in and gave us food
and friendship.

PHOTOGRAPH AND ILLUSTRATION CREDITS

Pages x & xi
Map by Guy Holt Illustration and Design

Illustrated section pages 8 & 9
Diagram by *Herald Sun*

Illustrated section page 12 (top)
Photograph by Lawrence Blair

All other photographs are from the author's private collection

ABOUT THE AUTHOR

Jesse Martin was destined for adventure. Born in Munich in 1981 while his parents were travelling through Europe in a kombi van, he spent his early years in the beautiful Daintree rainforest of north Queensland. By the time he was fourteen he had sailed a thousand kilometres along Australia's tropical coast on a flimsy catamaran and had trekked through South-East Asia and the Aboriginal communities of Central Australia. At sixteen he kayaked through remote islands of Papua New Guinea and then crewed on a yacht that sailed from Belize to Tahiti. In 1998 at the age of seventeen, Jesse set off from Melbourne on his record-breaking solo sail around the world.

After returning from Kijana, Jesse established an adventure sailing charter business in late 2004, cruising the islands of Papua New Guinea in a 38-foot Polynesian catamaran. For more information, visit <www.jessemartin.net>